Microsoft® Silverlight™ 3:
A Beginner's Guide

About the Author

Shannon Horn has been developing Microsoft Windows and web-based solutions, training, and authoring for over 14 years. He has been a featured speaker at many industry events, including Microsoft DevDays and the asp.netPRO "ASP.NET and Web Services Solutions" conference. He is a published author on subjects such as JavaScript, Silverlight, XML, the migration from Visual Basic 6 to Visual Basic .NET, JScript .NET, C#, ASP.NET, and SQL Server 2005.

Shannon speaks and trains for companies such as Microsoft, Batky-Howell, AppDev, and New Instruction, and has been a featured speaker on training videos with Microsoft and LearnKey. He has also worked with large corporate clients, including Microsoft, Excess Reinsurance, Universal Studios, MGM Studios, Monster.com/FlipDog.com, Intel, Polygram Pictures, Prudential, MicroAccounting Systems, Sky Harbor International Airport, and Evans Newton, Inc., on projects utilizing Microsoft technologies such as SQL Server, Silverlight, Visual FoxPro, Visual Studio .NET, C#, ADO.NET, and ASP.NET.

Shannon is currently pursuing his third-degree black belt in tae kwon do and trains in MMA and fights out of the Lion's Den Scottsdale (http://www.lionsdenaz.com). Shannon recently formed an athlete management company (http://www.SuperionManagement.com) and is a professional musician (bass guitar).

Microsoft® Silverlight™ 3:
A Beginner's Guide

Shannon Horn

New York   Chicago   San Francisco
Lisbon   London   Madrid   Mexico City
Milan   New Delhi   San Juan
Seoul   Singapore   Sydney   Toronto

The McGraw·Hill Companies

Cataloging-in-Publication Data is on file with the Library of Congress

McGraw-Hill books are available at special quantity discounts to use as premiums and sales promotions, or for use in corporate training programs. To contact a representative, please e-mail us at bulksales@mcgraw-hill.com.

Microsoft® Silverlight™ 3: A Beginner's Guide

1 2 3 4 5 6 7 8 9 0   FGR FGR   0 1 9

ISBN   978-0-07-159043-3
MHID   0-07-159043-9

Sponsoring Editor   Roger Stewart

Editorial Supervisor   Patty Mon

Project Manager   Vipra Fauzdar, Glyph International

Acquisitions Coordinator   Joya Anthony

Technical Editor   Robert Sponaugle

Copy Editor   Bart Reed

Proofreader   Julie Searls

Indexer   Claire Splan

Production Supervisor   Jean Bodeaux

Composition   Glyph International

Illustration   Glyph International

Art Director, Cover   Jeff Weeks

Cover Designer   Jeff Weeks

Contents at a Glance

Contents

Acknowledgments

I'd like to thank Roger and Joya for being patient with me in completing this book, and I'd also like to thank Robert for all of his work in editing.

Introduction

I compiled this book while working on several client projects that utilize Silverlight. Along that line, I have structured this book so that readers will learn Silverlight in a logical manner that closely follows the order in which a real-world application is developed. In particular, I was contacted by clients either to begin development of a Silverlight application from the ground up or to add a Silverlight user interface to an existing application infrastructure. In both scenarios, developers must be knowledgeable in all aspects of Silverlight application development so that they can hit the ground running with little or no ramp-up time.

In the case where a client requests an application to be created or redesigned from the ground up, life is easier for the developers because they have full control over all aspects of the software development project. On the other hand, in the case where a client requests that a Silverlight user interface be created for an existing application infrastructure, a developer must be prepared to design the Silverlight user interface to communicate with multiple types of web-enabled services that could be designed to communicate in a multitude of ways.

As an example, I was recently contacted by a client in North Carolina who uses a large custom application to manage all facets of their business. Their application is divided into several modules and was created using a development technology from the 1980s. Beginning with a selected module, I began redesigning the application to be based on SQL Server 2008, LINQ, C#, WCF services, and Silverlight 3.

On the opposite side of the coin, another client contacted me to design a Silverlight user interface for an existing application that utilized an ASP.NET user interface. Due to the existing ASP.NET user interface, some of the framework for the redesign was already in place. However, the improved Silverlight UI took advantage of better graphics and integrated media. The code that resided in the ASP.NET code-behind pages had to be migrated to the Silverlight code-behind pages. Thus, the code had to undergo some changes because not all the code was applicable to Silverlight or a client execution environment. Additionally, the existing ASP.NET pages communicated directly with business classes and then, in turn, the database and the application relied on automatic postbacks. In a Silverlight application, there are no automatic postbacks; hence, the code had to be modified to accommodate this change, and WCF services had to be created on the server to fulfill requests coming from the client.

Early chapters in this book introduce Silverlight and the path of technologies leading up to the development of Silverlight. Chapters progress to illustrate networking and accessing data with Silverlight. Finally, this book discusses how Silverlight can be used to display graphics and media. Here's a breakdown of what you'll encounter in each chapter:

- Chapter 1 gives a detailed overview of Silverlight and the history of Microsoft technologies that led up to the development of Silverlight. This chapter also introduces a simple application created using Silverlight and illustrates the display of the application in various browsers.

- Chapter 2 ventures out to describe and illustrate the latest technologies available in the .NET Framework, version 3.5. These technologies include Windows Presentation Foundation (WPF), Windows Communication Foundation (WCF), Windows Workflow Foundation (WF), Windows CardSpace, ASP.NET AJAX, and Language Integrated Query (LINQ).

- Chapter 3 takes a much closer look at the architecture of a Silverlight application as created using Visual Studio 2008. Topics in this chapter include how to install Silverlight 3, a quick overview of Visual Studio 2008 and Expression Blend, the most common languages used to code Silverlight applications, how to integrate Silverlight 3 media with existing ASP.NET AJAX pages, and how to quickly create a Silverlight 3 application and a Silverlight 3 animation.

- Chapters 4 and 5 delve deeper into displaying shapes and graphics using Silverlight. Chapter 4 also explains how animations are created in Silverlight and how to display very large, high-resolution graphics using Deep Zoom technology. Chapter 5 explores Expression Encoder and how to prepare media for display in Silverlight.

- Chapter 6 focuses on the networking capabilities available in Silverlight. Silverlight includes functionality for communicating with Web Services and WCF services using protocols such as POX, sockets, SOAP, JSON, REST, RSS, and ATOM.

- Chapter 7 discusses options for securing Silverlight applications. Although Silverlight is a subset of the .NET Framework, security options for Silverlight applications differ from the full gamut of security options available to other types of .NET Framework applications.

- Chapter 8 illustrates most of the controls available in Silverlight 3. Silverlight controls are commonly divided into categories of layout controls and data entry or user interface controls. Several third-party control vendors are actively creating control suites for Silverlight, and developers are able to customize all the controls that ship with Silverlight as well as create fully custom controls.

- Chapter 9 explores the options available in Silverlight for accessing and managing data. Silverlight can easily read and write data as XML as well as store and retrieve data in local Isolated Storage. The Silverlight framework includes functionality for accessing data using Language Integrated Query (LINQ), and virtually all control properties can be dynamically configured through data binding.

- Chapter 10 discusses how to improve performance in Silverlight applications by downloading large resources, such as media, asynchronously using the WebClient class. This chapter also explains the concepts of synchronous versus asynchronous processing.

- Chapter 11 explores the debugging, testing, and deployment of Silverlight applications. Common options for deploying Silverlight applications include to a locally hosted web server and to the Windows Live Silverlight Streaming service.

- Chapter 12 applies Silverlight development techniques learned to create line of business (LOB) rich internet applications (RIAs). This chapter illustrates many useful techniques that make Silverlight a viable development option for the everyday, real-world, business application developer.

I am constantly on the road training developers; as a result, my writing style and approach to learning follow the developer training paradigm closely. While writing this book, several interim versions and builds of Silverlight were released with each update, including changes and enhancements that, in several cases, broke existing Silverlight code. Hence, if you find yourself pulling your hair out trying to figure out why code in Silverlight is not functioning correctly, please contact me for assistance at shannonhorn@msn.com.

Chapter 1

The Road Leading to Silverlight

Key Concepts & Skills

- Gain an understanding of the history of the Microsoft software development technologies that lead to the development of Microsoft Silverlight

- Learn about the features included in Silverlight versions 1.0, 2, and 3

- Expound upon the platforms and browsers supported by Silverlight 3

- Briefly investigate how the Silverlight plug-in functions in contrast to how standard web applications and ASP.NET applications function

Silverlight is a recent technology developed by Microsoft that enables the development of rich interactive applications (RIAs) that target the Web. Silverlight is a cross-platform and cross-browser plug-in that is composed of a subset of the functionality included in Windows Presentation Foundation (WPF) and the .NET Framework. When designing and developing Silverlight, Microsoft took notice of the features being offered by all competitors and used that as a baseline for creating a new product. As a result, Silverlight includes many features and functionality not available from competing technologies.

Silverlight Features

Three versions of Silverlight are available: version 1.0, version 2, and version 3. Silverlight 1.0 was released late in 2007 and was an immediate success. It was a subset of the .NET Framework, version 3.5, and included a subset of Windows Presentation Foundation (WPF) features. Silverlight 1.0 also provided the following capabilities:

- Create and manage 2-D graphics and animation

- Handle mouse, keyboard, and ink input

- Deliver Windows Media Video (WMV), Windows Media Audio (WMA), and MP3 media

- Display JPEG (JPG) and PNG image formats

- Format and manipulate text

- Make same domain calls to services and download server resources using the HTTP downloader object

- Parse Extensible Application Markup Language (XAML) content

- Utilize the W3C Document Object Model (DOM) using JavaScript

Features included in Silverlight 1.0 were accessible by using JavaScript.

Silverlight was released in an interim beta version (version 1.1) between Silverlight 1.0 and Silverlight 2. However, due to the enormity of the features and functionality being added to Silverlight 2, Microsoft decided to make it a major version release instead of a build release. Silverlight 2 was released in September 2008.

Silverlight 2 included all features that were included in Silverlight 1.0 as well as the following features:

- Support for managed code, including code written in C#, Visual Basic, IronPython, and IronRuby

- Extensible Application Markup Language (XAML) extensibility

- Additional Windows Presentation Foundation (WPF) features, namely dynamic user interface layout support

- A multitude of user interface controls

- Improved and extended data access, data binding, and networking functionality

The first beta of Silverlight 3 was released at MIX09 in March 2009. In line with Silverlight 2, Silverlight 3 includes all the features available in Silverlight 2 as well as the following features:

- XAML elements can be used to directly data bind properties.

- Controls and data binding support data validation.

- Cascading styles are now natively supported.

- Externally defined resources are now supported so that resource libraries can be shared across applications.

- Out-of-browser applications are now supported so that Silverlight applications can be used offline with more access to local user resources.

- New controls are now included in the Silverlight SDK, including the File Save As dialog.

- Assemblies in the Silverlight framework are now cached locally on the user's machine to improve performance.

- Animation easing effects are built in that simplify animating objects, including bounce, elastic, circle, and cubic.

- Options are included for improving performance while animating text.

- An API and functionality are provided for programmatically modifying bitmap images.

- Pixel shader effects can be applied to graphics such as drop shadows and blurs.

- Perspective 3-D transformations can be applied to graphics to simulate a 3-D environment.

- Some support is provided for interaction with local graphics hardware (GPU).

- Deep Zoom performance has been improved.

- Developers can now create their own audio and video codecs for media playback.

- True high definition (HD) playback is offered in full-screen mode.

- Fonts can now be compressed and distributed in an application, and Silverlight applications can access locally installed fonts.

- The ability to easily determine whether an application is offline or has access to the Web has been added.

- Silverlight controls can easily communicate with other Silverlight controls.

- XML can be formatted using binary serialization to improve network performance.

- Some accessibility features have now been included in Silverlight.

- Silverlight applications can now be developed on the Macintosh operating system.

- A navigation framework is built in to the Silverlight framework.

An Ocean of Resources

Since the early community technology previews of Silverlight 1.0, the industry has been abuzz over Silverlight, and the Web is now flooded with Silverlight resources. The official Silverlight home page is located at http://www.silverlight.net/ and includes links for downloading Silverlight as well as a gamut of learning resources, tutorials, and videos. The Silverlight home page is shown in Figure 1-1.

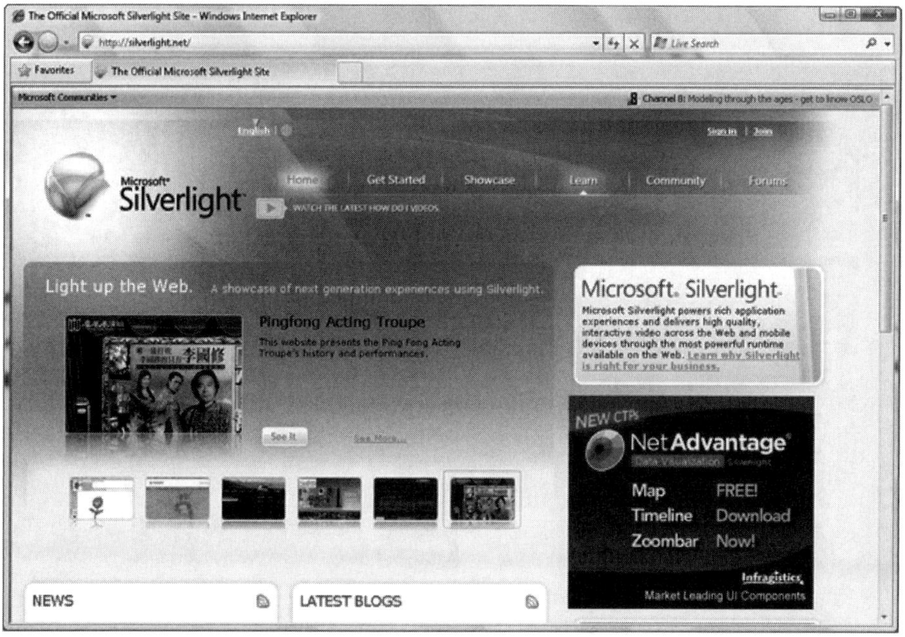

Figure 1-1   The Silverlight.net home page

Early Adopters

As a result of the mass developer following of Silverlight, many significant web presences have redesigned their websites to utilize Silverlight. Some of the early adopters are featured in this section.

The 2008 Olympics website was completely redesigned with Silverlight at its heart. The new Olympics website offered on-demand viewing of Olympic events, picture-in-picture, multiple camera angles, and DVD-style navigation controls. The 2008 Olympics website is shown in Figure 1-2.

The Hard Rock Cafe owns the largest rock-and-roll memorabilia collection in the world. The Hard Rock Cafe has utilized a new imaging technology based on Silverlight, called Deep Zoom technology, to display their memorabilia collection to the world in a unique manner over the Web. The Hard Rock Cafe rock-and-roll memorabilia website is shown in Figure 1-3.

The World Wrestling Entertainment (WWE) website was redesigned to offer streaming media and an impressive UI using Silverlight. The WWE website is shown in Figure 1-4.

These early adopter examples are just three of many. The library of websites that are registered early adopters can be reviewed by visiting the Silverlight website at http://silverlight.net/Showcase/. The Silverlight.net Showcase is shown in Figure 1-5.

Figure 1-2 The 2008 NBC Olympics website

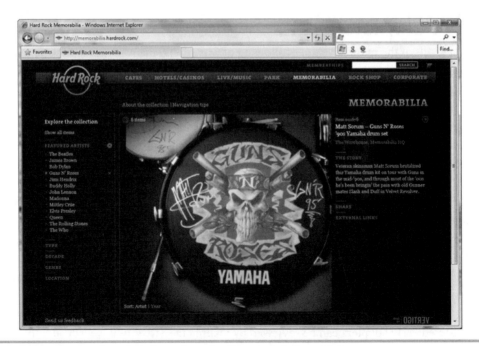

Figure 1-3 The Hard Rock Cafe rock-and-roll memorabilia website

Figure 1-4   The WWE website

Figure 1-5   The Silverlight.net Showcase

A Technological Evolution

Silverlight was not conceived by Microsoft as a completely new idea but rather was arrived at via a progression of technologies over several years. Prior to the year 2000, Microsoft offered three primary development environments for creating Windows applications and one primary development environment for creating web applications. However, Microsoft technologies were at a standstill and the company did not have a consolidated technology that could compete with the technologies being offered by other vendors such as Java. A major obstacle facing developers who developed applications using Microsoft technologies in the late 1990s was that the technologies and programming languages were very different and not compatible. In order to communicate between the languages, data had to be marshaled and prepared beforehand.

This section illustrates the progression of technologies that led up to the development of Silverlight.

Microsoft C++

C++ is Microsoft's powerhouse programming language for creating unmanaged code and applications. C++ offers developers a very low level of control over every minute aspect of an application. The power and level of control offered by C++ make it a very complex programming language to master, and many developers shy away from using it. Writing efficient and optimized code using C++ is considered a science. If a developer does not put forth the effort required to become a C++ guru, he or she can easily write code that performs poorly. Most platform-level applications created by Microsoft are written using C++ (Windows, SQL Server, Internet Information Services, and so on).

Microsoft Visual Basic

Visual Basic (version 6.0 and versions prior to Visual Basic .NET) was an incredibly popular programming language due to it simplifying most programming tasks. Visual Basic automated most of the low-level programming tasks that C++ developers had to endeavor to master. However, although Visual Basic did make life easier for developers, it sometimes did so at a slight cost. In many scenarios, applications created using Visual Basic could be created rapidly but were generally not as efficient or optimized as an application created using C++.

Microsoft Active Server Pages (ASP)

Microsoft's web development platform, prior to the release of the .NET Framework, was named Active Server Pages (ASP). ASP was extremely popular but could not really be extended any further than it had been extended in the late 1990s without being completely redesigned. ASP rendered web content dynamically by intermingling web markup with script code, executing the script code on the server, and generating and sending the result to the client's browser.

ASP was designed in the infancy of the Web and, as such, wasn't designed to accommodate the incredible bulk of traffic that emerged as the Web grew. ASP had several limitations that developers had to work around, and it faced stiff competition by other technologies, namely Java. Using Java, a developer can create applications using the Java programming language, build the Java code into an intermediate and portable format called bytecode, and then deploy, interpret, and execute the bytecode to any operating system that is running the Java Virtual Machine (JVM).

In the late 1990s, Microsoft decided that, in order to remain competitive in the industry, they needed to completely revamp their development technologies.

The .NET Framework

In order to compete with Java and other technologies, Microsoft revolutionized their development efforts by consolidating all their development technologies into a single framework called the .NET Framework. The .NET Framework was released to market in 2000 and accommodated all functionality offered by existing Microsoft and competing technologies as well as introduced new technologies, features, and functionality.

The .NET Framework enables application development using one or more programming languages. All programming languages that utilize the .NET Framework must comply with the Common Language Specification (CLS). The CLS mandates that all .NET-compliant languages must emit Intermediate Language (IL), a portable, low-level, text-based code format, and all .NET-compliant languages must support a common set of data types known as the Common Type System (CTS). The IL emitted from a .NET-compliant programming language is deployed, loaded, executed, managed, and unloaded by the Common Language Runtime (CLR). The CLR operates in a manner similar to the Java Virtual Machine (JVM). However, the CLR is a compiler whereas the JVM is a command interpreter.

Microsoft redesigned ASP into ASP.NET, which has become the most widely used and popular web development technology in the industry. Microsoft also upgraded its data access technologies into ADO.NET. The .NET Framework now proliferates all Microsoft technologies and is supported by and has had an impact on most competing technologies provided by other vendors.

Introducing Silverlight

Version 3.5 of the .NET Framework includes all the functionality provided in .NET Framework version 2.0 as well as some additional technologies. New .NET Framework 3.5 technologies include Windows Presentation Foundation (WPF), Windows Communication Foundation (WCF), Windows Workflow Foundation (WF), Windows CardSpace, ASP.NET AJAX, and Language Integrated Query (LINQ).

WPF is a focal point when discussing Silverlight because Silverlight is a subset of WPF. Prior to .NET Framework 3.0/3.5, the technologies included in the .NET Framework for creating Microsoft Windows applications closely resembled Visual Basic 6 Forms technology. What's more, the GDI+ libraries used to manipulate and display graphics, animations, and media were, literally, the same, unmanaged libraries used by C++ and technologies prior to the .NET Framework. As the .NET Framework grew in popularity, Microsoft began to redesign all their technologies and products around the .NET Framework. Microsoft redesigned the technologies used to create Windows applications and manage graphics into WPF. Using WPF, a developer can create user interfaces that were not possible by using its preceding technology.

In an effort to enable developers to create better-performing web applications, Microsoft integrated AJAX technology into ASP.NET. AJAX was originally created by Microsoft using an ActiveX control in the late 1990s and was, at that time, referred to as Remote Scripting. AJAX is now supported by all mainstream web browsers, and Microsoft defines AJAX as an acronym for Asynchronous JavaScript and XML. An ASP.NET page that utilizes AJAX sends data to and receives data from the web server asynchronously, and the user does not have to wait for the communication with the web server to complete before continuing to work on the page.

Although ASP.NET AJAX enables an improved user experience and an improved perceived performance gain, AJAX is implemented using JavaScript, XML, HTML, and other web technologies. Each browser may render markup and content in a manner different from other browsers; hence, when developing a web application using traditional web technologies, including the content rendered by ASP.NET and AJAX, the developer must trust that the browser will display content as the developer intended it to be displayed.

The only manner in which a developer can guarantee that content is displayed in a consistent manner across all platforms and across all browsers is to utilize a browser plug-in. A browser plug-in affords a developer an encapsulated environment where they can have complete control over processes and display. Adobe Flash is the most popular browser plug-in that is used to render and display graphics, animations, and media. In order to compete with Adobe Flash, Microsoft began working on a downloadable browser plug-in that not only could be used to render and display graphics, animations, and media, but could also implement a subset of WPF and .NET Framework functionality and features.

Microsoft Silverlight—originally called Windows Presentation Foundation/Everywhere (WPF/E)—is a free browser plug-in that functions in a restricted sandbox in a manner similar to the Java Virtual Machine (JVM).

Silverlight Architecture

Developers accustomed to developing standard web applications or applications by using ASP.NET will need to adjust to developing applications in Silverlight. Silverlight applications are downloaded and executed on the client's machine. A postback to the web server only occurs if it is initiated manually from the Silverlight application. Figure 1-6 compares Silverlight application processing to ASP.NET application processing.

When a user displays a page that contains a Silverlight control, if the Silverlight plug-in is not installed on the user's machine, the user will be prompted to download and install the plug-in. Once the plug-in is installed, the Silverlight control will be downloaded and executed. Upon subsequent requests to run the Silverlight control, the control will instantiate on the user's machine and then requests for resources from the web server will only be made manually, when necessary.

Silverlight Versions

Silverlight is currently available in version 3. Silverlight version 1.0 was released in 2007, supports Windows Media Services, and is used to create rich interactive applications (RIAs) by using JavaScript.

In the last quarter of 2007, Silverlight version 1.1 was released in beta. Silverlight version 1.1 extended Silverlight version 1.0 functionality to include more support

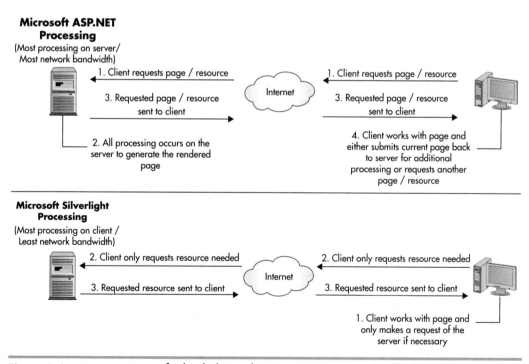

Figure 1-6   A comparison of Silverlight application processing and ASP.NET application processing

for .NET Framework functionality by using JavaScript or one of several managed programming languages such as C#, VB, IronRuby, or IronPython.

Due to the vast number of changes, enhancements, and updates that was planned to be included in Silverlight version 1.1, Microsoft decided to release the new version as a new version instead of a new build. Thus, version 1.1 was renamed to version 2. Figure 1-7 illustrates the major features included in Silverlight version 1.0 and Silverlight version 2. Silverlight 3 functionality expands upon the features shown in this figure.

Silverlight Hosting

Web applications are created and deployed to a location on a web server that is exposed to the Internet. Every resource available on the Internet is assigned a unique address. A user is then able to request a resource that is available online, typically by using a web browser. Most web application technologies require that the web server hosting the application meet minimal standards, possibly be equipped with particular hardware or software, and be configured in a particular manner.

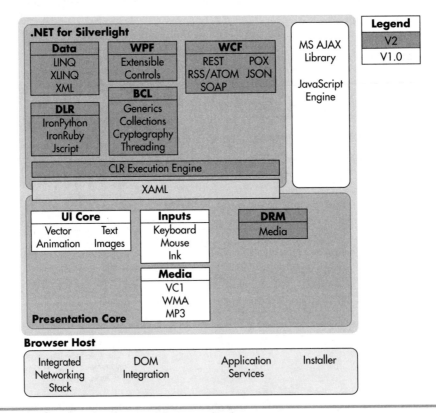

Figure 1-7 Silverlight features and functionality by version

Silverlight was designed to be server and client agnostic, meaning that it can, potentially, be hosted on any web server and executed on any web client. The reality is that a Silverlight application can be executed on web clients (as described in the next section) currently supported and can be hosted on virtually any web server. The server-side hosting requirements for a Silverlight application are negligible because the server only needs to be configured as it would be for hosting simple HTML applications. The two most commonly used web servers are Microsoft Internet Information Services (IIS) and Apache.

Supported Web Client Platforms

The server hosting a Silverlight application must only adhere to minimal requirements. However, the Silverlight plug-in can be downloaded and installed only on web client machines that are running an operating system (platform) on which the plug-in is designed to run. The goal is that, eventually, Silverlight will be available for all, or most, operating systems. Currently, the Silverlight plug-in is available for the following operating systems.

Microsoft Windows

Silverlight is available for the following versions of Microsoft Windows:

- Microsoft Windows Vista

- Microsoft Windows XP SP2

- Microsoft Windows 2000

- Microsoft Windows 2003

- Microsoft Windows 2008

Macintosh

Silverlight is available for the following versions of the Macintosh operating system:

- Mac OS 10.4.8+ (PowerPC)

- Mac OS 10.4.8+ (Intel based)

Linux

In an effort to make Silverlight available to more web client platforms, in 2007, Microsoft struck a deal with Novell to develop a version of the Silverlight plug-in for the Linux operating system. A version of the .NET Framework, known as the Mono project, runs on the Linux operating system. The version of the Silverlight plug-in that runs on Linux is called Moonlight. The open-source developers of the Mono project have done a phenomenal job of keeping Mono synchronized with the version of the .NET Framework developed by Microsoft, and they developed Moonlight in just 21 days!

Supported Web Browsers

Just as Silverlight will eventually be available for most operating systems, Silverlight will eventually be available for most web browsers. Silverlight is currently available for the following web browsers.

Microsoft Internet Explorer

Internet Explorer is Microsoft's web browser. Silverlight was available first for Internet Explorer and is currently supported by the following versions of Internet Explorer:

- Internet Explorer versions 7 and 8 on Windows Vista, Windows XP SP2, Windows Server 2003, and Windows Server 2008

- Internet Explorer version 6 on Windows XP SP2, Windows Server 2003, and Windows 2000

Figure 1-8 illustrates a simple Silverlight application as displayed in Internet Explorer version 8 on Windows Vista.

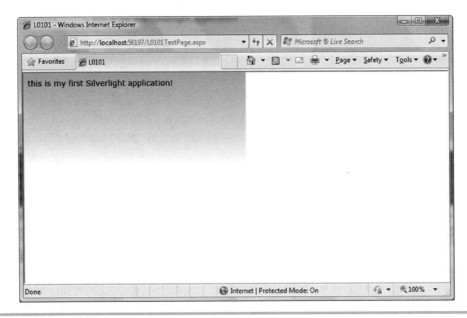

Figure 1-8   A Silverlight 3 application in Internet Explorer 8 on Windows Vista

Try This Build and Test a Simple Silverlight Application

Perform the following steps to quickly build and test a very simple Silverlight 3 application:

1. Start or open Visual Studio 2008.

2. Select File | New | Project to display the New Project dialog.

3. Under the .NET Framework programming language of choice (Visual C# as an example), select the Silverlight node in the Project Types pane on the left side of the dialog.

4. Select Silverlight Application from the Templates pane on the right side of the dialog.

5. At the bottom of the dialog, assign the project to be created a name and select a location to create the new project.

6. Click the OK button at the bottom of the dialog to create the new Silverlight application project. The process of creating the project may take a few seconds.

7. When prompted with the New Silverlight Application dialog, click the OK button to accept the default settings.

8. If the default name was assigned to the new Silverlight project, the project will be named something similar to SilverlightApplication1. In the Visual Studio 2008 Solution Explorer, right-click the MainPage.xaml file and select Open in Expression Blend from the context menu.

9. If a Security Warning dialog appears, click the Yes button.

10. Once the file is open in Expression Blend, select a TextBlock from the toolbox and drop it onto the Silverlight design surface. With the newly dropped TextBlock selected, adjust the properties of the TextBlock as desired.

11. Close Expression Blend and save the updated MainPage.xaml file.

12. When prompted by Visual Studio 2008 to reload the updated MainPage.xaml file, click the Yes button.

13. In Visual Studio 2008, select the green play button (Execute) from the toolbar or press F5 to execute the new Silverlight application.

14. When prompted to enable debugging for the project, click the OK button.

(continued)

15. The newly created Silverlight project should be displayed using Microsoft Internet Explorer.

16. Close Internet Explorer to return to Visual Studio 2008.

17. To view the Silverlight application using other browsers, right-click the SilverlightApplication1TestPage.aspx file in the Visual Studio 2008 Solution Explorer and select Browse With… from the context menu.

18. Select the desired browser from the list of registered browsers and then click the Browse button to view the application or click the Add button to register a new browser with Visual Studio 2008.

19. When finished exploring and viewing the Silverlight application, close Visual Studio 2008.

Mozilla Firefox
Silverlight is currently supported by Firefox versions 1.5, 2, and 3 on the following operating systems:

- Windows Vista
- Windows XP SP2
- Windows 2000
- Windows Server 2003
- Windows Server 2008
- Mac OS 10.4.8+ for the PowerPC
- Mac OS 10.4.8+ for the Intel-based PC

Figure 1-9 illustrates a simple Silverlight application as displayed in Firefox version 2 on Windows Vista.

Apple Safari
Silverlight is currently supported by Safari version 3 on the following operating systems:

- Mac OS 10.4.8+ for the PowerPC
- Mac OS 10.4.8+ for the Intel-based PC
- Windows Vista
- Windows XP SP2

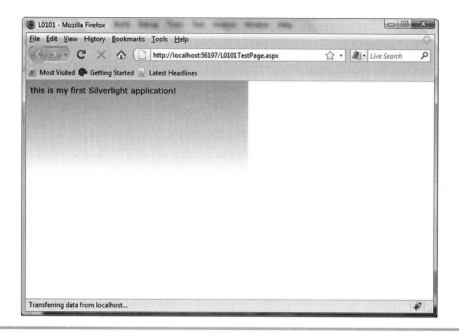

Figure 1-9   A Silverlight 3 application in Firefox 2 on Windows Vista

- Windows Server 2003

- Windows Server 2008

Figure 1-10 illustrates a simple Silverlight application as displayed in Safari version 3.1.1 on Windows Vista.

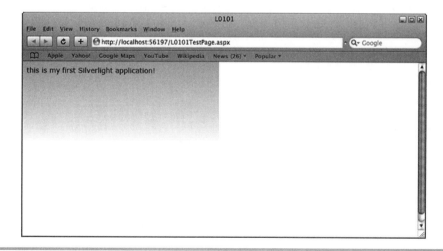

Figure 1-10   A Silverlight 3 application in Safari 3 on Windows Vista
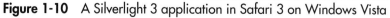

Opera

Silverlight 3 is not officially supported by the Opera browser. As a result, Silverlight applications may sporadically function in Opera even in Silverlight 3.

Conclusion

Microsoft has, once again, delivered a new technology that is already, even in its infancy, taking the industry by storm. Silverlight further extends the .NET Framework technologies, namely Windows Presentation Foundation (WPF), to the client's browser space, thus reinforcing the popularity and success of the .NET Framework. Silverlight is a downloadable plug-in that is optimized for the display of graphics, animations, and media and is platform and browser agnostic.

Chapter 2

.NET Framework 3.5

Key Concepts & Skills

- Gain a basic understanding of the technologies included in the .NET Framework, version 3.0 and version 3.5

- Explore the Extensible Application Markup Language (XAML)

- Examine the primary tools used to work with XAML, WPF, and Silverlight applications

- Learn how to create an application using Windows Presentation Foundation (WPF), the predecessor of Silverlight

- Understand the basics of creating a Windows Communication Foundation (WCF) service that can later be consumed by a Silverlight application

As mentioned in the previous chapter, the .NET Framework was originally released in 2000. Since that time, the .NET Framework has been continually upgraded, extended, and enhanced to provide developers with the latest technology available. The current version of the .NET Framework is version 3.5, Service Pack 1. The .NET Framework includes several technologies that aided in the development of Silverlight and can be utilized from Silverlight applications.

.NET Framework 3.5 Technologies

Version 2.0 of the .NET Framework was released in 2005 and included improvements and enhancements to the technologies that were included in earlier versions of the .NET Framework. Then, .NET Framework 3.0 built upon version 2.0 by adding new technologies to the mix. It introduced Windows Presentation Foundation (WPF), Windows Communication Foundation (WCF), Windows Workflow Foundation (WF, so as to not conflict with the WWF wrestling acronym), and Windows CardSpace. Version 3.5 of the .NET Framework built upon version 3.0 by introducing ASP.NET AJAX and Language Integrated Query (LINQ). The .NET Framework 3.5 Service Pack 1 grants many features and new technologies that have been under testing over the past year first-class citizen status in the .NET Framework. Likewise, Microsoft intends to release an update to the .NET Framework in the very

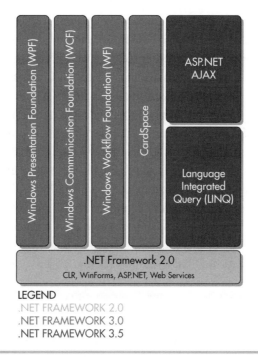

Figure 2-1 The .NET Framework versions

near future that will make Silverlight an integral part of the .NET Framework. Figure 2-1 illustrates the .NET Framework 3.5 technologies.

The Extensible Application Markup Language (XAML)

The Extensible Application Markup Language (XAML, pronounced *zammel)* is a custom XML grammar that Microsoft created for use in WPF.

In 2005, Microsoft realized the popularity of the .NET Framework as well as the popularity of integrating their other development products with the .NET Framework. As evidence, in that same year Microsoft had released SQL Server 2005, their premiere database server and one of the top three database management systems on the market. In redesigning SQL Server into SQL Server 2005, Microsoft designed SQL Server natively around .NET Framework 2.0. The decision to integrate the .NET Framework into SQL Server 2005 was an immediate hit with developers who were already familiar with the .NET development paradigm. In an effort to keep pace, both Oracle and IBM immediately released updates to their database management systems so that their systems could make external calls to .NET Framework assemblies.

Bolstered by community approval of recent design decisions around the .NET Framework, Microsoft began looking at other technologies in their fold that could benefit from being designed around and integrated into the .NET Framework. At that time, the technology available in the .NET Framework used to create Windows applications was called Windows Forms, and it was an immediate candidate for being redesigned. Along with the redesign of Windows Forms, Microsoft decided to redesign the graphics libraries, known as the GDI+ libraries, which resided in Windows and were used by developers for creating and managing graphics. The GDI+ libraries had never been redesigned for the .NET Framework and posed memory-management issues for developers who utilized them in the .NET Framework as they remained unmanaged libraries.

Microsoft decided to create the new Windows development technology using the same development paradigm and architecture that ASP.NET developers were already very familiar with. The existing ASP.NET architecture utilizes a file that contains markup and defines the layout of the user interface as well as a file that contains code written in C#, VB, or another managed language known as the *code-behind file.* The newly redesigned Windows development technology was called Windows Presentation Foundation (WPF). In order to build WPF using the same architecture as ASP.NET, Microsoft had to create a markup language that could be used to define WPF interfaces. The markup language created was XAML.

A XAML file is used to define user interface components and layout. A parser reads the XAML file and instantiates objects behind the scenes to build and lay out the interface indicated. As related to WPF, a XAML file may contain one of three document elements: the <Window> element, the <Page> element, or the <UserControl> element, depending on the type of WPF application created. If a standard WPF application is created, the XAML file will contain a <Window> document element. If a WPF XAML Browser application (XBAP) is created, the XAML file will contain a <Page> document element. XAML files are well formed with the exception that they do not contain an XML prolog (<?xml version="1.0"?>) by default. If an XML prolog is added to a XAML file, the XAML file should be readable and editable in any XML editor.

XAML Namespaces

A XAML document element contains two namespace references, by default. A XAML document may reference additional namespaces and custom assemblies as well. The two namespaces included in a XAML document by default are the WPF namespace and the XAML namespace.

The WPF namespace is configured as the default namespace because most markup contained in a WPF XAML file will be associated with the WPF namespace. The XAML namespace is typically assigned a prefix of "x," and when markup is included in a XAML document that should be associated with the XAML namespace, it is assigned the "x:" prefix. The following markup illustrates a default WPF XAML document:

```
<Window x:Class="L0201.Window1"
    xmlns="http://schemas.microsoft.com/winfx/2006/xaml/presentation"
    xmlns:x="http://schemas.microsoft.com/winfx/2006/xaml"
    Title="Window1" Height="300" Width="300">
    <Grid>

    </Grid>
</Window>
```

XAML Tools

The primary tools for creating and manipulating XAML documents are those tools available from Microsoft; however, several third-party XAML tools are on the horizon, including KaXAML.

Microsoft Visual Studio 2010

Microsoft Visual Studio 2010 is Microsoft's premiere development tool. All development tools from Microsoft have now been assimilated into Visual Studio. Figure 2-2 shows the Visual Studio 2010 start page.

Microsoft Expression Blend

Microsoft has developed and released an entire suite of tools, called the Microsoft Expression Suite, that is designed for preparing user interfaces, graphics, and media for WPF and Silverlight applications. The primary tool in the Expression Suite for creating and manipulating XAML files is Microsoft Expression Blend. Figure 2-3 shows Expression Blend.

Figure 2-2 Visual Studio 2010 start page

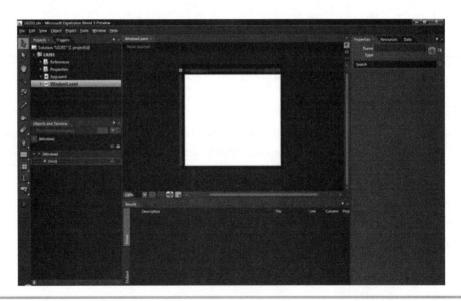

Figure 2-3 Expression Blend

NOTE
As mentioned, Visual Studio 2010 is Microsoft's primary development environment and will be the primary tool used by developers. The Expression Suite of tools was designed for designers. However, both tools share a common solution and project file format so that either tool can be used to create and manage Silverlight projects.

XAML Power Toys

XAML Power Toys is a third-party set of utilities used to extend Visual Studio 2010's XAML functionality. XAML Power Toys was developed by Karl Shifflett, a Microsoft developer, and is primarily used to ease the creation of line of business (LOB) XAML applications. XAML Power Toys offers the developer the following capabilities:

- Easily create a ViewModel class stub

- Automatically create a WPF or Silverlight DataGrid for a selected class

- Create a WPF ListView for a selected class

- Create a business form for a selected class

- Show a list of data members for a selected class

The XAML Power Toys menu is shown in Figure 2-4.

Figure 2-4   XAML Power Toys menu

For more information on XAML Power Toys, visit Karl Shifflett's website at http://karlshifflett.wordpress.com/xaml-power-toys/.

MoXAML Power Toys

MoXAML Power Toys was developed by Pete O'Hanlon as an extension to the XAML Power Toys and includes functionality for directly formatting XAML. MoXAML Power Toys provides the following functionality:

- Easy beautification and formatting of XAML markup

- Direct search the Web for a selected keyword

- The ability to mark selected XAML as a comment

- The ability to automatically add a status bar, toolbar, and menu to an application

The MoXAML Power Toys menu is shown in Figure 2-5.

For more information on MoXAML Power Toys, visit Pete O'Hanlon's blog at http://peteohanlon.wordpress.com/moxaml-power-toys/.

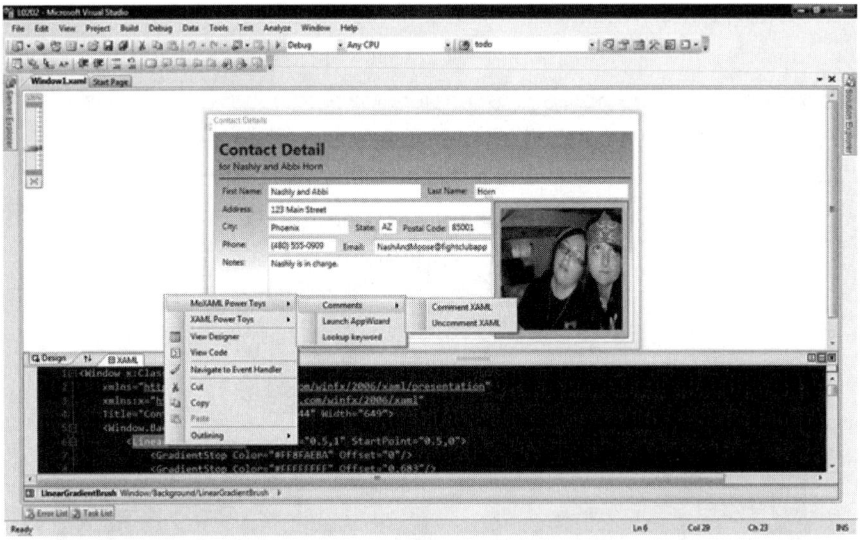

Figure 2-5 MoXAML Power Toys menu

Figure 2-6   KaXAML editor

KaXAML

KaXAML is a simple third-party XAML editor. KaXAML does not include all the functionality included in Visual Studio 2010 or Expression Blend but is simple and lightweight. Each new version of KaXAML released includes new features, but the goal of KaXAML is to remain lightweight. KaXAML is shown in Figure 2-6.

For more information on KaXAML, visit the KaXAML website at http://www.kaxaml .com/.

Windows Presentation Foundation (WPF)

Windows Presentation Foundation (WPF) is the redesigned and improved version of the .NET technology that is utilized for creating Windows applications and working with graphics, animations, and media. Windows Forms and GDI+ technologies will continue to be supported by Microsoft and can still be utilized, but they lack many of the media features available in WPF. Additionally, Windows Forms are created using a "VB style" of development, whereas WPF forms are built on the same file architecture as ASP.NET pages. WPF enables the creation of elaborate and dynamic rich user interfaces that were not possible using earlier technologies. Microsoft was very pleased with WPF and utilized it to create the user interface for Windows Vista.

Here are some points to note about WPF:

- WPF provides a common, .NET-centric environment for creating rich Windows applications and user interfaces that maintains compatibility with older presentation technologies. All presentation and user-interface development created in the future that targets a Microsoft or web client should be created by using WPF or Silverlight.

- WPF provides a proper separation of developer and designer roles. Due to Visual Studio and Expression Blend utilizing the same solution and project architecture, developers and designers can collaborate simultaneously on projects.

- WPF enables both Windows and web applications to be created using a common technology (through the use of Silverlight).

Here's a list of the technologies included in WPF:

- A complete application development framework that is integrated into the .NET Framework 3.0+

- Dynamic user interface layout management and a gamut of user interface controls that are fully extensible

- Complete support for styles and templates

- Advanced text formatting and display capabilities (using ClearType) that greatly increase text readability

- Support for both fixed and flow layout documents and the introduction of a brand-new fixed-layout document format known as XML Paper Specification (XPS)

- Dynamic display of image formats, video, audio, 2-D graphics, 3-D graphics, transformations, effects, and animations

- Advanced data binding capabilities

WPF Example

Although comprehensive coverage of WPF is beyond the scope of this book, a quick example of WPF directly relates to Silverlight because Silverlight is a subset of WPF technology. The following WPF form is a simple form prototype that illustrates displaying contact information.

Try This   Create a WPF Application

1. Start or open Visual Studio 2010.

2. Select File | New | Project to display the New Project dialog.

3. Under the .NET Programming language of choice, select the Windows node from the Project Types pane on the left side of the New Project dialog.

4. Select WPF Application from the Templates pane on the right side of the New Project dialog.

5. Assign a name to the new WPF application, select a location to create the new application, and click the OK button.

6. Use the visual WPF designer in Visual Studio 2010 to lay out and design a form similar to the one shown in Figure 2-7.

7. Drag controls from the Visual Studio 2010 Toolbox and drop them on the WPF form. Drag and resize the controls to design the form.

8. Use the XAML viewer at the bottom of the WPF designer to examine the XAML rendered as the WPF form is designed.

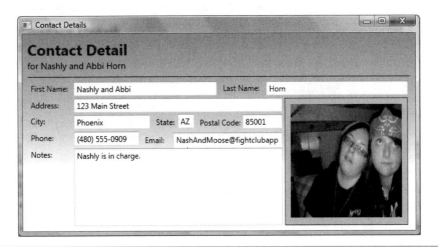

Figure 2-7   The contact information WPF form

(continued)

9. Click the green play button (Start Debugging) on the Visual Studio 2010 toolbar or press F5 to display the WPF form created.

10. When the form is complete, close Visual Studio 2010.

Alternatively, Microsoft Expression Blend can be used to directly create the WPF prototype form and application. However, bear in mind that Blend can be used only to design the visual aspect of the form and cannot be used to add code to the form.

The resultant WPF form is shown in Figure 2-7.

```
<Window x:Class="L0202.Window1"
    xmlns="http://schemas.microsoft.com/winfx/2006/xaml/presentation"
    xmlns:x="http://schemas.microsoft.com/winfx/2006/xaml"
    Title="Contact Details" Height="344" Width="649">
    <Window.Background>
        <LinearGradientBrush EndPoint="0.5,1" StartPoint="0.5,0">
            <GradientStop Color="#FF8FAEBA" Offset="0"/>
            <GradientStop Color="#FFFFFFFF" Offset="0.683"/>
        </LinearGradientBrush>
    </Window.Background>
    <Canvas>
        <TextBlock Width="617" Height="45" TextWrapping="Wrap"
        Canvas.Left="8" Canvas.Top="8" Text="Contact Detail"
        FontSize="24" FontWeight="Bold" Foreground="#FF252E6A"/>
        <TextBlock Width="617" Height="Auto"
        TextWrapping="Wrap" Canvas.Left="8" Canvas.Top="40">
        <Run FontSize="14" Text="for Nashly Horn"/>
        </TextBlock>
        <Path Width="617" Height="1" Fill="#FFFFFFFF"
        Stretch="Fill" Stroke="#FF000000" Canvas.Left="8"
        Canvas.Top="67" Data="M10,67 L624,67"/>
        <Label Width="Auto" Height="Auto"
        Content="First Name:" Canvas.Left="8" Canvas.Top="72"/>
        <TextBox Width="230" Height="Auto" Text="Nashly and Abbi"
         TextWrapping="Wrap" Canvas.Left="81.683" Canvas.Top="75"/>
        <Label Width="Auto" Height="Auto"
        Content="Last Name:" Canvas.Left="317" Canvas.Top="72"/>
        <TextBox Width="230" Height="Auto" Text="Horn"
        TextWrapping="Wrap" Canvas.Left="390.683" Canvas.Top="75"/>
        <Label Width="Auto" Height="Auto" Content="Address:"
        Canvas.Left="8" Canvas.Top="97.96"/>
        <TextBox Width="335" Height="Auto"
        Text="123 Main Street" TextWrapping="Wrap"
        Canvas.Left="81.683" Canvas.Top="100.96"/>
```

```
      <Label Width="Auto" Height="Auto" Content="City:"
      Canvas.Left="8" Canvas.Top="122.92"/>
      <TextBox Width="123.51" Height="Auto" Text="Phoenix"
      TextWrapping="Wrap" Canvas.Left="81.683" Canvas
          .Top="126.92"/>
      <Border Width="200" Height="199.04"
      Canvas.Left="420.683" Canvas.Top="100.96"
          Background="#FFBED8CA"
      BorderBrush="#FF252E6A" BorderThickness="1,1,1,1"/>
      <Label Width="Auto" Height="Auto"
      Content="State:" Canvas.Left="209.193" Canvas.Top="124.92"/>
      <TextBox Width="26.817" Height="Auto" Text="AZ"
      TextWrapping="Wrap" Canvas.Left="248.683"
          Canvas.Top="125.92"/>
      <Label Width="Auto" Height="Auto"
      Content="Postal Code:" Canvas.Left="279.5"
          Canvas.Top="125.92"/>
      <TextBox Width="63.693" Height="Auto" Text="85001"
      TextWrapping="Wrap" Canvas.Left="352.99"
          Canvas.Top="126.92"/>
      <Label Width="Auto" Height="Auto" Content="Phone:"
      Canvas.Left="8" Canvas.Top="148.88"/>
      <TextBox Width="105.51" Height="Auto"
      Text="(480) 555-0909" TextWrapping="Wrap"
          Canvas.Left="81.683"
      Canvas.Top="152.88"/>
      <Label Width="Auto" Height="Auto" Content="Email:"
      Canvas.Left="191.193" Canvas.Top="152.88"/>
      <TextBox Width="175.283" Height="Auto"
      Text="nash@fightclubfightgear.com" TextWrapping="Wrap"
      Canvas.Left="241.4" Canvas.Top="154.88"/>
      <Label Width="Auto" Height="Auto" Content="Notes:"
      Canvas.Left="8" Canvas.Top="174.84"/>
      <TextBox Width="335" Height="121.16"
      Text="Nashly is in charge." TextWrapping="Wrap"
      Canvas.Left="81.683" Canvas.Top="178.84"/>
      <Image Width="181" Height="177" Canvas.Left="430"
      Canvas.Top="111" Source="DSC03758.JPG"/>
    </Canvas>
</Window>
```

For more information on WPF, visit the WPF website located at http://msdn.microsoft.
com/en-us/netframework/aa663326.aspx.

Windows Communication Foundation (WCF)

The .NET Framework has always included the functionality for creating distributed applications. A *distributed application* is an application that is composed of components and services located on different physical machines and in different physical locations. The .NET Framework distributed technologies include creating, hosting, and consuming Web Services. A Web Service is a service, most commonly available over the Web, that complies with the service-oriented architecture (SOA). Web Services and SOA are industry standards for creating components that provide services, generally data-related services, and expose them over the Web for client applications to utilize, or consume.

Web Services are capable of receiving data from and sending data to client applications using several protocols. The protocol most commonly used when Web Services were first introduced was the Simple Object Access Protocol (SOAP). SOAP is an XML grammar that is useful for transporting data; however, SOAP can become bloated when large amounts of data or binary data is transported. A newer and more succinct communication protocol commonly in use is JavaScript Object Notation (JSON). Regardless of the data packaging protocol in use, Web Services generally send and receive messages over the Hypertext Transport Protocol (HTTP).

Due to Web Services using portable protocols over HTTP, in most scenarios Web Services are easily accessible even through firewalls and the SOAP, and JSON protocol standards are supported by most development environments. Regardless of the ease of use, due to Web Services utilizing portable protocols, they may not offer the best performance in all scenarios. If better performance is the goal, and a development team has control of or access to all servers that host components that comprise a distributed application, an alternative technology, known as .NET Remoting, could be implemented. When .NET Remoting is used, the .NET Framework must be installed on all host servers.

The support for Web Services and .NET Remoting was available when the .NET Framework was introduced. When Microsoft designed .NET Framework 3.0, they decided to consolidate, enhance, and improve the .NET Framework distributed technologies and thus delivered Windows Communication Foundation (WCF). Although Web Services can still be created by using the .NET Framework, WCF encompasses the ability to create web-based and standard server-based distributed applications.

WCF provides the following features:

- An advanced system for configuring endpoints in a distributed environment

- The ability to configure communication protocols to be used between endpoints

- A reliable system for sending and receiving messages between endpoints

- The ability to send messages asynchronously, secured and managed through transactions

- Functionality for serializing and deserializing primitive, complex, and binary data

In a nutshell, WCF is an elaborate system for creating distributed systems by using .NET Framework 3.0. For more information on WCF, visit the WCF website at http://msdn.microsoft.com/en-us/netframework/aa663324.aspx.

Windows Workflow Foundation (WF)

Windows Workflow Foundation (WF) is used to document workflows, both system based and human based, as well as a combination of both. A *workflow* is a real-world set of activities that can be documented in their order of precedence. WF is a layer on top of .NET Framework 3.0 and is created and maintained by using .NET programming languages. Visual Studio 2010 provides a designer for WF, and all future Microsoft products that implement a workflow of some type (this includes most products) will utilize and benefit from WF. Workflows are documented graphically by using the WF designer, and WF then mostly automates the creation of the underlying objects, code, and services.

In many scenarios, a workflow represents a process that may require human interaction at one or more points along the process in order for it to continue. Human interaction is an unknown *activity*. WF includes the ability to put a workflow to sleep for an indefinite amount of time. When a workflow is put to sleep, it is serialized to a data store, where it can persist indefinitely and even survive system reboots. When a workflow is sleeping, WF will listen for requests for the workflow. When a request is initiated, the workflow is awakened and reinstantiated to resume right where it left off when it was put to sleep.

WF provides the following features:

- A runtime engine and services for managing workflows. Workflow process steps may be represented by objects and services as well.

- Advanced design tools and a modeler through Visual Studio 2010.

- Indefinite persistence of workflows.

- Workflow management through transactions, tracking, timing, and threading.

WF can be integrated with Silverlight, but at the time of this writing it is not being implemented commonly in a Silverlight context. For more information on WF, visit the WF website located at http://msdn.microsoft.com/en-us/netframework/aa663328.aspx.

Windows CardSpace

Windows CardSpace is Microsoft's new digital identity management system. CardSpace is client-side software that is included with .NET Framework 3.0. CardSpace stores a user's digital identities and presents them to users in the form of visual cards, as shown in Figure 2-8.

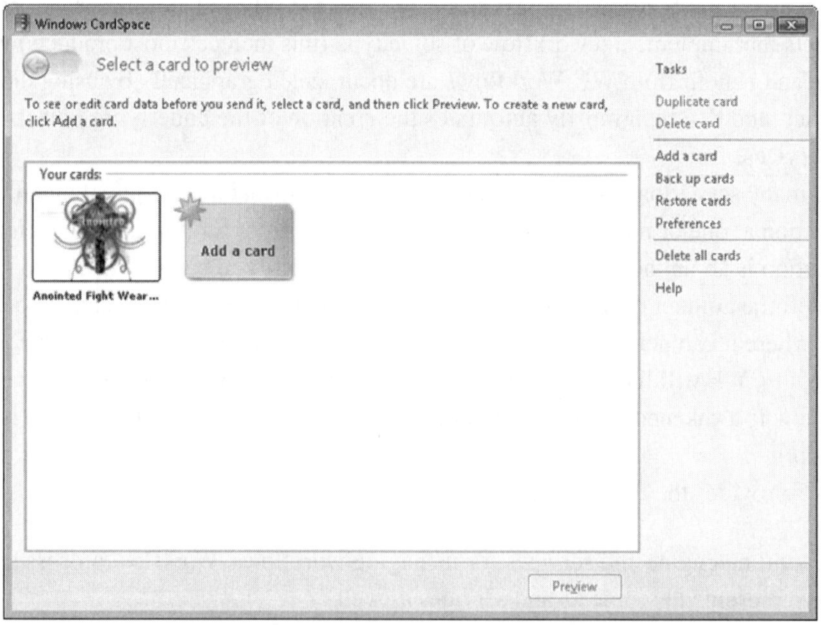

Figure 2-8 Windows CardSpace manager

CardSpace is used to identify users over the Web. Users can create their own identities and verify those identities through third-party vendors. When a website needs to authenticate a user, it can make a request of CardSpace. At that time, CardSpace will display the user's identities to the user as well as information on the website making the request. The user can then select the identity to use for authentication at the website. CardSpace can then contact the third-party vendor who issued the digital identity to the user to verify that the user identity is valid and, in turn, acquire a digitally signed XML token to send to the website for authenticating the user.

CardSpace is built on the latest Web Service (WS) protocols and provides the following features:

- A unified, secure, private, and interoperable method for managing digital identities

- Support for any digital identity system

- User control of digital identities

- Replacement of password-based web login mechanisms

- Improved user confidence in web security and authentication

For more information on CardSpace, visit the CardSpace website located at http://msdn.microsoft.com/en-us/netframework/aa663320.aspx.

ASP.NET AJAX

Through the progression of Microsoft's attempts to improve web development and offload more processing to the client's computer, Remote Scripting (RS) was introduced in 1997. Remote Scripting instantiated an ActiveX control, the XMLHTTPRequest object, through JavaScript to initiate asynchronous calls to the web server. This approach significantly improved web application responsiveness and performance. However, ActiveX controls are reliant upon the Microsoft Windows operating system; thus, RS through the use of an ActiveX control was not portable to non-Microsoft operating systems. To sidestep this limitation, Microsoft moved forward by building RS support into Internet Explorer itself. Hence, any operating system that supports Internet Explorer could then support RS. The idea and concept caught the attention of competing web browser developers and they, too, integrated support for the XMLHTTPRequest object into their browsers. RS functioned by using JavaScript to asynchronously send XML to and receive XML from the server; hence, Microsoft named RS technology Asynchronous JavaScript and XML (AJAX).

In 2006, Microsoft released ASP.NET AJAX, the implementation of Ajax integrated into ASP.NET. ASP.NET AJAX consists of three primary components: a client-side library or framework that significantly extends what client-side JavaScript is capable of doing, server-side programming and development extensions that allow ASP.NET AJAX to integrate nicely into Visual Studio, and a community-developed and supported toolkit. The ASP.NET AJAX architecture is illustrated in Figure 2-9. A nice feature included in the AJAX client-side library is the extension of JavaScript to enable many object-oriented development features by using JavaScript.

As Figure 2-9 illustrates, on the server side, the AJAX extensions provide a handful of AJAX controls, with the two primary controls being the ScriptManager and the UpdatePanel. Every ASP.NET Web Form that needs to be "AJAX enabled" must include one and only one ScriptManager control. The ScriptManager control instructs the ASP.NET

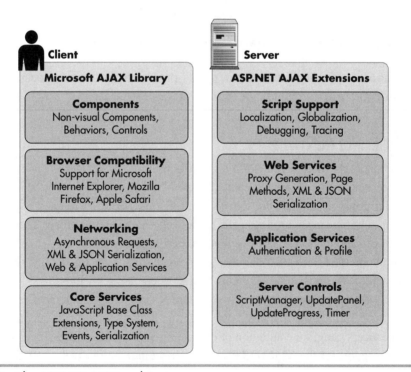

Figure 2-9 The ASP.NET AJAX architecture

engine to configure the outgoing response to the client for working with AJAX and to include the script library when sending the response. Each ASP.NET Web Form that needs to be AJAX enabled may contain one or more UpdatePanel controls. The UpdatePanel serves as a container for portions of the Web Form and controls that should utilize AJAX.

ASP.NET AJAX can be extended by downloading the ASP.NET AJAX Control Toolkit from http://www.codeplex.com. Furthermore, ASP.NET AJAX calls to the server can be improved by making them directly to a Web Service instead of posting back to the server. For more information on ASP.NET AJAX, visit the ASP.NET AJAX website located at http://www.asp.net/ajax/.

Language Integrated Query (LINQ)

The final major addition to the .NET Framework in version 3.5 is Language Integrated Query (LINQ). Most seasoned developers have mastered or are adequately familiar with the Structured Query Language (SQL). SQL is used to query relational database data. However, in many cases, SQL queries that pull data from a relational database schema are abstracted away from business logic and middle-tier code. Furthermore, data is generally represented at the business logic and code level through objects, arrays, and collections. Developers regularly have to search these constructs by using tailor-made loops.

Many programmers have long requested a language for querying data stored in programming constructs and object-oriented mechanisms. SQL is a stable and well-entrenched industry standard. It would be an insurmountable task to attempt to extend SQL so that it could be used to query programming constructs. However, Microsoft was determined to make things easier for programmers by creating a standard for querying data stored in coding constructs. The result of their efforts was a new query language that targets data stored in objects and collections—Language Integrated Query (LINQ). LINQ was also extended to query relational data stored in databases, XML data, and other data sources. However, data queried by using LINQ must be stored as objects. If data is queried from a relational data source using LINQ, it must first be represented using an object model.

Microsoft has released a bridge, called LINQ to SQL, that accommodates pulling data from SQL Server to be queried using LINQ. However, LINQ to SQL currently only supports connecting to SQL Server in the released version. Another option for developers to utilize LINQ with databases beyond SQL Server is to use the ADO.NET

Entity Framework. The ADO.NET Entity Framework adds an abstraction layer between code and a data source so that database entities can be treated as objects and in a consistent manner.

For more information on LINQ, visit the LINQ Project website located at http://msdn .microsoft.com/en-us/netframework/aa904594.aspx.

For more information on the ADO.NET Entity Framework, visit the MSDN article "ADO.NET Entity Framework Overview," located at http://msdn.microsoft.com/en-us/ library/aa697427(VS.80).aspx.

Down the Road: .NET Framework 4

Although documentation is limited, Microsoft is readying the world for the next rendition of the .NET Framework—version 4. Version 4 of the .NET Framework will include upgraded and enhanced versions of each of the contained technologies. Additionally, developers will be able to utilize version 4 using the new Visual Studio 2010. Visual Studio 2010 will include many new features and will focus heavily on delivering new modeling and testing features. Figure 2-10 shows the .NET Framework 4 technology poster prepared by Brad Abrams.

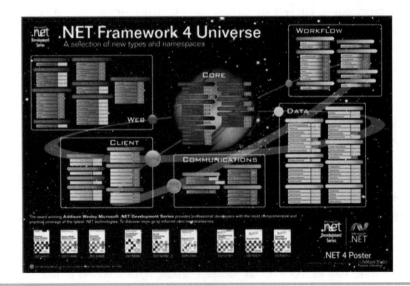

Figure 2-10   .NET Framework 4 technology poster

The .NET Framework 4 technology poster can be downloaded in PDF format by visiting Brad Abrams' website at http://blogs.msdn.com/brada/archive/2008/10/29/net-framework-4-poster.aspx.

Conclusion

Although Silverlight applications can be created without knowledge of prior and related technologies, having this knowledge will certainly increase the intellectual toolkit and effectiveness of a Silverlight developer. Furthermore, Silverlight applications can be enhanced and extended by utilizing .NET Framework 3.5 technologies such as WCF, LINQ, and ASP.NET AJAX.

Chapter 3

The Silverlight Framework

Key Concepts & Skills

- Learn about the architecture of a Silverlight application and how Silverlight compares to Windows Presentation Foundation (WPF)

- Explore how to install Silverlight

- Investigate the programming languages supported by Silverlight

- Gain an introductory understanding of the tools used to create Silverlight applications

- Integrate Silverlight content with ASP.NET AJAX

- Create a simple Silverlight application and a simple Silverlight animation

S ilverlight is the most recent major development technology to be offered by Microsoft. Developers who aspire to specialize in creating Silverlight applications must be fully aware of the steps and aspects involved. This chapter focuses on the process of creating Silverlight applications.

Overview

Silverlight is a logical progression of Microsoft technologies. Microsoft technologies progressed from separate technologies that were not designed to intercommunicate and were not designed for creating web applications to Active Server Pages (ASP), Microsoft's first dynamic web development technology. As mentioned somewhat in Chapter 1, in order to remain competitive in the industry, Microsoft decided to completely redesign and consolidate all their development technologies into a single platform, the .NET Framework. All Microsoft development technologies were not redesigned around the .NET Framework overnight, but all have been redesigned since the year 2000.

The .NET Framework is the most popular and the most commonly used development environment available. One facet of the .NET Framework is ASP.NET. ASP.NET is the .NET Framework version of Active Server Pages. ASP.NET is used to create extremely powerful, dynamic web applications where the bulk of the processing occurs on the server.

As the Web has evolved over the years, businesses and developers have adopted the Web as a primary development platform. A term was coined to describe the new era of web applications: *Web 2.0.* Web 2.0 specifies that web applications should be composed of original developer efforts and should consume services offered by other companies and developers. Web 2.0 applications are partially designed on the publisher-subscriber paradigm and integrate media and animation.

Over the years, web developers began to look at ways to improve web application performance. The Web is composed of millions of interlinked computers, again, with the bulk of processing occurring on servers. Web 2.0 indicates that networks, including the Internet, should be powered by a conglomeration of distributed computing power. The vast majority of computers on the Web, client computers, have been acting as dumb terminals for years. Developers have looked at methods for utilizing the untapped computing power available in client computers attached to the Web. Several methods, such as ASP.NET AJAX, have been developed that perform more processing on the client's computer than standard web applications. ASP.NET AJAX uses JavaScript to asynchronously pass data to a server in XML format, thus delivering a user-perceived improvement in performance and a better user experience. Web applications that work to improve performance to deliver a better user experience are referred to as *rich interactive applications (RIAs).*

The downside to standard RIA solutions is that they perform client-side processing using JavaScript. JavaScript is powerful but is executed directly by the user's browser and is therefore at the mercy of the browser's capacity to correctly execute the script.

Microsoft began experimenting to extend ASP.NET AJAX to further gain control over the client-side computing environment to improve the technology. Microsoft also wanted to determine how they could offer the ability to create incredible user interfaces using technology similar to Windows Presentation Foundation (WPF). As a result, Microsoft developed a new downloadable plug-in technology that extends ASP.NET AJAX and incorporates the functionality and rendering capabilities of WPF. The resultant technology was originally named *WPF/E (Windows Presentation Foundation/Everywhere)* and was eventually renamed *Silverlight.*

Silverlight is available in three versions: version 1.0, version 2, and version 3. Version 1.0 was fairly limited in functionality, and JavaScript was the only language supported. Version 2 includes a gamut of new features, and many .NET-compliant programming languages are now supported. Version 3 extends and fine-tunes the features and functionality of Silverlight 2.

Silverlight vs. WPF

Silverlight is a subset of Windows Presentation Foundation that also extends and utilizes many of the features and aspects of ASP.NET AJAX. With the bulk of software development today targeting the Web, many developers question why they need to create WPF applications at all now that Silverlight has arrived. Although that is a valid point, the answer is that both technologies have their strengths. Silverlight's strengths lie in its portability over the Web. However, Silverlight is cross-platform and cross-browser compliant, and as such it is platform agnostic and cannot take advantage of or be reliant upon any particular environment or platform. More advanced graphics features require hardware support and must take advantage of a platform's features. As such, WPF provides advanced 3-D graphics features that perform very well, whereas Silverlight is not able to fully provide these features at this time. Silverlight not being able to rely upon any particular hardware currently limits its ability to support advanced 3-D graphics, speech and voice recognition, recording, and so on, although several developers and third parties are working to simulate a 3-D environment using Silverlight.

Silverlight 3 is constricted somewhat by the same limitation in accessing local client hardware. However, Silverlight 3 introduces the ability to simulate a 3-D environment using 2-D images. The new 3-D simulation functionality is called perspective 3-D. Perspective 3-D is simple to implement by using a XAML element to adjust the viewer's "perspective" of the image being displayed. Perspective 3-D is illustrated in Chapter 4.

Silverlight must also function in the realm of a secure sandbox in order to provide a secure client environment. However, the sandbox does limit Silverlight's ability to directly interact with the host operating system and perform direct I/O functionality. Silverlight 3 extends some of the client-side I/O interaction functionality by including a Save As dialog and the ability for users to opt to run a Silverlight application as an out-of-browser (OOB) application. Using the Save As dialog and creating OOB applications are discussed in later chapters.

The powers and limitations of Silverlight and WPF are really a result of the environment in which each is designed to perform. Silverlight is a subset of WPF only because the full gamut of WPF functionality cannot be utilized in Silverlight's world.

Silverlight Performance

Silverlight has many obvious competitive advantages, including its blazing fast rendering engine and performance. A handful of performance test tools are available on the Web that can be used to illustrate the performance advantages of Silverlight. One such performance tool is the BubbleMark tool, which is located at http://bubblemark.com/ and can be used to compare the rendering speeds of the most popular competitive development environments. Figure 3-1 shows the BubbleMark home page.

BubbleMark.com has also introduced an example of simulating a 3-D environment using Silverlight, as shown in Figure 3-2.

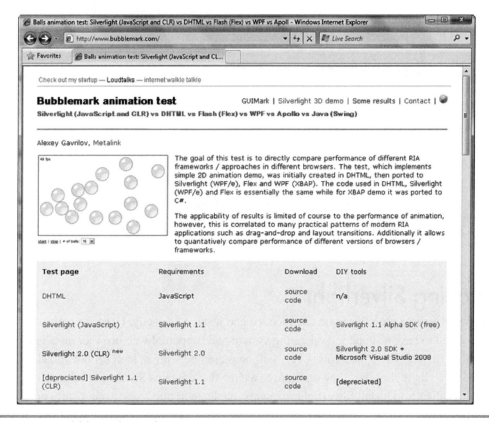

Figure 3-1   BubbleMark.com home page

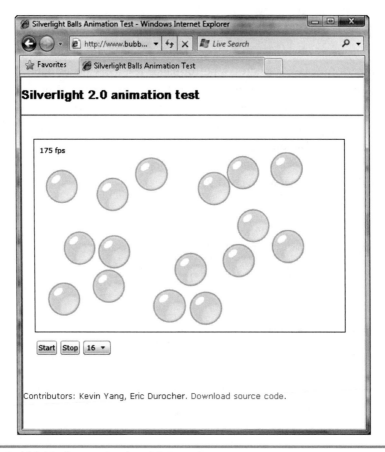

Figure 3-2 BubbleMark.com simulated 3-D environment

Installing Silverlight

The Silverlight plug-in can be downloaded and installed directly. Users are only required to have a supported operating system and supported web browser installed to utilize Silverlight applications. Users will be presented with an icon for downloading the Silverlight plug-in if they navigate to a page that contains Silverlight content. Alternatively, to install Silverlight manually, navigate to http://www.microsoft.com/ silverlight/resources/install.aspx and select the Silverlight download for Windows or Macintosh.

To get started as a Silverlight 3 developer, you have four components to install in Windows:

- Silverlight 3 Runtime

- Silverlight 3 Software Development Kit (SDK)

- Silverlight 3 Tools for Visual Studio

- Silverlight 3 Toolkit

Additionally, as an aspiring Silverlight developer, you will also want to install Expression Blend 3. Expression Blend is a component of the Expression Suite and is described in more detail later in this chapter.

Developers who anticipate developing Silverlight applications that utilize server-side data will want to install .NET RIA Services. .NET RIA Services is described in more detail in Chapter 12.

Silverlight 3 documentation can be viewed online or manually downloaded as a separate CHM help file.

Silverlight 3 Runtime

The initial Silverlight 3 Runtime installation screen for Windows is shown in Figure 3-3. From this screen, click the Install Now button to begin installation. The Silverlight 3 successful installation screen is shown in Figure 3-4. Once installation is complete, click the Close button.

Figure 3-3   The Silverlight 3 Runtime initial installation screen

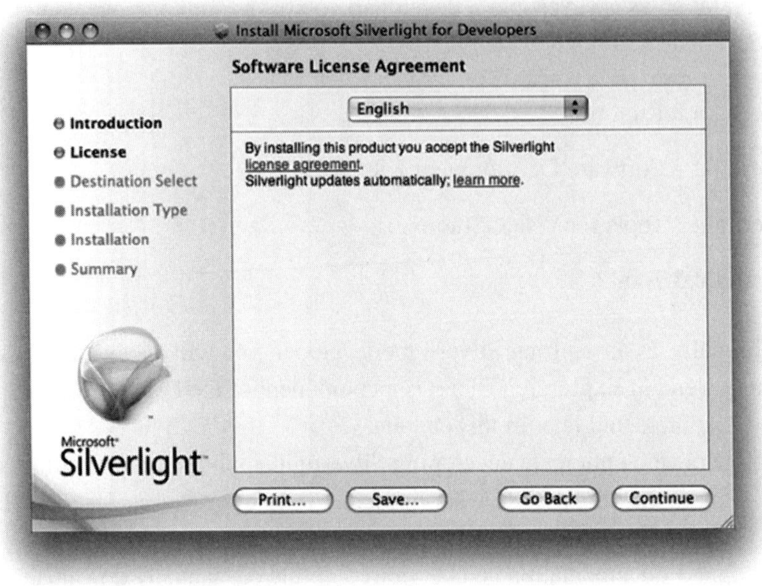

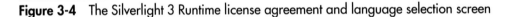

Figure 3-4   The Silverlight 3 Runtime license agreement and language selection screen

The Silverlight Runtime can also be installed on a Macintosh. The Silverlight 3 Runtime installation wizard includes a few additional steps and options when installing on Macintosh. The license agreement and language selection screen is shown in Figure 3-4.

Silverlight 3 Tools for Visual Studio

Silverlight developers using Windows with Visual Studio 2010 installed will want to download and install the Silverlight 3 Tools for Visual Studio 2010. The Tools for Visual Studio 2010 download includes the Silverlight 3 Runtime, the Silverlight 3 Software Development Kit (SDK), and the Tools for Visual Studio 2010. The Silverlight 3 Tools for Visual Studio 2010 installation wizard is shown in Figure 3-5. If you are installing Silverlight as a developer, the Tools for Visual Studio 2010 installation is the only one necessary.

The Silverlight 3 Tools for Visual Studio 2010 system requirements check screen is shown in Figure 3-6.

Figure 3-5   The Silverlight 3 Tools for Visual Studio 2010 initial installation screen

Figure 3-6   The Silverlight 3 Tools for Visual Studio 2010 system requirements check screen

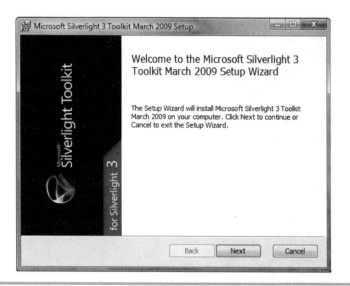

Figure 3-7   The Silverlight 3 Toolkit initial installation screen

Silverlight 3 Toolkit

The Silverlight 3 Toolkit is an upgraded and enhanced version of the Silverlight 2 Toolkit and includes additional Silverlight controls and themes. The Silverlight 3 Toolkit initial installation screen is shown in Figure 3-7.

Expression Blend 3

Expression Blend is one component of the Expression Suite of design tools from Microsoft. The Expression Suite of tools is used to prepare media, graphics, and user interfaces for WPF and Silverlight applications. Expression Blend is used to graphically design and lay out XAML user interfaces. The Expression Blend 3 initial installation screen is shown in Figure 3-8.

.NET RIA Services

.NET RIA Services is a new services platform that runs in the middle tier to control access to data, to provide a consistent and standardized means of creating RIA middle-tier and back-end code, and to consolidate the Silverlight and ASP.NET platforms. The .NET RIA Services initial installation screen is shown in Figure 3-9.

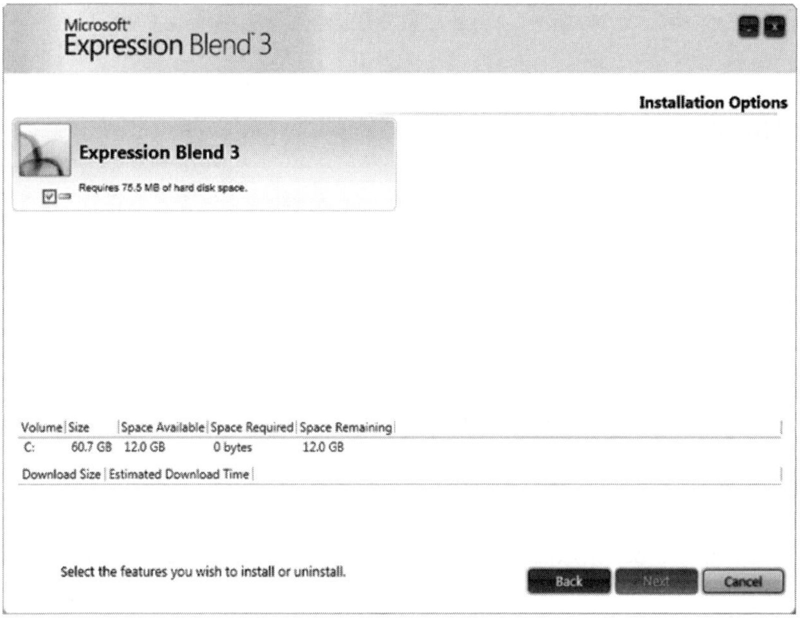

Figure 3-8   The Expression Blend 3 initial installation screen

Figure 3-9   The .NET RIA Services initial installation screen

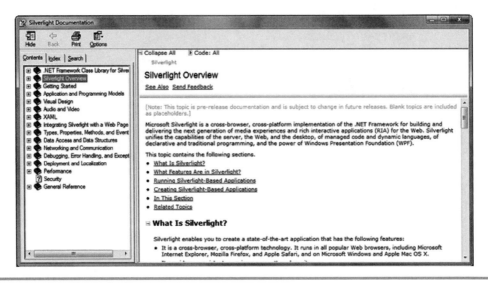

Figure 3-10 Silverlight documentation

Silverlight Documentation

Silverlight 3 documentation can be viewed online in the MSDN Library located at http://msdn.microsoft.com/en-us/library/cc838158(vs.96).aspx or it can be manually downloaded as a Microsoft Help CHM file. Figure 3-10 shows the Silverlight documentation as displayed in Windows.

2010 Silverlight Tools

Several vendors and developers are actively creating editors and design tools for use with Silverlight. The two primary Silverlight development tools are discussed in this section.

Microsoft Visual Studio 2010

Microsoft Visual Studio 2010 is Microsoft's premiere development tool. All development tools from Microsoft have now been assimilated into Visual Studio. Figure 3-11 shows the Visual Studio 2010 start page.

Visual Studio 2010 will be the primary tool used by Silverlight developers because Visual Studio 2010 is the only tool that can be used to easily write, test, and debug code for Silverlight. Visual Studio 2010 also offers the most control over physical file management in Silverlight projects.

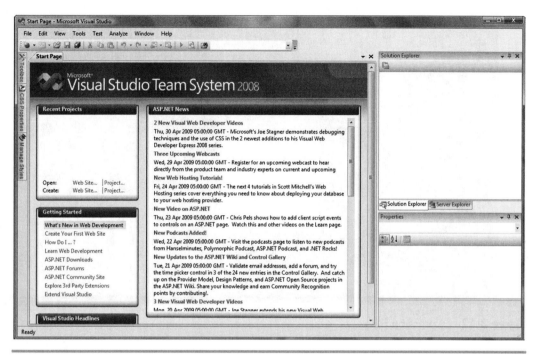

Figure 3-11 Visual Studio 2010 start page

Visual Studio 2010 is used to work with all other development technologies offered by Microsoft. Hence, Visual Studio 2010, by far, includes more features and functionality than any other Microsoft development tool or environment.

Microsoft Expression Blend

Microsoft has developed and released an entire suite of tools, called the Microsoft Expression Suite, designed for preparing user interfaces, graphics, and media for WPF and Silverlight applications. The primary tool in the Expression Suite for creating and manipulating Silverlight user interfaces is Microsoft Expression Blend. Figure 3-12 shows Expression Blend for Windows.

Although Visual Studio 2010 is the primary tool used by all Microsoft developers, Expression Blend was designed to cater to the needs of designers. Typically, application developers are very technical and prefer the straightforward interface presented by

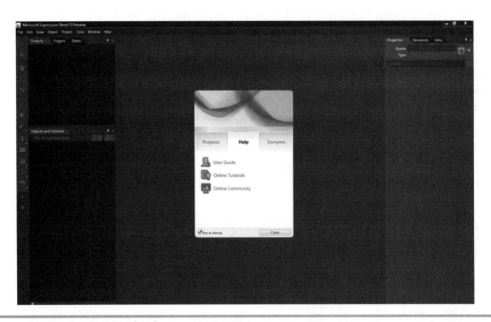

Figure 3-12 Expression Blend

Visual Studio 2010. Application designers, on the other hand, are very artistic by nature and prefer more impressive user interfaces. Expression Blend was designed with designers in mind.

As mentioned earlier, however, both Visual Studio 2010 and Expression Blend support the Silverlight project architecture and both can have a single Silverlight project opened simultaneously so that developers and designers can work side-by-side on project files.

Eclipse

Eclipse is a popular development editor for Windows and Macintosh. Eclipse is the first code editor developed by a vendor other than Microsoft that can be used to create Silverlight applications. Eclipse Tools for Silverlight can be found online at http://www .eclipse4sl.org. The Eclipse New Project dialog showing the option to create a new Silverlight project on the Macintosh is shown in Figure 3-13.

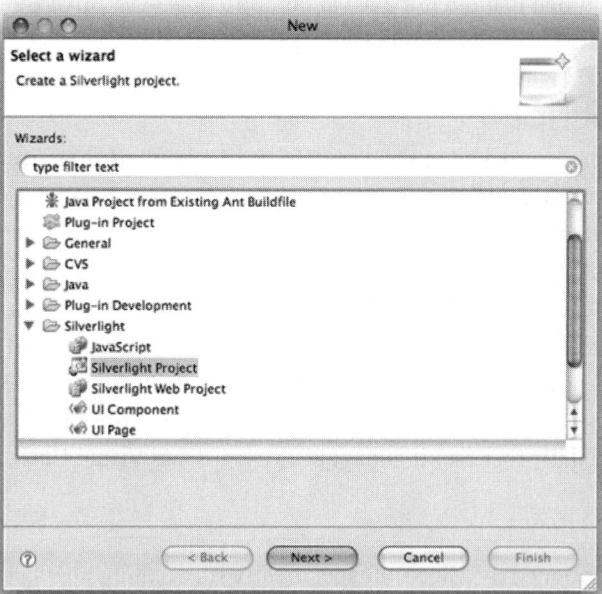

Figure 3-13   The Eclipse New Project dialog for a new Silverlight project

Silverlight Languages

Silverlight 3 includes a CLR execution environment and a subset of the .NET Framework base class library (BCL). Silverlight 2 also extends JavaScript and the standard browser script execution environment.

The three versions of Silverlight are version 1.0, version 2, and version 3. In version 1.0, the only language available is JavaScript. Version 2 extended the execution environment and provided the ability to program Silverlight applications using several more advanced programming languages. Furthermore, version 2 not only opened up the Silverlight CLR for use by more languages but also allowed the languages to seamlessly intercommunicate through the use of a Dynamic Language Runtime (DLR).

A dynamic programming language is one in which the language and the language runtime are designed to dynamically extend application capabilities at runtime. For instance, a dynamic language should be able to load, compile, and assimilate code that is read at runtime that did not exist at compile time. The Silverlight DLR enables Silverlight to take advantage of dynamic language functionality.

JavaScript

JavaScript was created in the early 1990s in a joint effort between Netscape and Sun Microsystems. JavaScript is not a subset of the Java programming language but, due to the popularity of the Java programming language at the time JavaScript was created, JavaScript was modeled after Java. JavaScript is a fully dynamic language that includes many object-oriented features. Although JavaScript is powerful, advanced development in the .NET Framework and, hence, Silverlight 3, does not lend itself to JavaScript. In lieu of using JavaScript in Silverlight, the more advanced .NET Framework programming languages can be used to take full advantage of the Silverlight framework. The most popular .NET programming languages are C# and Visual Basic.

C#

C# was designed by Microsoft specifically for creating applications using the .NET Framework and was originally named Visual C# .NET. Version 3.0 of C# is a fully dynamic language and is fully object oriented.

Visual Basic

Visual Basic has been around since the early 1990s when it was created as an improved version of the BASIC programming language and development environment. Visual Basic was completely redesigned for use in the .NET Framework and was renamed Visual Basic .NET at that time. Since then, all the .NET languages from Microsoft have dropped the ".NET" suffix from their name.

Visual Basic is currently in version 9.0 but does not fulfill the requirements of being a dynamic programming language yet. However, version 10.0 is currently being developed and will be named VBx. VBx will be a new dynamic version of Visual Basic that's much more streamlined for creating Silverlight applications. VBx is scheduled to be released with Visual Studio 2010.

IronPython

IronPython is a dynamic version of the Python programming language that was designed by Microsoft for use in the .NET Framework. The Silverlight 3 runtime supports the use of IronPython. Coverage of the IronPython programming language is beyond the scope of this book.

IronRuby

IronRuby is another dynamic programming language that was designed by Microsoft for use in the .NET Framework. The Silverlight 3 Runtime supports the use of IronRuby. Coverage of the IronRuby programming language is beyond the scope of this book.

Integrating Silverlight with ASP.NET AJAX

ASP.NET is the leading web development technology in use on the Web and has thoroughly saturated the market. A plethora of ASP.NET applications is currently deployed that integrate Silverlight controls or can be upgraded to fully utilize Silverlight. Microsoft realized the need to merge the two worlds of web computing and released some controls to do so in the ASP.NET 3.5 Extensions Preview package.

The Microsoft ASP.NET 3.5 Extensions Preview package includes new features and functionality that are being considered for integration into ASP.NET, ASP.NET AJAX, and ADO.NET and are made available for developers to begin experimenting with and adopting. Components that are released in ASP.NET 3.5 Extensions Preview are normally somewhat stable and are generally included in the next release of ASP.NET, ASP.NET AJAX, and ADO.NET.

asp:Silverlight Control

XAML files can be loaded, manipulated, and managed using a generic class included in the Silverlight Runtime. The ASP.NET 3.5 Extensions Preview package also includes a generic control for displaying Silverlight XAML files in an ASP.NET AJAX page—namely, the System.Web.UI.SilverlightControls.Silverlight control. The asp:Silverlight control loads and displays a Silverlight XAML file that can then be manipulated using JavaScript or server-side code.

The most important attribute of the asp:Silverlight control is the Source attribute. The Source attribute identifies the name of the XAML file the control should load, optionally including path information relative to the hosting ASP.NET AJAX page. The asp:Silverlight control exposes three minimal events, with one of those fired upon an error and one fired upon the XAML loading.

When you are creating a new Silverlight project using Visual Studio 2010, if the Add a New ASP.NET Web Project to the Solution to Host Silverlight option is selected from the Add Silverlight Application dialog, an ASP.NET AJAX page is created in the web application for testing your Silverlight content. The name of the ASP.NET AJAX page will be the same as the name of the Silverlight project with the string "TestPage" appended to the name. The ASP.NET AJAX test page created utilizes the asp:Silverlight control to display your Silverlight content.

The asp:Silverlight control can easily be added to an existing ASP.NET AJAX page either by dragging the control from the Visual Studio 2010 Toolbox and dropping it onto the page or by adding it declaratively through the markup for the page.

Try This Examine Silverlight Integrated into ASP.NET AJAX

Silverlight content can be integrated into existing ASP.NET AJAX pages using controls provided in Visual Studio as illustrated using the steps below.

1. Start or open Visual Studio 2010.

2. Select File | New | Project to display the New Project dialog.

3. Under the .NET Framework programming language of choice, select the Silverlight node in the Project types pane on the left side of the New Project dialog.

4. Select Silverlight Application in the Templates pane on the right side of the New Project dialog.

5. Assign the new project a name, select a location to create the new project, and then click the OK button.

6. When prompted with the New Silverlight Application dialog, click the OK button to accept the default settings.

7. Open the ASP.NET AJAX test page in the web project.

8. Locate the asp:Silverlight control in the page. Notice the `@Register` directive located at the top of the file and the asp:ScriptManager control in the page. The `@Register` directive is added to the page so that the asp:Silverlight control is available on the page. The asp:ScriptManager control is added to the page so that the page is AJAX enabled.

9. Modify the MainPage.xaml file in the Silverlight project in some fashion, such as by adding a TextBlock to the file.

10. Press F5 to test the application and display the Silverlight control on the ASP.NET AJAX page. If prompted to enable debugging for the project, click the OK button.

11. The Silverlight content should be displayed on the ASP.NET AJAX page. When this is done, close Visual Studio 2010.

An example of including XAML in an ASP.NET AJAX page by using the asp:Silverlight control is shown in the following code listing:

```
<%@ Page Language="C#" AutoEventWireup="true" %>

<%@ Register Assembly="System.Web.Silverlight"
  Namespace="System.Web.UI.SilverlightControls"
    TagPrefix="asp" %>

<!DOCTYPE html PUBLIC
"-//W3C//DTD XHTML 1.0 Transitional//EN"
"http://www.w3.org/TR/xhtml1/DTD/xhtml1-transitional.dtd">

<html xmlns="http://www.w3.org/1999/xhtml">
<head runat="server">
    <title>L0301</title>
    <style type="text/css">
    html, body {
          height: 100%;
          overflow: auto;
    }
    body {
          padding: 0;
          margin: 0;
    }
    </style>
</head>
<body>
    <form id="form1" runat="server" style="height:100%;">
        <asp:ScriptManager ID="ScriptManager1" runat="server">
            </asp:ScriptManager>
        <div  style="height:100%;">

            <asp:Silverlight ID="Silverlight1"
            runat="server" Source="~/ClientBin/L0301.xap"
            MinimumVersion="3.0.40307.0" Width="100%"
            Height="100%" />

        </div>
    </form>
</body>
</html>
```

The results of this code are shown in Figure 3-14. The example doesn't accomplish much at this point, but it does illustrate using the asp:Silverlight control.

(continued)

Figure 3-14 Simple Silverlight content included in an ASP.NET AJAX page using the asp:Silverlight control

asp:MediaPlayer Control

Audio, video, and media can be just as easily included in ASP.NET AJAX applications by using the asp:MediaPlayer control with Silverlight. The asp:MediaPlayer control is included in the ASP.NET Extensions Preview package. The asp:MediaPlayer control is designed to integrate Silverlight audio and video. The benefit of using the asp:MediaPlayer control is that it integrates Silverlight audio and video without the developer being required to have knowledge of XAML or JavaScript. The asp:MediaPlayer control allows for quick Silverlight integration into an ASP.NET or ASP.NET AJAX application while giving the developer time to get up to speed on the new technologies.

The asp:MediaPlayer control currently supports Windows Video (WMV), Windows Media Audio (WMA), and MP3 media formats. The asp:MediaPlayer control exposes events that can be handled by using JavaScript. Additionally, the asp:MediaPlayer control accommodates the display and navigation of chapters in media files and custom display skins. Figure 3-15 illustrates a media file being played in an ASP.NET AJAX web page using the asp:MediaPlayer control.

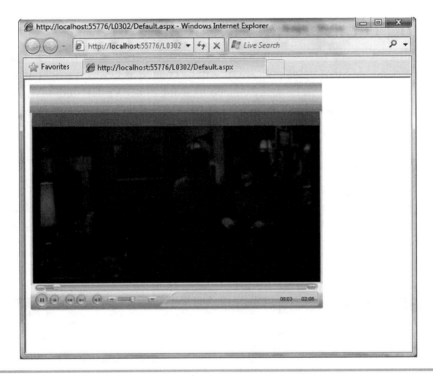

Figure 3-15   The asp:MediaPlayer control

Ask the Expert

Q: How can I change the skin being displayed for the asp:MediaPlayer control?

A: The skin is easy to change. The asp:MediaPlayer control ships with several built-in skins, and a custom skin can also be selected. To select a new skin, select the Design tab to display the ASP.NET AJAX page in Design view. Select the asp:MediaPlayer control, and a property extender button should be displayed on the control. Click the property extender button to display the MediaPlayer Tasks dialog. Click the Import Skin link and select a built-in skin or a custom skin.

Creating a Silverlight Application

Although existing applications can integrate Silverlight content and media, in most cases the most elaborate Silverlight applications will be created as new Silverlight applications. Silverlight applications can be easily created by using either Visual Studio 2010 or Expression Blend; however, Visual Studio 2010 offers more options when creating a new project.

The Silverlight Project

The first step in creating a Silverlight application is to create a new Silverlight project. Figure 3-16 shows the new Silverlight project dialog displayed when using Visual Studio 2010, and Figure 3-17 shows the new Silverlight project dialog displayed when using Expression Blend.

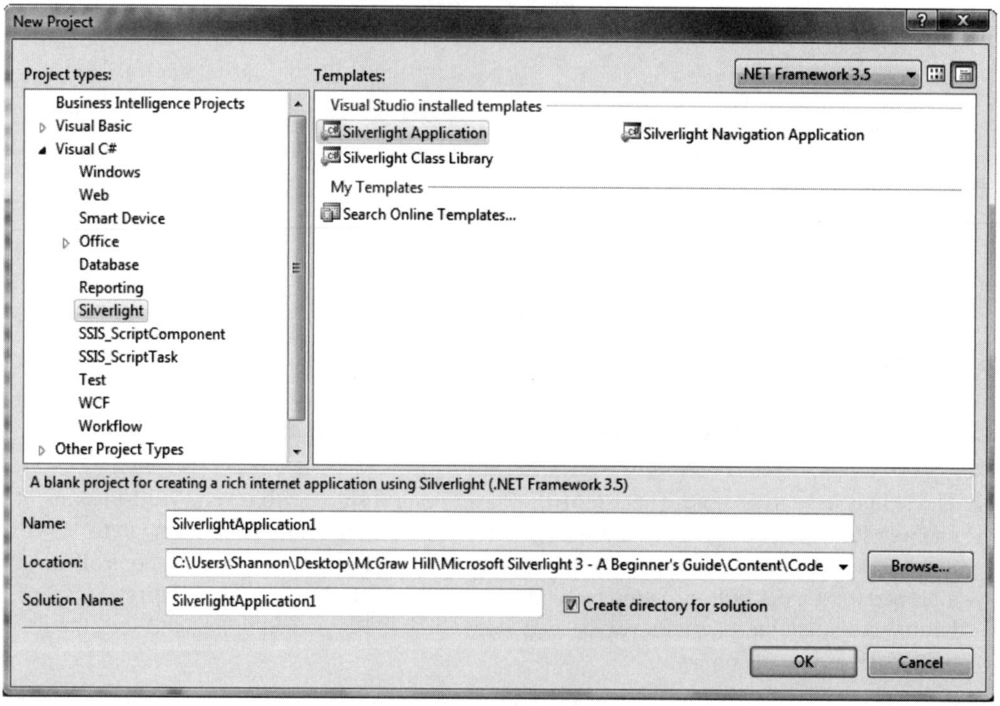

Figure 3-16 The Visual Studio 2010 New Project dialog for a new Silverlight project

Figure 3-17 The Expression Blend New Project dialog for a new Silverlight project

When a new project dialog is populated using Visual Studio 2010, another dialog prompts you for additional project configuration information that is not presented when creating a new Silverlight project using Expression Blend. Figure 3-18 shows the additional dialog displayed in Visual Studio 2010.

Here's a list of the New Silverlight Application dialog options:

• **Host the Silverlight application in a new Web site** This is the most commonly selected option. It will create an ASP.NET AJAX web project in addition to the Silverlight project. The ASP.NET AJAX web project created will serve as a test harness for the Silverlight application. Silverlight content is hosted in an HTML or ASP.NET page. This option instructs Visual Studio to create a page for testing the Silverlight application that the developer will have access to modify.

NOTE
A *test harness* is a project or file that exists for the purpose of testing another portion of an application. The ASP.NET AJAX web project created for a new Silverlight project contains files that are used to display and test your Silverlight content. Hence, the new web project acts as a test harness for the Silverlight project.

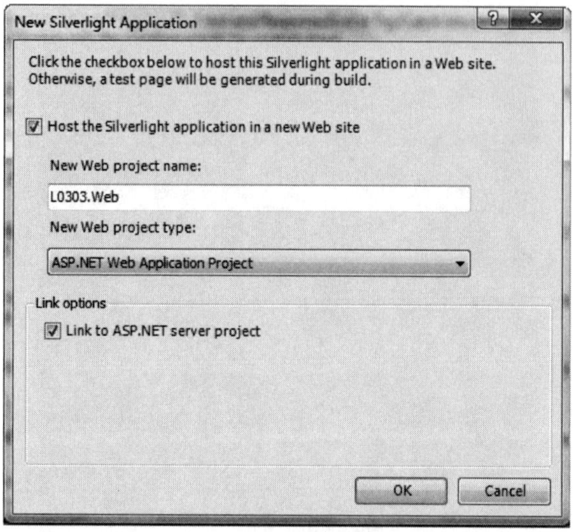

Figure 3-18 The Visual Studio 2010 New Silverlight Application dialog

- **Link to ASP.NET server project** This option is used to link a newly created Silverlight application to an existing website so that the existing website serves as the test harness for the newly created Silverlight application. This option differs from the first option in that the web application test harness project already exists instead of being newly created by Visual Studio.

Other options on the Add Silverlight Application dialog are available conditionally based on the option selected at the top of the dialog. The Project Type dropdown offers the option to create a website or a web application project. Finally, the Name text box offers the option to change the name of the newly created website from the default name supplied.

When the first option on the Add Silverlight Application dialog is selected, two projects will appear in the Solution Explorer, as shown in Figure 3-19.

In Figure 3-19, the first project shown is the web application test harness. The second project shown is the Silverlight application. In the Silverlight application, the only files of interest at this time are the MainPage.xaml file and the associated code-behind file, MainPage.xaml.cs. The MainPage.xaml file will be opened by default in Visual Studio for editing. The WPF Cider XAML designer was introduced to Silverlight in version 2 but is currently locked in read-only mode. Hence, Silverlight 3 applications created by using Visual Studio 2010 must be created through direct XAML coding. The alternative method

Silverlight project ———▶

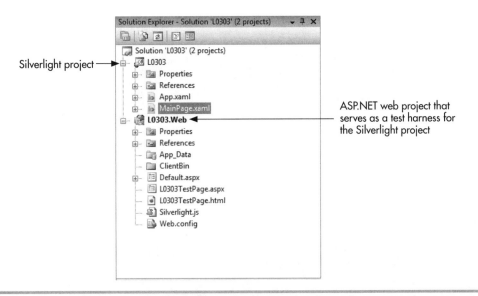

ASP.NET web project that
serves as a test harness for
the Silverlight project

Figure 3-19 A newly created Silverlight application and web application test harness project
in the Visual Studio 2010 Solution Explorer

for creating and designing a Silverlight application is to use Expression Blend. A Silverlight
application created in Visual Studio can easily be opened in Expression Blend as well.

Try This Open a New Silverlight XAML
File in Expression Blend

While Silverlight XAML files can be designed programmatically and by using the Cider
designer built into Visual Studio, Expression Blend makes visually designing XAML
much easier.

1. With the Silverlight project open in Visual Studio 2010, right-click the MainPage.xaml
   file in the Silverlight project in the Solution Explorer.

2. From the context menu, select Open in Expression Blend. The dialog shown in Figure 3-20
   may be displayed as a security precaution.

3. The MainPage.xaml file was intentionally opened from Visual Studio 2010. Therefore,
   it is safe to select Yes from the Security Warning dialog. The MainPage.xaml file will
   then be displayed by Expression Blend as shown in Figure 3-21.

(continued)

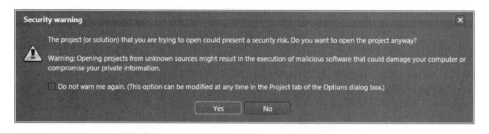

Figure 3-20 The Expression Blend Security Warning dialog displayed by default when a Silverlight XAML file is opened from Visual Studio 2010

Figure 3-21 A newly created Silverlight XAML file displayed in Expression Blend

Designing the Silverlight XAML

The initial sample application created in this section is a simple echo program that follows suit with most programming texts. The steps to create the simple Silverlight application are as follows:

1. With the MainPage.xaml open in Expression Blend, from the Objects and Timeline panel of the Interaction tab, select the LayoutRoot node.

2. Use the Brushes panel of the Properties tab to configure the background of the root Grid control to your liking. For example, you may change the background fill to a gradient fill.

3. From the vertical toolbox on the far-left side of Blend, drag and drop a TextBox control onto the Silverlight design surface.

4. Position the TextBox control toward the top of the design surface.

5. Assign the TextBox control a name, such as txtName, by typing the name in the Name text box at the top of the Properties tab.

6. With the newly dropped TextBox control selected, on the Properties tab, delete the string "TextBox" that appears in the Text Property text box.

7. From the toolbox, drag and drop a Button control onto the Silverlight design surface.

8. Position the Button control to the right of the TextBox control and assign the Button control a name, such as btnDisplayName, by typing the name in the Name text box at the top of the Properties tab.

9. With the newly dropped Button control selected, on the Properties tab, change the string "Button" in the Content Property text box to read "Display Name."

10. From the toolbox, drag and drop a TextBlock control onto the Silverlight design surface.

11. Position the TextBlock control below the TextBox control and the Button control and assign the TextBlock control a name such as tbName.

12. With the newly dropped TextBlock control selected, on the Properties tab, delete the string "TextBlock" that appears in the Text Property text box. The completed XAML design should resemble what's shown in Figure 3-22.

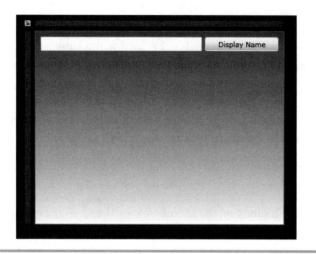

Figure 3-22   The completed Silverlight echo program XAML file as displayed in Expression Blend

Wiring Up an Event Handler

In order for the Button control to perform an action, it must identify when the action should be performed. Each control includes a series of events that can be initiated on the control. The most common user interface event that is fired in response to user interaction is the Click event. Once an event is identified, it must be directed to code, referred to as an *event handler,* to execute in response to the event being fired.

Event handlers can be wired up to Silverlight controls in multiple ways:

- When working in Visual Studio 2010, you can create an event handler directly in a code-behind file and then wire the event of a control to the existing handler. Additionally, if an event handler does not exist when you attempt to wire an event to a handler, a handler can be dynamically created at that time.

- When working in Expression Blend, you can create an event handler by selecting a control and then double-clicking the desired event in the Events panel of the Properties tab. Expression Blend will create an event handler for the selected control event.

The code for the event handler is shown in the following listing:

```
using System;
using System.Windows;
using System.Windows.Controls;
```

```
using System.Windows.Documents;
using System.Windows.Input;
using System.Windows.Media;
using System.Windows.Media.Animation;
using System.Windows.Shapes;

namespace L0303
{
    public partial class Page : UserControl
    {
        public Page()
        {
            InitializeComponent();
        }

        private void btnDisplayName_Click(object sender,
            RoutedEventArgs e)
        {
            tbName.Text = txtName.Text;
        }
    }
}
```

The results of the sample echo program are shown in Figure 3-23.

Silverlight Project Architecture

When you create a new Silverlight project using Visual Studio and select the option
Host the Silverlight application in a new Web site, two projects are created. One project
contains the actual Silverlight application, and the second project serves as a test harness
for the Silverlight application. When you create a Silverlight project using Expression
Blend, a test harness project is automatically created but it's not nearly as robust as the
Web application test harness project created by Visual Studio 2010.

A Silverlight project contains multiple Silverlight files. By default, a separate class file
is created to accompany each Silverlight XAML file. Microsoft designed Silverlight using
the same basic architecture as ASP.NET and many other Microsoft .NET development
technologies such as WPF. A Silverlight control is composed of a file containing XAML
(markup) and a separate class file containing code, or a *code-behind file* (most commonly
C# or Visual Basic). Regardless of which tool is used to create a Silverlight project, when
the Silverlight application is built, the code-behind files are compiled into an assembly
(a .dll file) and all the XAML files and the assembly are compressed into a single file with
a .xap extension (pronounced *zap*). The XAP file will be deployed to the hosting web
server. The project architecture described was illustrated previously in Figure 3-19.

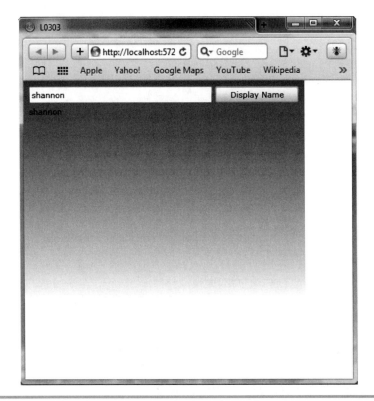

Figure 3-23 The sample echo program as displayed in Safari

Notice in the test harness project that three web pages are created. The Default.aspx page is not used in the test harness project. However, an ASP.NET page and an HTML page are created that are named after the Silverlight project. The HTML page includes the Silverlight control by using an <object> element, whereas the ASP.NET page includes the Silverlight control by using a new <asp:Silverlight> element.

Creating a Simple Silverlight Animation

Creating animations for Silverlight can be a simple process, depending on the animation you have in mind. Silverlight animations can be created using Visual Studio 2010 either programmatically or through XAML. However, the tool of choice for creating animation is Expression Blend. A standard, simple animation to get started with in Silverlight consists of a spinning circle (reminiscent of the one displayed in Windows Vista when waiting on a lengthy process to complete).

Try This   Create a Simple Animation

Using Expression Blend, Silverlight animations can be easily created using steps similar to those listed below.

1. Start or open Visual Studio 2010. Select File | New | Project to display the New Project dialog.

2. Under the .NET Framework programming language of choice, select the Silverlight node in the Project Types pane on the left side of the New Project dialog.

3. Select Silverlight Application in the Templates pane on the right side of the New Project dialog.

4. Assign the new project a name, select a location to create the new project, and then click the OK button.

5. When prompted with the New Silverlight Application dialog, click the OK button to accept the default settings.

6. Right-click the MainPage.xaml file in the Silverlight project in the Solution Explorer.

7. From the context menu, select Open in Expression Blend. The MainPage.xaml file will then be displayed in Expression Blend.

8. From the toolbox on the left side of Blend, drag an ellipse and drop it onto the Silverlight design surface.

9. With the newly dropped ellipse selected, use the Brushes panel of the Properties tab to apply a transparent fill to the ellipse.

10. From the Properties tab, set the StrokeThickness value to 20 or greater and apply a linear gradient stroke. The resultant XAML design is shown in Figure 3-24.

NOTE
When sizing an ellipse in Expression Blend, in order to maintain a perfect circle, hold down the SHIFT key while resizing.

11. On the Objects and Timeline pane, click the Add (+) button to create a new storyboard. The Create Storyboard Resource dialog should be presented, as shown in Figure 3-25.

12. Assign the new storyboard a name of sbSpin and click OK.

(continued)

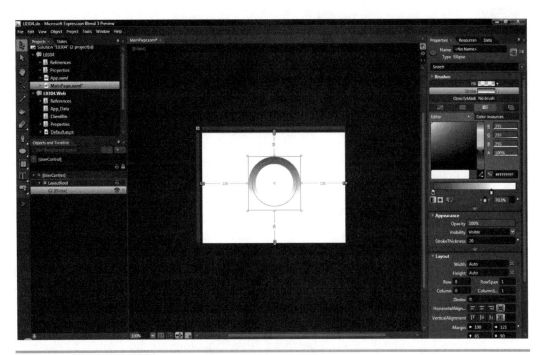

Figure 3-24 An ellipse configured on the design surface in Expression Blend

13. Select a point on the timeline and modify the ellipse in some manner. In this example, select a point on the timeline at about 2 seconds and then grab the corner anchor of the ellipse using the mouse and spin the ellipse around several times.

14. You can test the animation by clicking the Play button on the Timeline pane.

15. If the animation should be assigned a name or should loop forever, in Expression Blend select the timeline and in the Properties panel assign a name to the storyboard or set the RepeatBehavior to "Forever."

16. Save the page, close Expression Blend, and then go back to Visual Studio 2010.

Figure 3-25 A new storyboard created using Expression Blend

NOTE

To get the animation to start, you must call the Begin method of the storyboard. In order to call the Begin method of the storyboard, you need to assign the storyboard a name. Assuming that the storyboard was assigned a name in Expression Blend, the Begin method can be called from the Silverlight code-behind file. However, the call to the Begin method must also occur from an event handler fired by an element in the XAML file. The animation can start immediately when the XAML file is loaded if the Begin method is called from the Loaded event.

17. To easily create a new event handler that is wired to the XAML Loaded event, open the XAML file in Visual Studio and position the cursor at the end of the opening <UserControl> document element. Press the spacebar to display the IntelliSense member selector and highlight Loaded. Press the equals (=) key to assign a new event handler.

18. Right-click the Silverlight XAML design surface and select View Code.

19. Locate the newly created Loaded event handler and add a call to the Begin method of the storyboard, as illustrated in the following code snippet:

```
private void UserControl_Loaded(object sender, RoutedEventArgs e){
  sbSpin.Begin();
}
```

The resultant animation should be displayed in a browser instance, as shown in Figure 3-26.

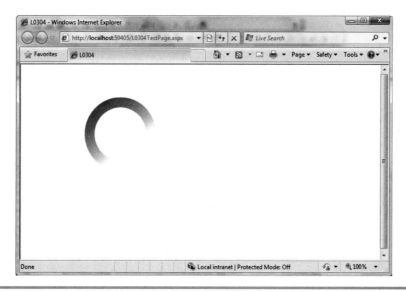

Figure 3-26   A simple Silverlight animation

Ask the Expert

Q: Why does my animation play a single time and then stop animating?

A: The number of times that an animation repeats itself is controlled by the RepeatBehavior attribute. The default setting for the RepeatBehavior attribute is 1. You may assign any positive integer value to the RepeatBehavior attribute or assign a string value of "Forever" to cause the animation to repeat forever.

Conclusion

Although creating Silverlight applications should be very familiar to veteran .NET developers, there are significant differences between developing ASP.NET applications and Silverlight applications. Due to the popularity, proven stability, and success of the ASP.NET architecture—and in order to make it easier for developers to quickly learn to create Silverlight applications—Microsoft designed Silverlight using the same design paradigm as ASP.NET. Each Silverlight control is composed of a markup file containing XAML and an associated code-behind file that handles events fired by the XAML markup. Silverlight animations can be easily created using Expression Blend.

Chapter 4

Animating Silverlight

Key Concepts & Skills

- Get an idea of the importance of an impressive user interface in an application

- Learn how to draw two-dimensional shapes and apply three-dimensional effects in Silverlight

- Experiment with brushes and transformations

- Gain an understanding of Silverlight animations

- Use Deep Zoom technology to create an elaborate photo display

One of the key features originally built into Silverlight is the ability to host media and animation to provide the user with an incredible web application experience. Silverlight applications will, in many cases, be constructed by a team of designers and developers. Whereas in the past the duties and responsibilities of the designer and developer roles were fairly well defined and isolated, Silverlight brings the designer and developer worlds together. Silverlight developers may not create complex graphics, media, and animations, but they must have an understanding of how animations function so that they can control animations declaratively through XAML or imperatively through code.

Chapter 3 illustrated how to create a simple spinning animation. This chapter covers 2-D shapes, effects, and animation in greater detail.

The Importance of an Impressive User Interface

Microsoft and other companies have invested millions of dollars in software research and development. The primary factors that affect and influence end users are performance and the user interface. The factors that influence the end user are referred to as the *user experience (UX)*. Software developers are on a continual quest to improve application performance; however, new rules and guidelines have recently been introduced that define higher standards for the creation of user interfaces. The new guidelines were primarily released by Microsoft and coincided with the release of Windows Vista, WPF, and, in turn, Silverlight.

Basically, the more impressed users are with the overall user experience an application provides, the more impressed they will be with the application and the more likely they will be to refer the application to others. For more information on Microsoft UX guidelines, visit the MSDN article "Designing with Windows Presentation Foundation," located at http://msdn.microsoft.com/en-us/library/aa511329.aspx#guidelines.

Drawing Graphics

Silverlight implements many of the features included in WPF. For instance, Silverlight provides the ability to draw two-dimensional (2-D) graphics in applications. Graphics of this caliber are more than adequate for most user interfaces and applications, particularly business applications. However, some applications require more elaborate graphics capabilities—namely, three-dimensional graphics (3-D). For example, an engineering application may benefit tremendously from 3-D graphics in the user interface. Whereas WPF provides 3-D graphics, Silverlight currently does not. Silverlight 3 does, however, provide perspective transformations that simulate 3-D graphics.

In order to provide true 3-D graphics, an application must utilize the hardware of the local workstation and the facilities of the local operating system. Silverlight is designed to be cross-platform and cross-browser compliant. With that in mind, it cannot be tied to any particular hardware configuration, operating system, or browser.

Drawing in Silverlight is accomplished through the use of a graphic element such as an ellipse or a rectangle. All graphic elements in Silverlight extend the Shape type. As a result, all Shape type objects in Silverlight include some common functionality, as listed next:

- **Stroke**   The stroke defines the brush used to paint the outline of the shape.

- **StrokeThickness**   The stroke thickness defines the thickness of the outline of the shape.

- **Fill**   The fill defines how the interior of the shape is filled or painted.

Lines

To draw lines in Silverlight, use the Line object. A line can easily be drawn using Blend, can be created directly in XAML using Visual Studio 2008, and can be created programmatically. A line is defined through the definition of two points. Each point is composed of an X coordinate and a Y coordinate.

The markup snippet shown here is used to render a red diagonal line from 50,50 to 200,200:

```
<Line
  X1="50" Y1="50"
  X2="200" Y2="200"
  Stroke="Red"
  StrokeThickness="2"
  RenderTransformOrigin="0.595,0.416" />
```

The result of this XAML is shown in Figure 4-1.

TIP

The Line object is used to draw straight lines in Silverlight. If you need to draw a curved line, use the Path class, described later.

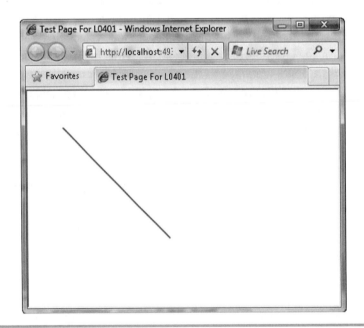

Figure 4-1 A red diagonal line in Silverlight

Ellipses

An Ellipse object is used to draw circles and round objects in Silverlight. The circular characteristics of an ellipse are defined by specifying the height and width of the ellipse. The markup snippet shown next renders an oval Ellipse object with a blue gradient fill and a stroke of 5:

```
<Ellipse
  Width="226"
  Height="124"
  Stroke="Black"
  StrokeThickness="5"
  Canvas.Left="8"
  Canvas.Top="8">
  <Ellipse.Fill>
    <LinearGradientBrush
    EndPoint="1,0.5"
    StartPoint="0,0.5">
    <GradientStop
    Color="#FFD9EAF0"
    Offset="0"/>
    <GradientStop
    Color="#FF126D8E"
    Offset="1"/>
  </LinearGradientBrush>
  </Ellipse.Fill>
</Ellipse>
```

The ellipse rendered by this XAML is shown in Figure 4-2.

TIP

When you're drawing an ellipse in Expression Blend, if you want the ellipse to be rendered as a perfect circle, hold down the SHIFT key as you draw it.

Rectangles

The Rectangle class is used to draw rectangles in Silverlight. The following markup snippet illustrates drawing two rectangles—a larger blue rectangle in the background and a smaller orange rectangle on top:

```
<Rectangle
  Width="240"
  Height="120"
  Stroke="#FF000000"
```

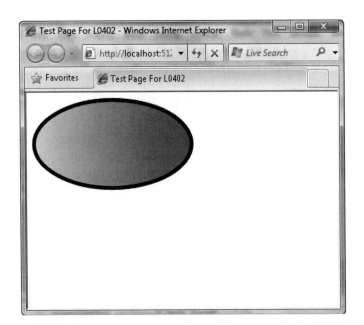

Figure 4-2 A Silverlight ellipse

```
Canvas.Left="40"
Canvas.Top="40">
<Rectangle.Fill>
<LinearGradientBrush
EndPoint="1,0.5"
StartPoint="0,0.5">
<GradientStop
Color="#FF000000"
Offset="0"/>
<GradientStop
Color="#FF6867D2"
Offset="1"/>
</LinearGradientBrush>
</Rectangle.Fill>
</Rectangle>
<Rectangle
Width="72"
Height="72"
Stroke="#FFF28C12"
```

```
Canvas.Left="200"
Canvas.Top="80">
<Rectangle.Fill>
<LinearGradientBrush
EndPoint="1,0.5"
StartPoint="0,0.5">
<GradientStop
Color="#FFF28C12"
Offset="0"/>
<GradientStop
Color="#FFFFFFFF"
Offset="1"/>
</LinearGradientBrush>
</Rectangle.Fill>
</Rectangle>
```

The rectangles generated from this XAML are shown in Figure 4-3.

TIP
When you're drawing a rectangle in Expression Blend, if you want the rectangle to be rendered as a perfect square, hold down the SHIFT key while drawing it.

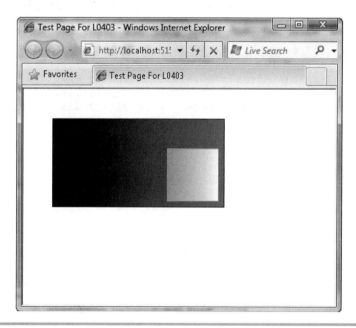

Figure 4-3   Rectangles in Silverlight

Paths and Geometries

The Path object also derives from the Shape object; however, the Path object has no defined shape. Instead, a Path object accepts an indirect or abstract definition of a shape to define how the path is rendered. The Geometry class is used to define how a shape is rendered. There is only one Path class but many types of Geometry classes. The Geometry class itself is an abstract class that cannot be directly instantiated, but one of its child classes must be instantiated.

The Path class can be used to define simple shapes such as lines, ellipses, and rectangles in the same manner as the Line, Ellipse, and Rectangle classes; however, the PathGeometry class is used to create more complex shapes. Creating a path can be rather tricky by hand-coding the path coordinates directly in XAML. When using a design tool such as Blend, you can create a path as a combination of simpler elements or freehand by using a pen/pencil tool. The following markup snippet shows several path elements rendered in Blend when a sketchy little stick man was quickly drawn with the pencil tool.

```
<Path Height="65.285" HorizontalAlignment="Left" Margin=
"91.3889999389648,11.8640003204346,0,0" VerticalAlignment="Top"
Width="82.611" Data="M173,39 C142.05241,26.256876 136.00845,
7.1175995 103,36 C100.25935,38.398071 97.748062,41.251938 95,44
C90.541801,48.458199 90.216232,49.852882 94,57 C96.2285,61.209385
99.469162,65.407486 101,70 C103.17303,76.519089 102.84608,76 112,76
C130.1981,76 138.42952,77.647919 155,70 C159.83434,67.768768
165.34642,66.307159 168,61 C170.94823,55.103531 170.00436,48.912659
164,44 C152.33842,34.458714 160.87141,26 142,26 C136.65819,26
131.72868,26.026575 127,24 C119.91907,20.965315 118,22.116327 118,12
C116.66666,12 115.29767,11.693663 114,12 C113.27458,12.171247
112.64546,13.372733 112,13" Fill="#FFFFFFFF" Stretch="Fill"
Stroke="#FF000000"/>
<Path Height="10" HorizontalAlignment="Left" Margin="124,8,0,0"
VerticalAlignment="Top" Width="7" Data="M119,23 C121,20 123,17 125,14"
Fill="#FFFFFFFF" Stretch="Fill" Stroke="#FF000000"/>
<Path Height="6" HorizontalAlignment="Left" Margin="145,37,0,0"
VerticalAlignment="Top" Width="1" Data="M145,37 C145,38 145,39 145,40
C145,40.666668 145,41.333332 145,42" Fill="#FFFFFFFF" Stretch="Fill"
Stroke="#FF000000"/>
<Path Height="8" HorizontalAlignment="Left" Margin="120,38,0,0"
VerticalAlignment="Top" Width="2" Data="M120,38 C120.55189,40.759438
120.78797,42.243656 121,45" Fill="#FFFFFFFF" Stretch="Fill"
Stroke="#FF000000"/>
<Path Height="7.278" HorizontalAlignment="Left" Margin="106,62,0,0"
VerticalAlignment="Top" Width="55" Data="M106,63 C114.78552,64.730484
123.33023,67 132,67 C142.79189,67 149.71115,71.349182 160,64
```

```
C159.33333,63.333332 158.66667,62.666668 158,62" Fill="#FFFFFFFF"
Stretch="Fill" Stroke="#FF000000"/>
<Path HorizontalAlignment="Left" Margin="80,77,0,110" Width="51.136"
Data="M130,77 C129.8295,81.262527 128.65659,89.313187 130,92
C129.33333,92.333336 128.66667,92.666664 128,93 C128.33333,93.333336
128.66667,93.666664 129,94 C119.24112,108.63832 130,124.69832 130,143
C130,152.48851 132.07855,165.96727 120,171 C106.10215,176.79077
92.163834,181.92285 80,189" Fill="#FFFFFFFF" Stretch="Fill"
Stroke="#FF000000"/>
<Path Height="34" HorizontalAlignment="Left" Margin="127,0,0,100"
VerticalAlignment="Bottom" Width="28" Data="M127,166 C138.52354,
177.00563 146.48206,185.11092 154,199" Fill="#FFFFFFFF" Stretch="Fill"
Stroke="#FF000000"/>
<Path Height="7" HorizontalAlignment="Left" Margin="92,109,0,0"
VerticalAlignment="Top" Width="71" Data="M92,109 C114.64909,109.59603
138.18405,115 160,115 C160.24759,114.38101 159.64951,113.5671 160,113
C160.39186,112.36596 161.26834,112.14227 162,112" Fill="#FFFFFFFF"
Stretch="Fill" Stroke="#FF000000"/>
```

The result of the preceding XAML is shown in Figure 4-4.

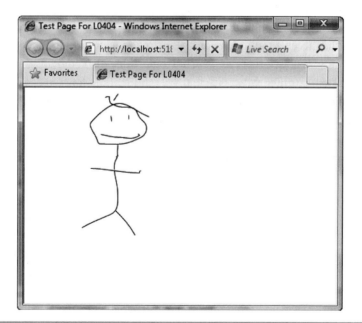

Figure 4-4   A series of paths in Silverlight

Ask the Expert

Q: The Path markup language is complex and confusing. How can I easily create a path?

A: The easiest way to create paths and geometries in Silverlight is to use Expression Blend. Blend includes tools such as the pencil tool that you can use to easily create paths. Using the pencil tool, you can create whatever shape or drawing you desire and Blend will render the correct Path markup language. Furthermore, if you need to create more advanced graphics for your application and would like them rendered as XAML, check out Expression Design. Design is a tool in the Expression suite use to create professional graphics.

Several types of geometries can be utilized with a path, including LineGeometry, RectangleGeometry, EllipseGeometry, and PathGeometry. The PathGeometry can compile complex shapes from multiple path segments. Path segments include arcs, Beziers, lines, and variations of each.

The preceding use of PathGeometry is in shorthand form. The Path object includes a Data attribute that accepts multiple coordinates to define points along the path. Upon a closer look, you will notice that the Data attribute value also contains characters such as M and C. The Data attribute value is actually a mini markup language, and the characters are very meaningful as well as case-sensitive. For instance, an uppercase M signifies a move command and the coordinates that follow indicate the movement of the path. For more information on the XAML Path markup language, visit the MSDN article "Path Markup Syntax," located at http://msdn.microsoft.com/en-us/library/ms752293.aspx.

Brushes

Brushes are used to paint the internal area contained by a surrounding stroke or the stroke itself. For instance, a brush can be used to paint the interior space of a rectangle. In fact, in the rectangles example shown in Figure 4-3, a gradient brush is used to paint the interior of the rectangle. Brushes can be used to paint solid colors, gradients, images, and even video. The ability to paint with images is fairly common among graphic design tools; however, the ability to paint with video is only available in a very few elite graphic design tools. Expression Blend currently supports the display of image and video brushes in design mode for WPF applications but not for Silverlight applications. However, it's fairly easy to create an image brush fill, as shown in the following markup snippet:

```
<Ellipse
  Width="184"
  Height="184"
  Stroke="#FFD89623"
  StrokeThickness="3"
  Canvas.Left="8"
  Canvas.Top="8">
  <Ellipse.Fill>
  <ImageBrush
  ImageSource="gingerbread.jpg" />
  </Ellipse.Fill>
</Ellipse>
```

The filled ellipse resulting from the preceding XAML is shown in Figure 4-5.

Video can be used as a brush source in the same manner that images can be used, although a little more XAML is involved in painting with video. First, a VideoBrush does not directly play video but rather utilizes video from another source, such as a

Figure 4-5   An image brush used to fill an ellipse

MediaElement object. In the following example, video is being played as the foreground of text. The TextBlock.ForeGround utilizes a VideoBrush that, in turn, utilizes video from a MediaElement object.

```
<MediaElement
  Source="axe_murderer.wmv"
  Opacity="0"
  x:Name="myMovie" />
<TextBlock
  Margin="45,81,40,126"
  TextWrapping="Wrap"
  FontSize="72"
  FontWeight="Bold"
  Text="Silverlight">
  <TextBlock.Foreground>
  <VideoBrush SourceName="myMovie" />
  </TextBlock.Foreground>
</TextBlock>
```

The resultant TextBlock is shown in Figure 4-6 as filled with video using the preceding XAML.

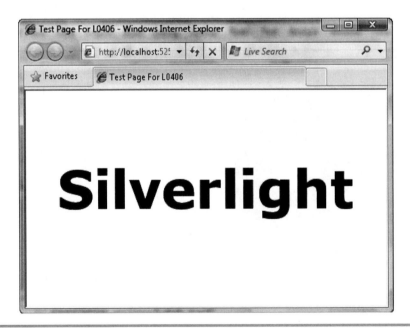

Figure 4-6   Using a video brush in Silverlight

Transformations

Transformation objects are used to transform other Shape objects. There are various types of transformations, including rotations, scales, skews, and translations. A scale is a resize. A skew transformation skews the shape of the Shape object. A translation moves a shape. The following markup snippet illustrates applying a 45-degree rotation to a TextBlock:

```
<TextBlock
  RenderTransformOrigin="0.5,0.5"
  Width="320"
  Height="80"
  Canvas.Left="80"
  Canvas.Top="104"
  TextWrapping="Wrap">
  <TextBlock.RenderTransform>
  <TransformGroup>
  <ScaleTransform ScaleX="1" ScaleY="1"/>
  <SkewTransform AngleX="0" AngleY="0"/>
  <RotateTransform Angle="45"/>
  <TranslateTransform X="0" Y="0"/>
  </TransformGroup>
  </TextBlock.RenderTransform>
  <Run
  FontFamily="Segoe UI"
  FontSize="48"
  Text="McGraw Hill"/>
</TextBlock>
```

Figure 4-7 illustrates the result of the preceding XAML.

Perspective Transformations

As mentioned, Silverlight is currently not able to deliver a true 3-D rendering engine due to the lack of coupling with local client hardware. Silverlight developers have been asking Microsoft for a 3-D engine of some type since version 1.0 was in beta. Silverlight 3 introduces a new feature called *perspective transformations.*

A perspective transformation is not a true 3-D engine but accommodates transforming the perspective of a graphic element along the X-axis, the Y-axis, and the Z-axis, resulting in a 3-D visual effect. Perspective transformations can be implemented using code but can also be easily implemented using XAML.

A perspective transformation can be easily illustrated by starting with a simple image. The following XAML is used to display the image shown in Figure 4-8:

```
<UserControl x:Class="L0408.MainPage"
    xmlns="http://schemas.microsoft.com/winfx/2006/xaml/presentation"
```

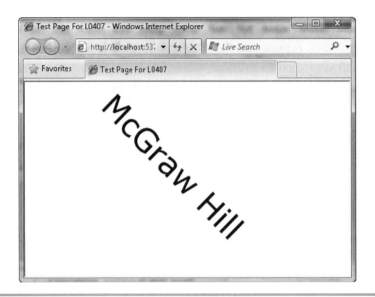

Figure 4-7 A TextBlock with a transformation applied to it

```
xmlns:x="http://schemas.microsoft.com/winfx/2006/xaml"
Width="400" Height="300">
<Grid x:Name="LayoutRoot" Background="White">
    <Image Source="gingerbread.jpg" Height="200">
    </Image>
</Grid>
</UserControl>
```

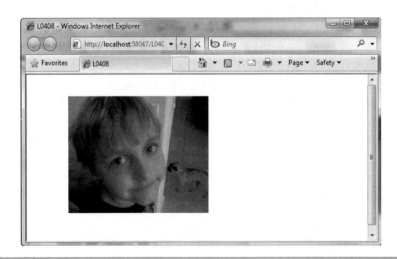

Figure 4-8 A simple image

The XAML UIElement element includes a new sub-element named Projection that is used to define a perspective transformation. The Projection element contains an element named PlaneProjection. The PlaneProjection element contains several attributes that are used to rotate a graphic element along the X-axis, Y-axis, and Z-axis. For example, to rotate the image along the X-axis, assign a value to the RotationX attribute, as shown in the following markup snippet and in Figure 4-9:

```
<Image Source="gingerbread.jpg" Height="200">
  <Image.Projection>
    <PlaneProjection RotationX="45" />
  </Image.Projection>
</Image>
```

Rotation angles may be combined so that a graphic element is rotated along multiple axes simultaneously, as shown in the following markup snippet and illustrated in Figure 4-10:

```
<Image Source="gingerbread.jpg" Height="200">
  <Image.Projection>
    <PlaneProjection RotationX="45" RotationY="25" />
  </Image.Projection>
</Image>
```

Perspective transformation rotation angles may also be bound to the property values of other elements and may be configured using a storyboard and animation. Additionally, the PlaneProjection element includes attributes to configure the center of rotation, the local offset, and the global offset.

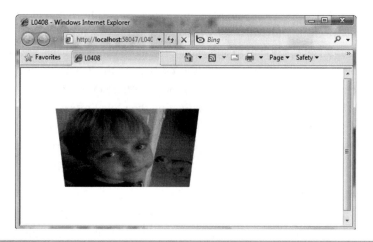

Figure 4-9   An image rotated 45 degrees along the X-axis

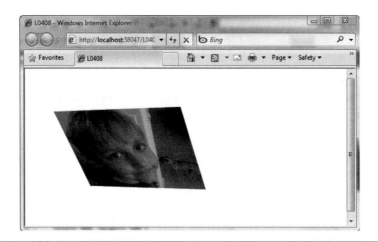

Figure 4-10 An image rotated along multiple axes

NOTE

By default, when the RotationX, RotationY, and RotationZ properties are adjusted, the center point where the visual element is rotated is in the center of the element. However, the center point that the visual element is rotated around may be adjusted by changing the CenterOfRotationX and CenterOfRotationY properties.

The LocalOffsetX, LocalOffsetY, and LocalOffsetZ properties are used to move a visual element along the X-axis, the Y-axis, and the Z-axis, respectively. The local offset properties move the visual element relative to any rotation adjustment also applied to the visual element. Adjusting the local offset properties makes the visual element appear to be turning toward or away from the user when combined with a rotation adjustment.

The GlobalOffsetX, GlobalOffsetY, and GlobalOffsetZ properties are also used to move a visual element along the X-axis, the Y-axis, and the Z-axis, respectively. If the visual element is not rotated using the RotationX, RotationY, or RotationZ property, adjusting the local offset properties and adjusting the global offset properties has the same effect. However, the global offset properties move the visual element irrespective of any rotation adjustment applied to the visual element. Adjusting a global offset property makes the entire visual element appear to be moving along the respective axis.

Pixel Shaders

Silverlight 3 also includes pixel shaders. A *pixel shader* is an object that transforms the pixel level output after it is rendered by Silverlight but before it is displayed to the user. Silverlight 3 ships with two pixel shaders: blur effect and drop shadow effect. Additionally, you can create custom pixel shaders. A pixel shader can be applied to any visual element displayed by Silverlight 3.

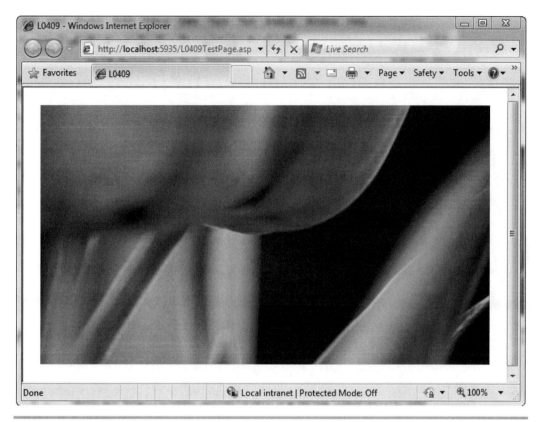

Figure 4-11   An unaltered image displayed using Silverlight 3

Pixel shaders are applied to a visual element by using the Effect sub-element, and each visual element may have a single effect associated with it. The effects are easy to apply. To illustrate pixel shaders, Figure 4-11 shows an unaltered image displayed using Silverlight 3.

In the following code listing, a blur effect has been added to the image displayed and a radius of 20 is applied. The radius attribute of the BlurEffect element controls how blurry the image appears. The higher the value assigned to the Radius attribute, the blurrier the image appears. Figure 4-12 shows the results of the blur effect.

```
<Image Source="tulip.jpg" Margin="24" Stretch="Fill">
  <Image.Effect>
    <BlurEffect Radius="20" />
  </Image.Effect>
</Image>
```

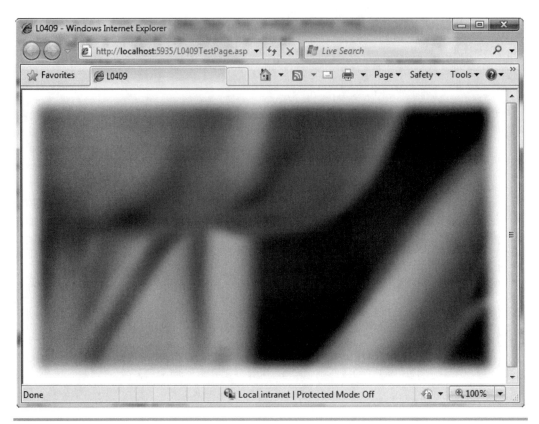

Figure 4-12 The image with a blur effect applied

The second pixel shader effect that ships with Silverlight 3 is the drop shadow effect. The drop shadow effect includes four properties of note: BlurRadius, Color, Direction, and ShadowDepth. The BlurRadius property determines how blurry the drop shadow is, the Color property determines the color of the drop shadow, the Direction property determines the direction that the drop shadow should appear, and the ShadowDepth property determines how far away from the visual element the drop shadow should appear. In the following code listing, a green drop shadow is displayed behind the image, as illustrated in Figure 4-13.

```
<Image Source="tulip.jpg" Margin="24" Stretch="Fill">
  <Image.Effect>
    <DropShadowEffect BlurRadius="20" Color="ForestGreen"
ShadowDepth="10" />
  </Image.Effect>
</Image>
```

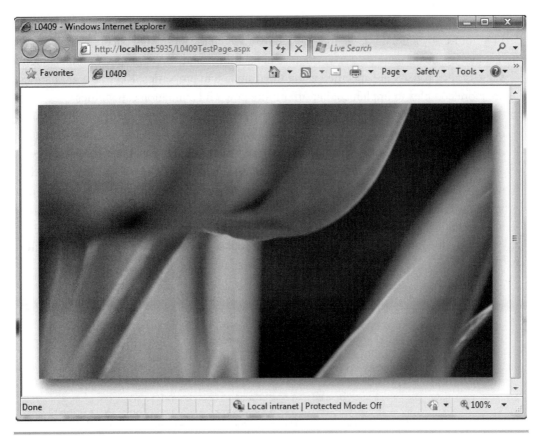

Figure 4-13   A green drop shadow displayed behind the image

Bear in mind that pixel shader visual effects can be applied to any visual element, including controls.

Animation

All elements in Silverlight XAML represent objects in the .NET Framework and Silverlight. Objects have properties with values that can be modified. An animation in software occurs through the progressive modification of a property value over a period of time. For example, the angle property of a rotation transformation can be progressively modified over a period of seconds to cause text affected by the transformation to spin.

The two categories of animations are from-to-by animations and keyframe animations. In a from-to-by animation, the time period over which the animation occurs is typically handled by the duration property, whereas the starting value of the property and the ending value of the property are specified using the from and to properties. Keyframe animations are more complex to implement but offer more powerful animation capabilities.

The various types of animations are implemented in Silverlight through animation objects. All animation objects derive from the Timeline object. Only properties with a value of type double, Color, or Point can be animated. As such, the derived animation object types are DoubleAnimation, ColorAnimation, and PointAnimation. A DoubleAnimation object is used to animate an object property value of the double type. In turn, a ColorAnimation object is used to animate an object property value of type Color, and a PointAnimation object is used to animate an object property value of type Point.

The following markup listing increases the font size of the text in the tbMcGrawHill TextBlock from 12.0 to 60.0 over a period of 5 seconds:

```
<UserControl x:Class="L0408.Page"
    xmlns="http://schemas.microsoft.com/winfx/2006/xaml/presentation"
    xmlns:x="http://schemas.microsoft.com/winfx/2006/xaml"
    Width="614" Height="300" Loaded="UserControl_Loaded">
    <UserControl.Resources>
        <Storyboard x:Name="sbGrow">
            <DoubleAnimation BeginTime="00:00:00"
            Storyboard.TargetName="tbMcGrawHill"
            Storyboard.TargetProperty="(TextBlock.FontSize)"
            From="12.0" To="60.0" Duration="0:0:5"/>
        </Storyboard>
    </UserControl.Resources>
    <Grid x:Name="LayoutRoot" Background="White">
        <TextBlock Height="Auto" Margin="27,38,0,0"
        VerticalAlignment="Top" Text="McGraw Hill" TextWrapping="Wrap"
        Width="Auto" HorizontalAlignment="Left" FontSize="12"
        x:Name="tbMcGrawHill"/>
    </Grid>
</UserControl>
```

As illustrated in the preceding markup, a DoubleAnimation must be contained inside a <StoryBoard> element. A <StoryBoard> may contain more than one animation. The animation in the preceding markup is initiated by a call to the Begin method of the animation from the Loaded event handler for the <UserControl> element.

The behavior of an animation may be further controlled by using additional attributes. For instance, the animation in the preceding markup will play a single time. If an animation should continue to play multiple times, the RepeatBehavior may be set to the number of iterations desired. If the animation should continue to play indefinitely, the RepeatBehavior should be set to "Forever". An animation may also be configured to animate in reverse once it completes by setting the AutoReverse property to "True".

Animation Easing

Although the primary types of animations are from-to-by and keyframe, it is difficult to simulate true extended animation and natural movement using these animation types. To reiterate, from-to-by animations are used to animate a single property of a single object, whereas keyframe animations are used to animate multiple properties of multiple objects simultaneously. However, even the simplest animation is difficult to simulate. Silverlight 3 introduces *animation-easing* effects that are used to assist in making animations appear much more fluid and natural. The animation-easing effects in Silverlight 3 include the following:

- **BackEase**   The BackEase effect "backs up" an animated item slightly before beginning the animation.

- **BounceEase**   The BounceEase effect makes an animation appear to "bounce."

- **CircleEase**   The CircleEase effect makes an animation appear to move along a circular path.

- **CubicEase**   The CubicEase effect moves an animated item along a path determined using a cubic equation.

- **ElasticEase**   The ElasticEase effect makes an animation appear to be on an elastic path, where it bounces back and forth in smaller increments until it comes to rest.

- **ExponentialEase**   The ExponentialEase effect moves an animated item along a path determined using an exponential equation.

- **PowerEase**   The PowerEase effect moves an animated item along a path determined using a power equation.

- **QuadraticEase**   The QuadraticEase effect moves an animated item along a path determined using a quadratic equation.

- **QuarticEase**   The QuarticEase effect moves an animated item along a path determined using a quartic equation.

- **QuinticEase**   The QuinticEase effect moves an animated item along a path determined using a quintic equation.

- **SineEase**   The SineEase effect moves an animated item along a path determined using a sine equation.

To implement an animation-easing effect, add an EasingFunction sub-element to an animation such as the DoubleAnimation element. Although each animation-easing effect includes properties that are relevant to only that effect, the EasingMode property is common to all animation-easing effects.

The EasingMode property may be assigned one of the following values:

- **EaseIn**   The effect occurs at the beginning of the animation.

- **EaseOut**   The effect occurs at the end of the animation.

- **EaseInOut**   The effect occurs at the beginning and end of the animation.

In the following code listing, a BounceEase animation-easing effect is applied to a simple keyframe animation. In itself, the keyframe animation moves the sphere from the top of the control to the bottom and then rotates it. With the addition of the easing effect, the sphere bounces once it reaches the bottom of the control. It's impossible to illustrate the animation using a screenshot, but Figure 4-14 shows the sphere bouncing during animation.

```
<UserControl x:Class="L0410.Page"
    xmlns="http://schemas.microsoft.com/winfx/2006/xaml/presentation"
    xmlns:x="http://schemas.microsoft.com/winfx/2006/xaml"
    xmlns:d="http://schemas.microsoft.com/expression/blend/2008"
    xmlns:mc="http://schemas.openxmlformats.org/markup-
compatibility/2006"
    mc:Ignorable="d"
    d:DesignHeight="300" d:DesignWidth="400" Loaded="UserControl_
Loaded">
        <UserControl.Resources>
            <Storyboard x:Name="sbBounce">
                <DoubleAnimationUsingKeyFrames BeginTime="00:00:00"
                Storyboard.TargetName="ellipse"
                Storyboard.TargetProperty="(UIElement.RenderTransform).
                (TransformGroup.Children)[3].(TranslateTransform.X)">
                    <EasingDoubleKeyFrame KeyTime="00:00:02.1000000"
                        Value="82">
                    <EasingDoubleKeyFrame.EasingFunction>
                        <BounceEase />
```

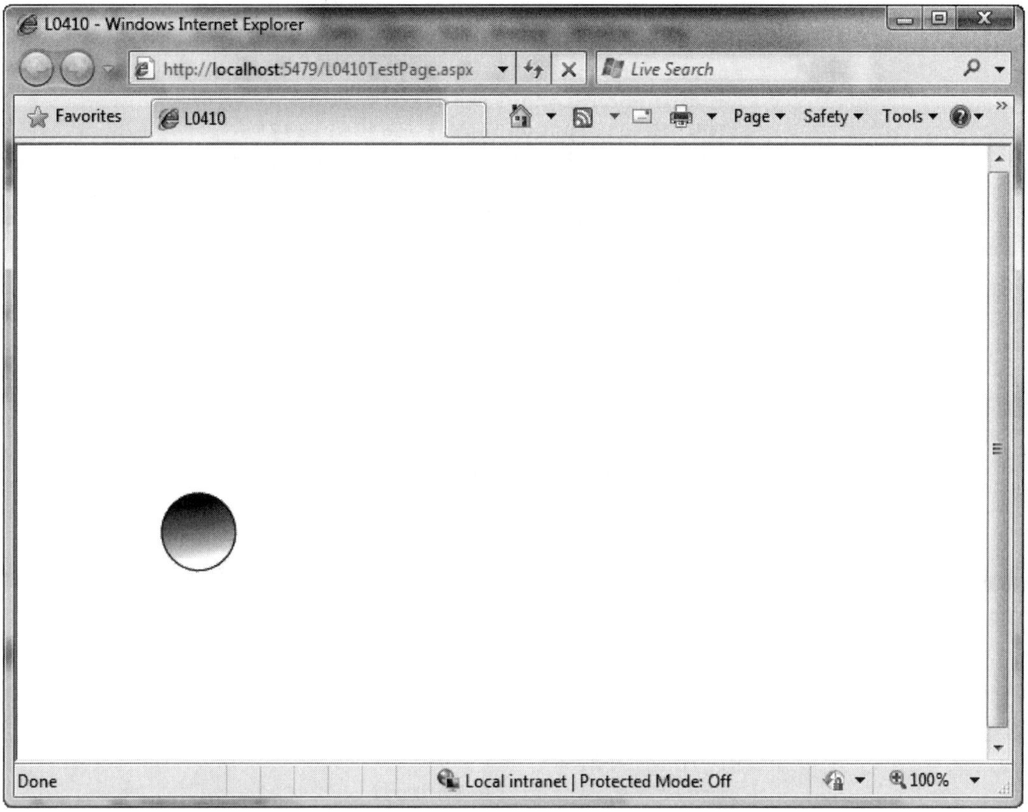

Figure 4-14   A sphere bouncing during animation using a BounceEase animation-easing effect

```
        </EasingDoubleKeyFrame.EasingFunction>
        </EasingDoubleKeyFrame>
</DoubleAnimationUsingKeyFrames>
<DoubleAnimationUsingKeyFrames BeginTime="00:00:00"
Storyboard.TargetName="ellipse"
Storyboard.TargetProperty="(UIElement.RenderTransform).
(TransformGroup.Children)[3].(TranslateTransform.Y)">
        <EasingDoubleKeyFrame KeyTime=
            "00:00:02.1000000" Value="236">
        <EasingDoubleKeyFrame.EasingFunction>
            <BounceEase />
        </EasingDoubleKeyFrame.EasingFunction>
        </EasingDoubleKeyFrame>
</DoubleAnimationUsingKeyFrames>
<DoubleAnimationUsingKeyFrames BeginTime="00:00:00"
```

```
                    Storyboard.TargetName="ellipse"
                    Storyboard.TargetProperty="(UIElement.RenderTransform).
                    (TransformGroup.Children)[2].(RotateTransform.Angle)">
                        <EasingDoubleKeyFrame KeyTime=
                        "00:00:02.1000000" Value="359.342">
                        <EasingDoubleKeyFrame.EasingFunction>
                            <BounceEase />
                        </EasingDoubleKeyFrame.EasingFunction>
                        </EasingDoubleKeyFrame>
                    </DoubleAnimationUsingKeyFrames>
                </Storyboard>
        </UserControl.Resources>

    <Grid x:Name="LayoutRoot" Background="White">
        <Ellipse x:Name="ellipse" Stroke="#FF000000"
        Height="54" HorizontalAlignment="Left" Margin="22,8,0,0"
        VerticalAlignment="Top" Width="54" RenderTransformOrigin="0.5,
        0.5">
            <Ellipse.RenderTransform>
                <TransformGroup>
                    <ScaleTransform/>
                    <SkewTransform/>
                    <RotateTransform/>
                    <TranslateTransform/>
                </TransformGroup>
            </Ellipse.RenderTransform>
                <Ellipse.Fill>
                <LinearGradientBrush EndPoint="0.5,1"
                    StartPoint="0.5,0">
                        <GradientStop Color="#FF000000"/>
                        <GradientStop Color="#FFFFFFFF"
                            Offset="0.836"/>
                </LinearGradientBrush>
                </Ellipse.Fill>
        </Ellipse>

    </Grid>
</UserControl>
```

Deep Zoom

Deep Zoom is an imaging technology that was released by Microsoft in March 2008. Deep Zoom is based on Silverlight 2 and later and allows for quickly viewing incredibly detailed and large images over the Web. Deep Zoom functions in a manner very similar to online mapping applications by sending the image data only for the portion of the image actually being viewed to the client. Deep Zoom is a great concept that's based on the same concept as a web search engine. A search conducted by a client may return a million hits. It would take considerable time to return a million hits to the client's machine so that they could scroll through them. However, a search engine returns the results in pages, generally 10 at a time. Returning 10 hits to the user's machine takes very little time. Furthermore, it is proven that if users don't find a match for a search in the first page of hits, they will modify their search and move on. Hence, search engines return only a portion of the hits being viewed by the client, thus optimizing search engine performance. Likewise, Deep Zoom can offer the display of incredibly detailed and large images over the Web with great performance by sending the data only for the portion of the image being viewed to the user's machine.

The Deep Zoom Composer is a free download and is used to prepare large images and collections of images for viewing in Deep Zoom mode. The Deep Zoom Composer is shown in Figure 4-15. The Deep Zoom Composer can be downloaded at http://www.microsoft.com/downloads/details.aspx?FamilyID=457B17B7-52BF-4BDA-87A3-FA8A4673F8BF&displaylang=en.

Figure 4-15 The Microsoft Deep Zoom Composer

Try This Use the MultiscaleImage Control
in Deep Zoom Composer

1. Navigate to http://www.microsoft.com/downloads/details.aspx?FamilyID=457B17B7-52BF-4BDA-87A3-FA8A4673F8BF&displaylang=en to download the Deep Zoom Composer.

2. At the Deep Zoom Composer download page, click the Download button.

3. When prompted with the File Download dialog, click the Run button to install the Deep Zoom Composer.

4. Click the Next button all the way through the Deep Zoom installer to accept all the default settings.

5. Once Deep Zoom Composer is installed, start or open it.

6. When prompted by the Deep Zoom Composer startup screen, select the link to create a new project.

7. When the New Project dialog is displayed, assign the new project a name and select a location for creating the project. Click the OK button.

8. The Deep Zoom Composer presents three tabs across the top of a project: Import, Compose, and Export.

9. With the Import tab selected, click the Add Image … button from the pane on the right side of the Deep Zoom Composer window. Add one or more images to the project.

10. Click the Compose tab.

11. Drag the images from the All Images pane, drop them on the design palette, and arrange them as desired.

12. Click the Export tab.

13. From the pane on the right side, you can select to export the project to a PhotoZoom account or export the project using custom settings. A Windows Live PhotoZoom account is free to create using your Windows Live ID.

14. When the project is exported, select the option to preview it in the browser.

15. After previewing the project, close the Deep Zoom Composer. You may explore the Deep Zoom Composer project by opening the solution in Visual Studio 2008.

The output of a Deep Zoom Composer project may also be manually displayed by using the Silverlight MultiscaleImage control. The MultiscaleImage control includes several properties and events that can be utilized to control viewing of a Deep Zoom image in incredible ways.

Figure 4-16 shows the Silverlight 2 developer reference diagram as displayed using Deep Zoom technology.

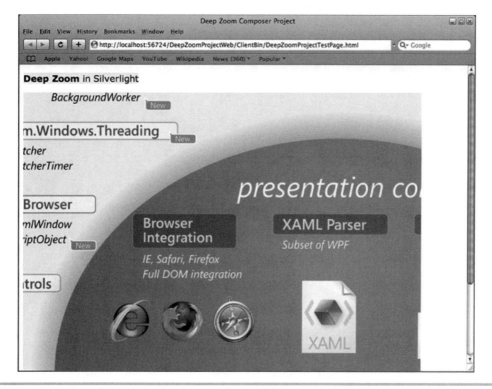

Figure 4-16 The Silverlight 2 developer reference diagram using Deep Zoom technology

Conclusion

In order for developers to be accomplished at creating Silverlight applications, they must have a thorough understanding of creating, managing, and controlling graphics and animations in Silverlight. Two-dimensional graphics can easily be created and have effects applied to them, but Silverlight currently does not support a true 3-D rendering engine. Any graphical element displayed in Silverlight can be animated over a timeline, and Deep Zoom technology can be used to render very large, high-resolution images in Silverlight applications while offering great performance.

Chapter 5

Preparing Media for Use in Silverlight

Key Concepts & Skills

● Learn how to integrate media into a Silverlight application

● Gain an understanding of how to create the "wet floor" effect using video files

● Review the media types supported in Silverlight

● Explore the Expression Encoder

In addition to displaying incredible graphics and animation, Silverlight is able to display on-demand and live streaming audio and video media, giving the user complete playback control. Although a media stream does not have to be specifically prepared for playback using Silverlight, Silverlight only supports the display of certain media formats. Also, when media is prepared for display using Silverlight, the media is able to take advantage of Silverlight-specific functionality and features.

Integrating Multimedia

The key feature available in Silverlight from its inception has been the ability to display streaming and on-demand media over the Web. Silverlight was designed to be platform independent and browser independent, and as such it must not be dependent on an external player or a particular codec. Silverlight is able to display media using an embedded media player so that the client system does not need to have a player installed. Most media technologies require that the client have a particular media player installed. With Silverlight, once the Silverlight plug-in is installed, all Silverlight features are accessible, including media playback.

Chapter 3 illustrated how to integrate multimedia into an ASP.NET AJAX application through the use of the ASP.NET Extensions asp:MediaPlayer control. The asp:MediaPlayer control is an implementation of the Silverlight <MediaElement> element. The <MediaElement> element is used to connect to multimedia sources from Silverlight. The following markup snippet is used to display a simple video in WMV format:

```
<MediaElement Width="500" Height="500" Canvas.Left="40"
Canvas.Top="40" Source="axe_murderer.wmv" Stretch="Fill"/>
```

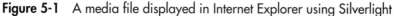

Figure 5-1   A media file displayed in Internet Explorer using Silverlight

Figure 5-1 shows the media file displayed using Internet Explorer.

A slight modification to the preceding markup renders control over media playback through mouse interaction. The MediaElement should have a name assigned to it, and it can then be accessed using code. In the following markup snippet, the MediaElement has been modified to assign a name to the element and fire the event associated with the MouseLeftButtonUp method:

```
<MediaElement Width="500" Height="500" Canvas.Left="40"
Canvas.Top="40" Source="axe_murderer.wmv" Stretch="Fill"
x:Name="myVideo" MouseLeftButtonUp="MediaElement_MouseLeftButtonUp"/>
```

The next snippet shows the code included in the method associated with the MouseLeftButtonUp event, which is used to toggle the current state of the media between play and pause:

```
if (myVideo.CurrentState == MediaElementState.Playing){

  myVideo.Pause();
} else {

  myVideo.Play();
  }
```

Try This Create a Wet Floor Effect

A popular visual effect when playing video using Silverlight or WPF is the "wet floor" effect. This effect can easily be accomplished by using Expression Blend. It consists of displaying a video twice—once for display and once for reflection. This effect can be easily accomplished by using two MediaElement elements. However, taking this approach will load the media file into memory twice, and the two copies playing may become out of sync with each other. The preferred approach is to display the playing media by painting it onto a rectangle using a VideoBrush and then displaying the media reflection via the actual MediaElement. Hence, the media file will only be loaded into memory a single time, and the media display and reflection will not display out of sync. Here are the steps to follow to create the wet floor effect:

1. Start or open Microsoft Expression Blend.

2. When prompted with the Blend startup screen, select the option to create a new project.

3. In the New Project dialog, select Silverlight 3 Application, assign the new application a name, select a location to create the new application, select a programming language, and click OK.

4. Select the Project tab from the pane on the right side of Blend.

5. In the Files panel, right-click the newly created project and select Add Existing Item....

6. From the Add Existing Item dialog, navigate to and select a video media file to use for the wet floor effect.

7. Once you have added this file to the project, from the Files panel, drag the newly added media file and drop it onto the Silverlight design area. The video file should appear in the design area.

8. Press F5 to test the application in the default browser to ensure that the media file plays as expected. Close the browser and return to Blend.

9. From the toolbox on the far left side of Blend, drag a Rectangle and drop it onto the design area. Configure the newly dropped Rectangle to be the same size as the media file display.

10. In the design area, select the XAML tab to display the Silverlight XAML.

11. Locate the XAML for the newly dropped Rectangle. Modify the fill of the Rectangle so that it includes a VideoBrush that refers to the media element, as shown here:

```
<Rectangle Margin="27,18,108,178" Stroke="#FF000000">
  <Rectangle.Fill>
    <VideoBrush SourceName="axe_murderer_wmv" />
  </Rectangle.Fill>
        </Rectangle>
```

12. In the design area, select the Design tab to display the Silverlight design area.

13. Maneuver the Rectangle and media element so that the media element is displayed below the Rectangle.

14. Press F5 to test the application in the default browser. You should now see two copies of the media file playing. Close the browser and return to Blend.

15. Select the media element.

16. Using the Transform panel of the Properties tab, select the Flip Y Axis option from the Flip tab on the panel to flip the media element upside down.

17. Using the Brushes panel of the Properties tab, select the Gradient Brush tab.

18. Select the dark gradient stop that is set all the way to the left and configure the Alpha value for the gradient stop to 0.

19. Drag the gradient stop to the right some to adjust the opacity of the media element. Figure 5-2 identifies the gradient and alpha value settings.

(continued)

Figure 5-2 The Expression Blend gradient palette.

20. Press F5 to test the application in the default browser. You should see the wet floor effect in action. Close the browser to return to Blend.

21. Save the project and exit Blend.

The XAML shown next is used to generate the wet floor effect using the same video file illustrated previously:

```
<UserControl x:Class="L0502.Page"
    xmlns="http://schemas.microsoft.com/winfx/2006/xaml/presentation"
    xmlns:x="http://schemas.microsoft.com/winfx/2006/xaml"
    Width="594" Height="424">
    <UserControl.Background>
        <LinearGradientBrush EndPoint="0.5,1" StartPoint="0.5,0">
            <GradientStop Color="#FF000000"/>
            <GradientStop Color="#FFFFFFFF" Offset="1"/>
        </LinearGradientBrush>
    </UserControl.Background>
```

```
<Grid x:Name="LayoutRoot">
  <Grid.Background>
      <LinearGradientBrush EndPoint="0.5,1" StartPoint="0.5,0">
          <GradientStop Color="#FFB7936B"/>
          <GradientStop Color="#FFFFFFFF" Offset="0.469"/>
      </LinearGradientBrush>
  </Grid.Background>
  <MediaElement Height="181" Margin="114,0,149,30"
  VerticalAlignment="Bottom" Source="axe_murderer.wmv"
  x:Name="myVideo" RenderTransformOrigin="0.5,0.5">
    <MediaElement.OpacityMask>
     <LinearGradientBrush EndPoint="0.499000012874603,0"
     StartPoint="0.500999987125397,1"> <GradientStop
        Color="#FF000000"/>
     <GradientStop Color="#00FFFFFF" Offset="0.531"/>
            </LinearGradientBrush>
        </MediaElement.OpacityMask>
        <MediaElement.RenderTransform>
          <TransformGroup>
               <ScaleTransform ScaleY="-1"/>
               <SkewTransform/>
               <RotateTransform/>
               <TranslateTransform/>
          </TransformGroup>
        </MediaElement.RenderTransform>
  </MediaElement>
  <Rectangle Height="181" HorizontalAlignment="Stretch"
  Margin="114,31,149,0" VerticalAlignment="Top"
  Stroke="#FF000000">
            <Rectangle.Fill>
          <VideoBrush SourceName="myVideo" />
        </Rectangle.Fill>
        </Rectangle>
    </Grid>
</UserControl>
```

The result of the preceding XAML is displayed in Figure 5-3.

The code in this listing implements the wet floor effect that is ubiquitous with Web 2.0 applications. *Web 2.0* is a commonly used term that describes applications being created

(continued)

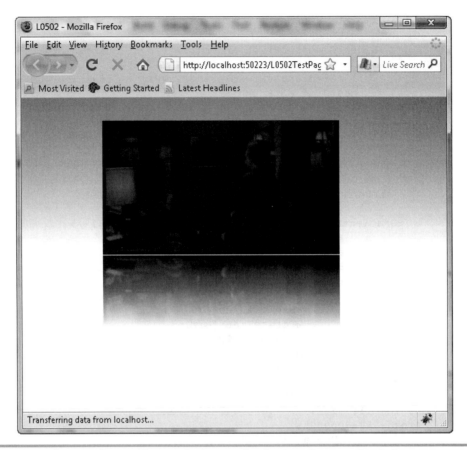

Figure 5-3   The "wet floor" effect applied to media displayed using Silverlight

that utilize the Web as a primary business platform instead of as a nicety. In the preceding code, the myVideo media element is used to load the media and display it. The rectangle fill is set to reflect what is displayed by the media element. The media element has a gradient fill applied to it, with an Opacity setting used to fade the media on one side. The media element is also transformed so that it is rotated upside-down.

Supported Media Types

Silverlight 3 supports the types of media listed in this section.

Server-Side Playlist (SSPL) formats:

- Advanced Stream Redirector (ASX) playlist file format. A playlist resides, or is generated, on the server and is used to group a collection of media elements and determine the order in which the media elements should be viewed. Silverlight supports ASX when the source of a media element is set to the ASX file (in the same manner as media is displayed using a media element).

Audio formats:

- Windows Media Audio 7 (WMA 7)

- Windows Media Audio 8 (WMA 8)

- Windows Media Audio 9 (WMA 9)

- ISO/MPEG Layer 3–compliant data stream input (MP3)

Video formats:

- Windows Media Video 7 (WMV 1)

- Windows Media Video 8 (WMV 2)

- Windows Media Video 9 (WMV 3)

- Windows Media Video Advanced Profile, non-VC1 (WMVA)

- Windows Media Video Advanced Profile, VC1 (WMVC1)

- H.264

The VC1 media types are used to display media that is encoded for high definition (HD), whereas the other media types listed are best suited for displaying video media encoded for smaller formats.

Microsoft Expression Encoder

Audio and video—and the combination of the two—are generically referred to as *media*. Media may exist in various formats. Most media vendors, such as Microsoft, Apple, and Real, distribute and save media in proprietary formats. Most media players will play media in multiple formats. There are also industry-standard media formats that most players also support. Media may be stored in a particular format when it is saved after being recorded or may be converted from one format to another using a conversion tool.

When media is prepared for playback in a particular format, the process is referred to as *media encoding*. During the encoding process, the stream of media bits may also be manipulated and modified. For instance, via a media encoder, a media (video/audio) stream may be played to a certain point and then another media source may be interjected. Television production studios perform this type of encoding action to interject a commercial into a live or recorded media stream (television show) that is being broadcast.

Microsoft released the Expression Encoder (EE) with the Expression Suite of tools that target designers. EE offers advanced media editing and encoding functionality, including the ability to encode and stream media from the file system or media being recorded live, overlay media elements, and add closed captioning to streamed media. Expression Encoder is shown in Figure 5-4.

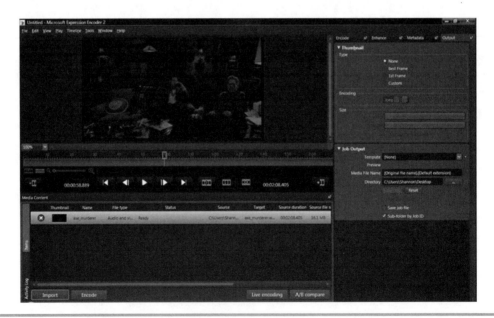

Figure 5-4 Microsoft Expression Encoder

Media Content Panel

The Expression Encoder Media Content panel is used to import and maintain media streams that are being manipulated in Expression Encoder. For instance, if a media file is to be imported, modified, and then saved in that modified format, the media file will be imported using the Media Content panel. The Media Content panel includes two tabs: the Items tab and the Activity Log tab. The Items tab displays the media streams that have been imported for use in Expression Encoder, and the Activity Log tab displays status messages that result from actions taken. Any media streams that are displayed on the Items tab may be removed by clicking the button labeled "Remove item from job."

The Media Content panel also includes four buttons that are displayed across the bottom of the panel:

- **Import**   This button is used to import media streams into Expression Encoder.

- **Encode**   This button is used to export, or save, the compilation of work that has been completed using Expression Encoder into a single resultant media file that is ready for use.

- **Live Encoding**   This button is used to enter into a separate mode within Expression Encoder that is designed for capturing multiple live audio and video feeds, on-demand feeds, manipulating those feeds, and rendering a new media file that is displayed in the Items tab of the Media Content panel once Live Encoding mode has been exited.

- **A/B Compare**   This button is used to display a media stream using two different playback quality settings in a side-by-side display mode so that the designer can compare the two visually and determine which quality setting should be used.

Expression Encoder also includes an active display and design area where the currently selected media stream is displayed. Figure 5-5 shows the active display area and the Media Content panel.

Side Panels

Expression Encoder offers the display of up to four side panels for use in working with a selected media stream. The side panels are named Encode, Enhance, Metadata, and Output. The Encode panel is used to determine and configure audio and video encoding

Figure 5-5   The Expression Encoder Media Content panel and active display area

settings for a selected media stream. The Enhance panel is used to configure a selected media stream by adding overlays, a leader, and a trailer. The Metadata panel is used to add descriptive metadata information that should be encoded into a media stream (such as the author and copyright information), add markers (or chapters) to a selected media stream, and add script commands to a selected media stream. The Output panel is used to determine the destination name and location of the resultant encoded output once the Encode button has been clicked. Figure 5-6 shows the side panels.

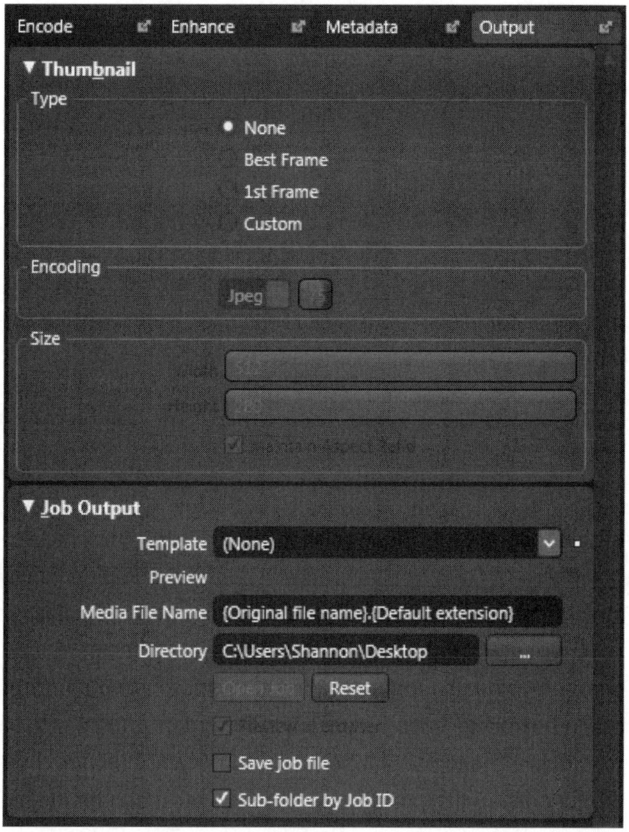

Figure 5-6   The Expression Encoder side panels

Conclusion

Silverlight supports the display of audio and video media streams in many different formats. Silverlight also supports the display of on-demand media streams as well as live media streams. The Expression Suite of design tools is used to create and manipulate XAML and media for use with WPF and Silverlight. Expression Encoder is used to manipulate and configure media streams and includes functionality for merging media streams as well as adding leaders, trailers, markers, script commands, and overlays. Expression Encoder is also capable of capturing multiple live audio and video media streams.

Chapter 6

Communicating with the Outside World

Key Concepts & Skills

- Gain a high-level understanding of sockets programming

- Learn about service-oriented architecture (SOA), Web Services, and WCF services

- Explore the networking and syndication protocols supported by Silverlight

- Observe how to create an RSS feed reader using Silverlight

Developing applications in a Silverlight world may present a mental obstacle to veteran ASP.NET developers. Developers who have web development experience will have the concept of continual postbacks deeply engrained into their minds. A Silverlight application executes within a plug-in environment, and as such there are no automatic postbacks to the server where the Silverlight application originated. If a call to a server is necessary from a Silverlight application, the call must be manually initiated by the developer.

Silverlight 3 supports several different networking protocols that enable communications with a server, as described in the following sections.

Sockets

Silverlight 3 supports sockets programming through the System.Net.Sockets namespace. A *socket* is a low-level communication channel that is generally configured using TCP/IP. Silverlight 3 supports asynchronously sending data back and forth across a socket over TCP ports, ranging from 4502 to 4534. Be aware that sockets programming is low level, requires more code to implement, and lacks the more robust features of some of the other networking standards. Also, Silverlight 3 supports socket communications between a Silverlight application and any server as long as a cross-domain policy implementation is in place on the server.

Sockets are most commonly used to push data from the server to a client. A socket, when used in this manner, eliminates the need to poll the server for updates on a timed basis and creates a client/server relationship based on the publisher/subscriber paradigm. Another benefit of using sockets is that when a client polls the server and data has not been updated, the client request to the server is a wasted effort. By pushing data from the server to the client, there are no wasted network communications.

For more information on Silverlight 3 and sockets programming, visit the MSDN article entitled "Working with Sockets," located at http://msdn.microsoft.com/en-us/library/cc296248(VS.96).aspx.

Service-Oriented Architecture

Service-oriented architecture (SOA) is an industry-accepted architecture that defines how an object should be created so that the methods of the object are accessible over the Web and can be consumed by using well-supported web standards such as HTTP, XML, SOAP, and WSDL.

For more information on SOA, visit the Open Group SOA Definition located at http://www.opengroup.org/projects/soa/doc.tpl?gdid=10632.

Serialization

The Web is a stateless environment. In a typical web communication scenario, a request for a resource is made by a client passing a message to the web server. The web server, in turn, replies to the client by sending a response message. Messages continue to be sent back and forth between the client and server to conduct the communications necessary to deliver an application. The messages that are sent between the client and the server contain simple text. If the messages used to conduct communications over the Web contain only text, how do more complex items such as images, graphs, animations, and multimedia get transported from a web server to a client? The answer is that all items transported over the Web are first converted to text, then transported over the Web, and then re-created from the text representation of the item into their original form. The process of converting a complex item to a text representation is called *serialization*.

To convert an item from a text representation back to the original object is called *deserialization*. The most common formats for an item to be converted to for transportation over the Web are XML, SOAP, and JSON. The .NET Framework and Silverlight both include facilities for serializing and deserializing data.

NOTE
Most classes in the .NET Framework are serializable. However, when a custom class is serialized, it must be marked as serializable using the [Serializable] attribute, must include a default (parameter-less) constructor, and must include a public property for each data member to be exposed outside of the class. To circumvent inherent issues mentioned here, when you're developing a custom class, the class may implement the ISerializable interface or IXmlSerializable interface.

Web Services

A common implementation of SOA is a Web Service. Developers have been able to create Web Services by using the .NET Framework since the .NET Framework was originally released. An easy way to build a Web Service that can be consumed by a Silverlight application is to select the option "Add a new Web to the solution" when creating a new Silverlight project in Visual Studio. The new website that is created serves as a test harness project for the Silverlight application. A Web Service will not exist in the new Web by default but can easily be added by right-clicking the web project and selecting Add New Item. From the Add New Item dialog, select Web Service. Figure 6-1 illustrates the project as displayed in the Solution Explorer once the new Silverlight project is created and a new Web Service is added to the project. The example illustrated here creates a Web Service that reads weather forecast data from a database.

The sample Web Service will act as a very simple customer management system. When accessed from a Silverlight application, a Web Service acts as a business facade tier of an application. However, the business facade tier is typically divided between the Web Service on the server and the Silverlight application, and business objects are serialized, deserialized, and transported over the Web. Figure 6-2 illustrates the simple Customers ERD, which contains a single table.

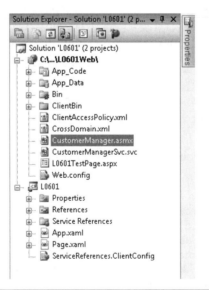

Figure 6-1 A Web Service in a Visual Studio 2010 project as displayed in the Solution Explorer

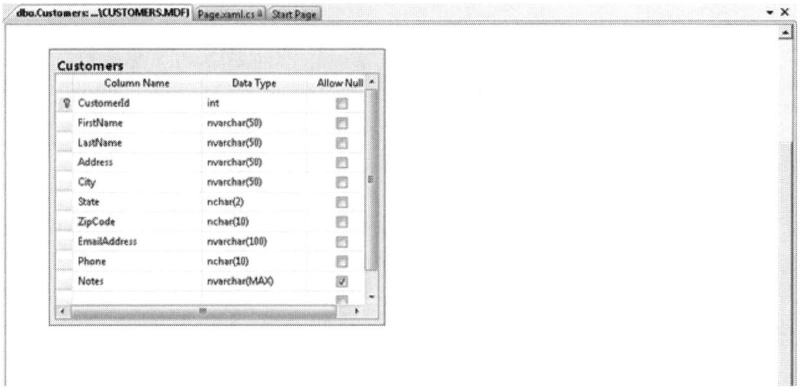

Figure 6-2 The sample Customers database diagram

The code in this sample Web Service contains two web methods at this point. The first web method returns a single Customer object and will be used to display a single customer. The single customer to be returned will be determined based on a customer ID supplied as an input parameter to the web method. The second web method will return a generic list of Customer objects and will be used to display a list of customers.

Each web method will retrieve customer information from the database by calling a stored procedure. The code for the stored procedures is shown in the following listing:

```
/*
  this stored procedure returns all customer profiles.
*/
create procedure dbo.GetCustomers
as

begin
     set nocount on

     -- retrieve customers.
     select

       CustomerId,
       FirstName,
       LastName,
       Address,
       City,
       State,
```

```
            ZipCode,
            EmailAddress,
            Phone,
            Notes

        from

            Customers
end


/*
this stored procedure returns a single customer profile based on a
supplied id.
*/
CREATE procedure dbo.GetCustomerById

 @customerId as int
as


begin
        set nocount on

        -- retrieve customers.
        select

          CustomerId,
          FirstName,
          LastName,
          Address,
          City,
          State,
          ZipCode,
          EmailAddress,
          Phone,
          Notes

        from

          Customers

        where

          CustomerId = @customerId
end
```

In order for a class to be able to be serialized, transported over the Web, and then deserialized, the class must contain a default constructor and must be marked up by using the [Serializable] attribute. The following listing shows the code for the Customer class:

```
using System;

 [Serializable]
public class Customer
{

    // default properties.
    public int CustomerId { get; set; }
    public string FirstName { get; set; }
    public string LastName { get; set; }
    public string Address { get; set; }
    public string City { get; set; }
    public string State { get; set; }
    public string ZipCode { get; set; }
    public string EmailAddress { get; set; }
    public string Phone { get; set; }
    public string Notes { get; set; }

    public Customer(){}
}
```

In a typical client/server environment, a business facade class, such as the Customer class, would include methods for inserting new customers, updating existing customers, deleting customers, and selecting customers. However, in order to design the class and Web Service correctly for a Silverlight application, the Customer class will simply contain customer data, and the methods used to manage customer data will be parsed out and added to the Web Service itself. The Web Service is shown in the next code listing and includes two web methods for retrieving all customers and a single customer by using the customer ID. In a real-world example, the Web Service would be more robust and include web methods to insert, update, and delete customers as well.

The following code utilizes simple ADO.NET to call the stored procedures and handle the data. Code that accesses data may also utilize Language Integrated Query (LINQ) or the new ADO.NET Entity Framework (more specific data-access code will be covered in a later chapter).

```
using System;
using System.Collections;
using System.Collections.Generic;
using System.Web;
using System.Web.Services;
```

```csharp
using System.Web.Services.Protocols;
using System.Data;
using System.Data.SqlClient;
using System.Configuration;

[WebService(Namespace = "http://tempuri.org/")]
[WebServiceBinding(ConformsTo = WsiProfiles.BasicProfile1_1)]
public class CustomerManager : System.Web.Services.WebService
{

    // create a connection to the database.
    SqlConnection cn = new SqlConnection(ConfigurationManager
        .ConnectionStrings["customerDB"].ConnectionString);

    public CustomerManager()
    {

        //Uncomment the following line if using designed components
        //InitializeComponent();
    }

    [WebMethod]
    public List<Customer> GetCustomers()
    {

        // create a new list for storing customers.
        List<Customer> customers = new List<Customer>();

        try
        {

            // open the connection.
            cn.Open();

            // process the stored procedure.
            using (SqlCommand cmd =
                new SqlCommand("GetCustomers", cn))
            {

                cmd.CommandType = CommandType.StoredProcedure;

                // execute the command and store the results into a
                // datareader.
                SqlDataReader rdr = cmd.ExecuteReader();

                // were any rows returned?
                if (rdr.HasRows)
```

```csharp
                {
                    Customer customer;
                    while (rdr.Read())
                    {
                        customer = new Customer();
                        customer.CustomerId =
                            int.Parse(rdr["CustomerId"].ToString());
                        customer.FirstName = rdr["FirstName"]
                            .ToString();
                        customer.LastName = rdr["LastName"]
                            .ToString();
                        customer.Address = rdr["Address"].ToString();
                        customer.City = rdr["City"].ToString();
                        customer.State = rdr["State"].ToString();
                        customer.ZipCode = rdr["ZipCode"].ToString();
                        customer.EmailAddress = rdr["EmailAddress"]
                            .ToString();
                        customer.Phone = rdr["Phone"].ToString();
                        customer.Notes = rdr["Notes"].ToString();
                        customers.Add(customer);
                    }
                }
            }

            return customers;
        }
        catch (Exception ex)
        {

            return customers;
        }
        finally {

            cn.Close();
            cn.Dispose();
            cn = null;
        }
    }

[WebMethod]
public Customer GetCustomerById(int customerId) {

    // create a new customer.
    Customer customer = new Customer();

    try
```

```
    {
        // open the connection.
        cn.Open();

        // process the stored procedure.
        using (SqlCommand cmd =
            new SqlCommand("GetCustomerById", cn))
        {

            cmd.CommandType = CommandType.StoredProcedure;

            // prepare the input parameter.
            SqlParameter parm = new SqlParameter();
            parm.ParameterName = "@customerId";
            parm.SqlDbType = SqlDbType.Int;
            parm.Value = customerId;
            cmd.Parameters.Add(parm);

            // execute the command and store the results into a
            // datareader.
            SqlDataReader rdr = cmd.ExecuteReader();

            // were any rows returned?
            if (rdr.HasRows)
            {

                while (rdr.Read())
                {

                    customer.CustomerId =
                        int.Parse(rdr["CustomerId"].ToString());
                    customer.FirstName = rdr["FirstName"]
                        .ToString();
                    customer.LastName = rdr["LastName"]
                        .ToString();
                    customer.Address = rdr["Address"].ToString();
                    customer.City = rdr["City"].ToString();
                    customer.State = rdr["State"].ToString();
                    customer.ZipCode = rdr["ZipCode"].ToString();
                    customer.EmailAddress = rdr["EmailAddress"]
                        .ToString();
                    customer.Phone = rdr["Phone"].ToString();
                    customer.Notes = rdr["Notes"].ToString();
                }
            }
        }
```

```
        return customer;
    }
    catch (Exception ex)
    {

        return customer;
    }
    finally
    {

        cn.Close();
        cn.Dispose();
        cn = null;
    }
  }
}
```

Once the Web Service has been completed and tested, it can be consumed by a Silverlight application. Consuming a Web Service from a Silverlight application is straightforward and normally problem-free when done within Visual Studio 2010. Silverlight supports, by default, calling services that reside at the same domain where the Silverlight control is hosted. However, consuming a Web Service that is hosted at a domain other than the domain where the Silverlight control is hosted can present challenges.

ClientAccessPolicy.xml File

In order to protect Web Services from being called by malicious Silverlight controls, Microsoft added a configuration file to Web Services so that access to the service from a control can be configured. A Web Service that is to be consumed by a Silverlight application should include a ClientAccessPolicy.xml file in the root of the virtual directory where the Web Service is hosted. The ClientAccessPolicy.xml file includes information pertaining to the controls and domains that are allowed to call a service. A standard ClientAccessPolicy.xml file is shown here:

```
<?xml version="1.0" encoding="utf-8" ?>
<access-policy>
  <cross-domain-access>
    <policy>
      <allow-from http-request-headers="*">
        <domain uri="*" />
      </allow-from>
      <grant-to>
        <resource path="/" include-subpaths="true"/>
      </grant-to>
```

```
    </policy>
  </cross-domain-access>
</access-policy>
```

CrossDomain.xml File

The ClientAccessPolicy.xml file was created by Microsoft for use with Silverlight and Web Services. However, there is an industry standard, the CrossDomain.xml file, already in place that is being used in a similar manner for accessing server resources from other RIA technologies such as Adobe Flash. The CrossDomain.xml file is used to determine which domains may make a call to a service. Silverlight supports a subset of the CrossDomain standard.

If a CrossDomain.xml file is used, it should be placed in the root of the virtual folder that hosts the service, just like the ClientAccessPolicy.xml file. It should be noted that if both a CrossDomain.xml file and a ClientAccessPolicy.xml file are used, the ClientAccessPolicy.xml file will take precedence over the CrossDomain.xml file when accessed by Silverlight. Both files may be used to support Silverlight as well as other technologies such as Adobe Flash. A sample CrossDomain.xml file is shown next:

```
<?xml version="1.0" encoding="utf-8" ?>
<!DOCTYPE cross-domain-policy SYSTEM
"http://www.macromedia.com/xml/dtds/cross-domain-policy.dtd">
<cross-domain-policy>
  <allow-http-request-headers-from domain="*" headers="*" />
</cross-domain-policy>
```

Try This Add a Service Reference

1. Start or open Visual Studio 2010.

2. Ensure that the Silverlight project where the reference should be added is open.

3. In the Visual Studio 2010 Solution Explorer, right-click the Silverlight project and select Add Service Reference from the context menu.

4. From the Add Service Reference dialog, select the Discover button to automatically discover all services hosted in the current solution.

5. Locate the service that should be consumed by the Silverlight application and assign it a namespace.

6. Click the OK button. Figure 6-3 shows the Add Service Reference dialog.

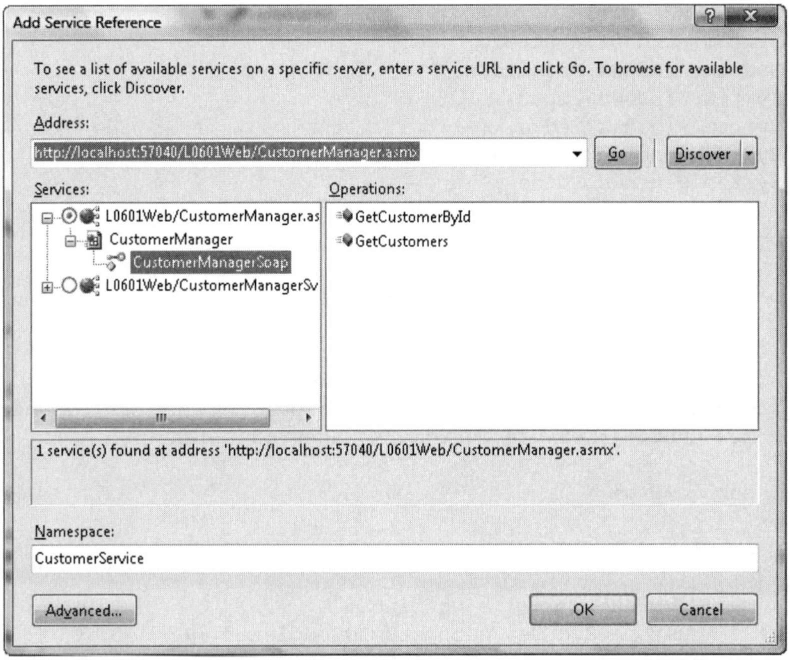

Figure 6-3   The Add Service Reference dialog

When a service reference is added in Visual Studio 2010, Visual Studio inspects the service and creates a proxy class for communicating with the service. The proxy class contains definitions for any classes that will be serialized, deserialized, and transported to and from the service.

Once a service reference has been successfully added, reference it in code in order to consume it. Silverlight 3 only supports asynchronous network calls. Both synchronous and asynchronous processing are discussed in detail in Chapter 10. To summarize, in the code-behind file of the Silverlight control that will consume the service, an instance of the service class must be created, a callback method must be created, and a call to a method must occur. In the following code listing, the Customer Web service is consumed and then the customer's name is displayed in a TextBlock to illustrate success:

```
using System;
using System.Collections.Generic;
using System.Linq;
using System.Net;
```

(continued)

```
using System.Windows;
using System.Windows.Controls;
using System.Windows.Documents;
using System.Windows.Input;
using System.Windows.Media;
using System.Windows.Media.Animation;
using System.Windows.Shapes;

namespace L0601
{
    public partial class Page : UserControl
    {

        // create an instance of the customer manager service.
        CustomerService.CustomerManagerSoapClient customerSvc =
        new CustomerService.CustomerManagerSoapClient();

        public Page()
        {
            InitializeComponent();

            // create a callback method.
            customerSvc.GetCustomerByIdCompleted +=
            new EventHandler<L0601.CustomerService
            .GetCustomerByIdCompletedEventArgs>
            (customerSvc_GetCustomerByIdCompleted);
            customerSvc.GetCustomerByIdAsync(1);
        }

        void customerSvc_GetCustomerByIdCompleted(object
        sender, L0601.CustomerService.GetCustomerByIdCompletedEventArgs e)
        {

            // capture the customer class.
            CustomerService.Customer customer = e.Result;

            // display the customer name.
            tbOutput.Text = "customer name is " + customer.FirstName +
            " " + customer.LastName;
        }
    }
}
```

Figure 6-4 illustrates the resultant customer name displayed in a Silverlight TextBlock control.

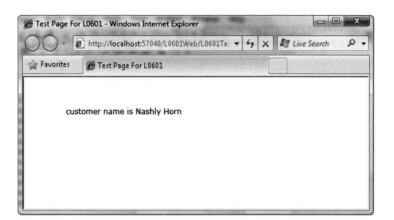

Figure 6-4   Customer information displayed in Silverlight

Windows Communication Foundation (WCF)

Windows Communication Foundation (WCF) is the latest distributed application development technology from Microsoft. WCF consolidates Web Services and .NET Remoting into a single technology. Creating a WCF service is very similar to creating a Web Service; however, the programming steps more closely follow object-oriented (OO) principles.

Every WCF service class must implement an interface. An interface defines the contract (guaranteed internal schema and design) that a class must adhere to when the interface is implemented. If a developer knows that a class implements a particular interface, the developer can rest assured that the class implements a particular internal structure. When a WCF service is consumed, the interface is read to determine the structure of the WSDL file.

NOTE
WCF presents a much more object-oriented environment. As such, when a custom class is being prepared to be serialized from a WCF service, the use of the [Serializable] attribute and public properties is not necessary. Instead, methods in the class are marked up using the [DataOperation] attribute and data members are marked up using the [DataMember] attribute.

WCF Example

Beyond improved design concepts implemented to comply with OO principles, creating a WCF service is very similar to creating an ASP.NET Web Service. The following code listing illustrates the interface implemented by the WCF service:

```
using System;
using System.ServiceModel;
using System.Collections;
using System.Collections.Generic;

[ServiceContract]
public interface ICustomerManagerSvc
{
    [OperationContract]
    Customer GetCustomerById(int customerId);

    [OperationContract]
    List<Customer> GetCustomers();
}
```

The next code listing shows the WCF service file that implements the interface:

```
using System;
using System.Collections;
using System.Collections.Generic;
using System.Configuration;
using System.Data;
using System.Data.SqlClient;
using System.Runtime.Serialization;
using System.ServiceModel;

public class CustomerManagerSvc : ICustomerManagerSvc
{
    // create a connection to the database.
    SqlConnection cn = new
    SqlConnection(ConfigurationManager.ConnectionStrings["customerDB"]
    .ConnectionString);

    public Customer GetCustomerById(int customerId) {

        // create a new customer.
        Customer customer = new Customer();

        try
        {
```

```csharp
// open the connection.
cn.Open();

// process the stored procedure.
using (SqlCommand cmd =
    new SqlCommand("GetCustomerById", cn))
{

    cmd.CommandType = CommandType.StoredProcedure;

    // prepare the input parameter.
    SqlParameter parm = new SqlParameter();
    parm.ParameterName = "@customerId";
    parm.SqlDbType = SqlDbType.Int;
    parm.Value = customerId;
    cmd.Parameters.Add(parm);

    // execute the command and store the results into a
    // datareader.
    SqlDataReader rdr = cmd.ExecuteReader();

    // were any rows returned?
    if (rdr.HasRows)
    {

        while (rdr.Read())
        {

            customer.CustomerId =
                int.Parse(rdr["CustomerId"].ToString());
            customer.FirstName = rdr["FirstName"]
                .ToString();
            customer.LastName = rdr["LastName"]
                .ToString();
            customer.Address = rdr["Address"].ToString();
            customer.City = rdr["City"].ToString();
            customer.State = rdr["State"].ToString();
            customer.ZipCode = rdr["ZipCode"].ToString();
            customer.EmailAddress = rdr["EmailAddress"]
                .ToString();
            customer.Phone = rdr["Phone"].ToString();
            customer.Notes = rdr["Notes"].ToString();
        }
    }
}

return customer;
}
```

```
        catch (Exception ex)
        {

            return customer;
        }
        finally
        {

            cn.Close();
            cn.Dispose();
            cn = null;
        }
    }

    public List<Customer> GetCustomers() {

        // create a new list for storing customers.
        List<Customer> customers = new List<Customer>();

        try
        {

            // open the connection.
            cn.Open();

            // process the stored procedure.
            using (SqlCommand cmd = new SqlCommand("GetCustomers", cn))
            {

                cmd.CommandType = CommandType.StoredProcedure;

                // execute the command and store the results into a
                // datareader.
                SqlDataReader rdr = cmd.ExecuteReader();

                // were any rows returned?
                if (rdr.HasRows)
                {

                    Customer customer;
                    while (rdr.Read())
                    {

                        customer = new Customer();
                        customer.CustomerId =
                            int.Parse(rdr["CustomerId"].ToString());
```

```
                    customer.FirstName = rdr["FirstName"]
                        .ToString();
                    customer.LastName = rdr["LastName"]
                        .ToString();
                    customer.Address = rdr["Address"].ToString();
                    customer.City = rdr["City"].ToString();
                    customer.State = rdr["State"].ToString();
                    customer.ZipCode = rdr["ZipCode"].ToString();
                    customer.EmailAddress = rdr["EmailAddress"]
                        .ToString();
                    customer.Phone = rdr["Phone"].ToString();
                    customer.Notes = rdr["Notes"].ToString();
                    customers.Add(customer);
                }
            }
        }

        return customers;
    }
    catch (Exception ex)
    {

        return customers;
    }
    finally
    {

        cn.Close();
        cn.Dispose();
        cn = null;
    }
  }
}
```

Although WCF has been available for a while now and it will replace ASP.NET Web Services, at the time of this writing, some aspects of WCF remain in their infancy and are not yet fully supported.

Supported Networking Protocols

Silverlight supports network communication and formatting data using several industry protocols, as described in this section. Accessing data local to a Silverlight application is covered in more detail in Chapter 9.

Plain Old XML (POX)

Plain Old XML (or simple, well-formed, and valid XML documents and XML fragments) can be programmatically sent and received over the Web to enable communication with services. In most cases, passing data over the Web by using POX will require more coding for the developer but offers the developer the ability to fully customize the schema of the XML being sent. Additionally, there may be scenarios where a service being consumed does not fully support all web standards and therefore XML must be used to exchange data with the service.

Simple Object Access Protocol (SOAP)

Simple Object Access Protocol (SOAP) is the default data transport protocol used to communicate between Silverlight and a Web Service or WCF service. SOAP is a custom XML grammar used to fully describe data being transported between a Web Service and a service consumer, and it has been the default transport protocol since the inception of Web Services. SOAP is extremely portable; however, due to SOAP being an XML grammar, it is also very bloated. The following markup shows the SOAP schema returned by the customer manager Web Service:

```xml
<?xml version="1.0" encoding="utf-8"?>
<soap12:Envelope xmlns:xsi=
"http://www.w3.org/2001/XMLSchema-instance"
xmlns:xsd="http://www.w3.org/2001/XMLSchema"
xmlns:soap12="http://www.w3.org/2003/05/soap-envelope">
  <soap12:Body>
    <GetCustomerByIdResponse xmlns="http://tempuri.org/">
      <GetCustomerByIdResult>
        <CustomerId>int</CustomerId>
        <FirstName>string</FirstName>
        <LastName>string</LastName>
        <Address>string</Address>
        <City>string</City>
        <State>string</State>
        <ZipCode>string</ZipCode>
        <EmailAddress>string</EmailAddress>
        <Phone>string</Phone>
        <Notes>string</Notes>
      </GetCustomerByIdResult>
    </GetCustomerByIdResponse>
  </soap12:Body>
</soap12:Envelope>
```

JavaScript Object Notation (JSON)

JavaScript Object Notation (JSON) is a very succinct and to-the-point communication protocol and is very simple to read. JSON, as its name implies, is used most commonly by applications that utilize JavaScript. However, JSON can be used by any application type or programming language that supports it. The following code snippets illustrate various JSON data configurations:

```
// single name / value pair.
{"Name":"Shannon"}

// multiple name / value pairs.
{"Name":"Shannon","Gender":"Male"}

// more elaborate data construct similar to an array or object.
({"Customers",["Name":"Shannon",
"Name":"Benny","Name":"Sean","Name":"Tom","Name":"Matt"]})
```

Representational State Transfer (REST)

Representational State Transfer (REST) is a method of transporting domain-specific data over HTTP without also transporting additional metadata or a containing transport protocol such as HTML or SOAP. Silverlight supports communicating with services through REST.

HTTP is an acronym for Hypertext Transport Protocol and is the standard protocol used to communicate over the Web. HTTP consists of request and response messages that are transported over the Web between computers, with one generally acting as a client and the other acting as a server. HTTP messages are referred to as *HTTP packets* and contain a head section and a body section. The head section of an HTTP packet contains information that is used by the application that receives and processes the HTTP packet, whereas the body section contains the data that is being transported using HTTP, such as an HTML document. The content of the body section is referred to as the *payload*. In turn, the content of the payload (for example, an HTML document) typically contains subsections of its own, such as content to display on an HTML document or scripts.

REST was designed by the same people who designed HTTP, and it eliminates the extra layer of transport protocol. The head section of an HTTP packet can contain commands and instructions such as GET or POST, which are read and executed by the application that processes the packet. The commonly used HTTP commands are GET, POST, PUT, and DELETE. These commands are analogous to the SQL DML commands, which are also referred to as NURD (new, update, read, delete) or CRUD (create, read, update, delete).

The POST command is used to issue create, update, or delete commands. The GET command is used to issue a read command. The PUT command is used to issue create and overwrite commands. The DELETE command is used to issue a delete command. Through the aforementioned commands, REST supports code on demand, and it also supports embedded hyperlinks.

Applications that communicate over the Web by using REST are referred to as "RESTful" applications. REST also eliminates, or extremely reduces, the need to manage state. The Web is, by nature, a stateless environment. When a server receives an HTTP request, it fulfills the request and returns an HTTP response. Once the response is sent, the server forgets about the request and moves on to the next request. The server's lack of ability to remember who a client is between calls is referred to as *stateless*. The ability for a server to remember clients between requests is referred to as *managing state*. In most modern web development technologies, servers manage state by using cookies. The REST standard discourages the use of cookies due to security and navigation precautions.

The most commonly used method of communicating between a client application and a server over the Web is currently via a Web Service. Web Services are designed based on a remote procedure call (RPC), where client applications must have knowledge about a service in order to be able to consume it (by using WSDL). REST can use hyperlinks to fully describe a service, thus eliminating the need for additional discovery technologies, such as WSDL, and it can use hyperlinks to manage state information.

Syndication Protocols

Silverlight also supports the two most commonly used syndication protocols: RSS and Atom. The syndication protocols can be used to create a syndication feed reader using Silverlight.

Really Simple Syndication (RSS)

Really Simple Syndication (RSS) is an XML grammar that is used to syndicate frequently updated content sources such as blogs. An RSS document is referred to as an *RSS feed*. RSS was originally created by Netscape in 1999 and has since gained widespread popularity. An RSS document defines a collection of channel elements. Each channel represents a particular publication channel, such as a blog. Each channel element contains a collection of items. Each item represents a particular publication entry, such as a blog entry.

RSS documents can be easily and automatically updated once created, and they typically have an .rss file extension. Just as a web browser reads and parses HTML documents, an RSS feed reader (or news reader) reads and parses RSS documents. The primary benefit of using RSS is that users can subscribe to an RSS feed to be automatically notified when new content is published instead of being required to manually check the site for updates periodically. Several versions of RSS have been released, but the current official version is version 2.0. The following markup illustrates an RSS document:

```
<?xml version="1.0" encoding="utf-8" ?>
<rss version="2.0">
<channel>
<title>My Training Blog</title>
<link>http://localhost/myTrainingBlog</link>
<description>I blog about my experiences in
training to fight professionally</description>
<item>
<title>Training at the Lion's Den</title>
<link>http://localhost/myTrainingBlog/Item1</link>
<description>Want to read about the Den?</description>
</item>
<item>
<title>Training with the Elite Team</title>
<link>http://localhost/myTrainingBlog/Item2</link>
<description>Training with the Elite Team is Awesome</description>
</item>
</channel>
</rss>
```

As mentioned, RSS documents are well-formed XML documents. Hence, in the preceding RSS markup listing, the first line of the markup is the XML declaration. The document element is the channel element. The channel element contains a collection of elements, with each defining a separate RSS syndication source. Each channel must define the title of the channel and the link to the channel, as well as provide a description of the channel. Each element contains a collection of elements, with each defining a single item to be published. Each item must define the title of the item and the link to the item, as well as provide a description of the item.

An RSS feed reader, also known as an *aggregator,* can read the document and provide updated information with links to the user as the RSS document is updated.

To create an RSS reader using Silverlight 3, create a new Silverlight project using Visual Studio 2010. Next, right-click the Silverlight project in the Solution Explorer and select Add Reference. Scroll to and select the System.ServiceModel.Syndication namespace.

Design the Page.xaml file to include a method of collecting the feed URL and a button to trigger the request. Additionally, include a TextBlock or other control for displaying the feed results. The sample XAML is shown in the following markup:

```
<UserControl x:Class="L0602.Page"
    xmlns="http://schemas.microsoft.com/winfx/2006/xaml/presentation"
    xmlns:x="http://schemas.microsoft.com/winfx/2006/xaml"
    Width="573" Height="343">
    <Canvas x:Name="LayoutRoot">
        <Canvas.Background>
            <LinearGradientBrush
                EndPoint="0.282999992370605,0.155000001192093"
                StartPoint="0.717000007629395,0.845000028610229">
                <GradientStop Color="#FFAA9563"/>
                <GradientStop Color="#FFFFFFFF" Offset="0.527"/>
            </LinearGradientBrush>
        </Canvas.Background>
        <TextBlock Height="Auto" Width="Auto" Canvas.Left="8"
            Canvas.Top="8" Text="Enter the URL for the RSS feed to
            acquire below" TextWrapping="Wrap" x:Name="tbHeading"/>
        <TextBox Height="Auto" Width="428" Canvas.Left="8"
            Canvas.Top="34.537" Text="" TextWrapping="Wrap"
                x:Name="txtURL"/>
        <Button Height="20.772" Width="125" Canvas.Left="440"
            Canvas.Top="34.537" Content="Acquire Feed"
                x:Name="btnAcquire"
            Click="btnAcquire_Click" />
        <ScrollViewer Height="275.691" Width="557"
            Canvas.Left="8" Canvas.Top="59.309" x:Name="svResults"
            HorizontalScrollBarVisibility="Auto"
            VerticalScrollBarVisibility="Auto">
            <TextBlock Height="Auto" Width="Auto"
            Text="no feed results to display..." TextWrapping="Wrap"
            x:Name="tbResults"/>
        </ScrollViewer>
    </Canvas>
</UserControl>
```

The results of the preceding markup, as displayed in Internet Explorer 8, are shown in Figure 6-5.

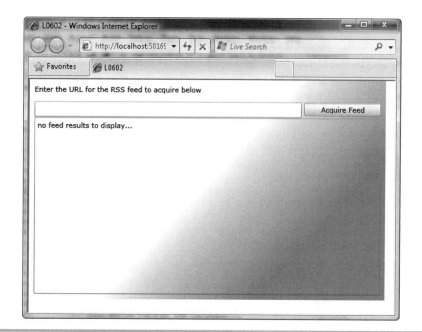

Figure 6-5   The Silverlight RSS feed reader display

Silverlight 3 ships with a class designed for working with syndication feeds—the System.ServiceModel.Syndication.SyndicationFeed class. However, prior to you working with a feed using the SyndicationFeed class, the feed contents must first be requested, read into memory, and parsed into the correct format. Furthermore, when a syndication feed is requested, a cross-domain call is being made, so the server where the feed resides must have a CrossDomain.xml file in place to allow a cross-domain request. The upcoming code listing illustrates asynchronously requesting the contents of a feed, parsing the feed contents into XML, and loading the contents into a SyndicationFeed class.

An additional step must be taken to display the results. When the request is made for the feed contents and the callback method is invoked, the callback method is functioning in the context of a background worker thread. The background worker thread is used when networking requests are being handled. The Silverlight user interface is managed using a separate thread of execution, commonly referred to as the *UI thread*. Silverlight prevents attempts in the background worker thread from directly interacting with the UI thread. Hence, it will be difficult or impossible to directly update the Silverlight UI from the callback method that handles the loading and parsing of the syndication feed contents.

Silverlight 3 includes a class called the Dispatcher class that is used to communicate between Silverlight threads. If the Dispatcher class is not used and an attempt is made to directly update the UI thread from the background worker thread, Silverlight will throw an exception, stating that unauthorized cross-thread access has been attempted. The following well-documented code listing illustrates a request for syndication feed contents:

```
using System;
using System.Collections.Generic;
using System.Linq;
using System.Net;
using System.Windows;
using System.Windows.Controls;
using System.Windows.Documents;
using System.Windows.Input;
using System.Windows.Media;
using System.Windows.Media.Animation;
using System.Windows.Shapes;
using System.Xml;
using System.ServiceModel;
using System.ServiceModel.Syndication;

namespace L0602
{
    public partial class Page : UserControl
    {

        // create an instance to represent the uri.
        Uri uri;

        public Page()
        {
            InitializeComponent();
        }

        /// <summary>
        /// this method makes the request.
        /// </summary>
        /// <param name="sender"></param>
        /// <param name="e"></param>
        private void btnAcquire_Click(object sender, RoutedEventArgs e)
        {

            // store the URL of the feed.
            uri = new Uri(txtURL.Text);

            // create a request.
```

```
        HttpWebRequest request = (HttpWebRequest)HttpWebRequest
            .Create(uri);

        // make the request.
        request.BeginGetResponse(new AsyncCallback(displayFeed),
            request);
    }

/// <summary>
/// this method handles the callback.
/// </summary>
/// <param name="asyncResult">the result of the request.
/// </param>
void displayFeed(IAsyncResult asyncResult) {

        // nab the request.
        HttpWebRequest request = (HttpWebRequest) asyncResult
            .AsyncState;

        // nab the response.
        HttpWebResponse response =
        (HttpWebResponse)request.EndGetResponse(asyncResult);

        // parse the response to xml.
        XmlReader reader = XmlReader.Create(response
            .GetResponseStream());

        // load the feed.
        SyndicationFeed feed = SyndicationFeed.Load(reader);

        // call to the UI thread to update the UI.
        Dispatcher.BeginInvoke(delegate {

            // clear the results textblock.
            tbResults.Text = "";

            // display the feed items.
            foreach (SyndicationItem item in feed.Items)
            {

                tbResults.Text += item.Title.Text + Environment
                    .NewLine;
            }
        });
    }
  }
}
```

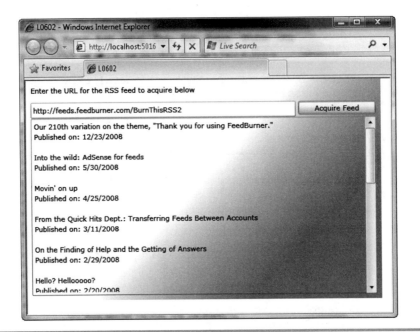

Figure 6-6 The results of an RSS feed

The results of making a valid RSS request using the preceding code and markup are displayed in Figure 6-6.

TIP
If you have a difficult time locating an RSS feed that supports Silverlight consumption, look into converting an RSS feed using FeedBurner. FeedBurner is located at http://www.feedburner.com.

Atom

An inherent problem with RSS is that although Netscape is primarily credited with creating it, other individuals released additional RSS standards that are not compatible with the version of RSS released by Netscape. In an effort to resolve the incompatibilities and inconsistencies among the various versions of RSS, a new syndication standard named Atom was created. Atom is divided into two technologies: the Atom Syndication Format and the Atom Publishing Protocol.

The Atom Syndication Format is a custom XML grammar that serves much the same purpose as the RSS XML grammar. An Atom Syndication Format file is a text-based XML file with an .atom file extension. The following markup listing illustrates the Atom version of the training blog entry:

```
<?xml version="1.0" encoding="utf-8" ?>
<feed xmlns="http://www.w3.org/2005/Atom">
<title>My Pet Blog</title>
<subtitle>I blog about my pet here for now</subtitle>
<link href="http://localhost/myPetBlog" />
<updated>2008-01-30T09:30:00Z</updated>
<author>
<name>Shannon Horn</name>
<email>shannonhorn@msn.com</email>
</author>
<entry>
<title>Ladybird Found</title>
<link href="http://localhost/myPetBlog/Item1"/>
<updated>2008-01-30T09:30:00Z</updated>
<summary>Want to read about how we found LadyBird?</summary>
</entry>
</feed>
```

The Atom Publishing Protocol is a query language very similar to the Structured Query Language (SQL) that's designed for exclusive use with the Atom Syndication Format. The Atom Publishing Protocol consists of four primary commands: GET, POST, PUT, and DELETE. The GET command is analogous to the SQL select statement, the POST command is analogous to the SQL insert statement, the PUT command is analogous to the SQL update statement, and the DELETE command is analogous to the SQL delete statement.

Conclusion

Silverlight executes in an isolated environment on the client's machine. As such, postbacks to the server do not automatically occur; rather, calls are made to a service residing on a web server to retrieve server resources. Silverlight supports only asynchronous networking calls. Silverlight supports several networking protocols, including POX, SOAP, JSON, REST, RSS, and Atom.

Chapter 7

Who Goes There? Securing Silverlight Applications

Key Concepts & Skills

● Learn the basic concepts of software security

● Understand the importance of properly managing and protecting user credentials

● Explore how users are authenticated in SOA scenarios

● Illustrate how to use the classes in the Silverlight System.Security namespace to protect data through cryptography

Traditionally, web applications have been considered difficult to secure. Silverlight applications are rich interactive applications (RIAs), an application type that runs locally on a client machine but utilizes the Web as a transport and communication mechanism. Hence, Silverlight applications are faced with all the security challenges of a standard web application. However, whereas most commonly used web development frameworks, such as ASP.NET, include intrinsic server-side security features, Silverlight applications include only minimal security features that execute on the client.

Silverlight applications communicate with a server through a server-side Web Service or WCF service. Web Services do not include security features as advanced as full web development frameworks. The following sections describe common solutions for securing Silverlight applications.

Software Security Basics

It has been said that in today's economy, data is money—and this is true. Data is vital to businesses today. Data is at the heart of all business software. Additionally, data pertaining to a user's identification is a foundational component of ecommerce. In ecommerce and business today, a business must be able to trust data related to a user and the user's identity. As such, identity theft is growing to be one of the top crimes perpetrated. With that said the need to protect data managed by software is of prime importance and should be considered in the conceptual and logical software design phases. In fact, a formal security plan should be compiled that includes a plan for determining a user's identity, what tasks a user is allowed to perform in an application, and how data is to be secured while being transported and stored.

In software security, all applications typically perform the two "A" words: authentication and authorization. *Authentication* is the process of determining a user's identity. A user's identity is generally determined via credentials that are unique to a particular user, such as a username and password. Once a user's identity is determined, an application must determine what the user has permission to perform. *Authorization* is the process of determining a user's permissions within an application.

The method used to secure data that is being transported and stored varies based on the type of application being created. For instance, a Windows application that is not exposed to the Web can rely on internal network security to protect data, whereas a web application must take many precautions to guard against malicious attacks.

In a web application environment, data is transported from a client's computer, over the Web, to a web server. A client computer that accesses a web application may be composed of any operating system and any web browser; therefore, it is nearly impossible to impose strict security mechanisms on the client's computer in a traditional web application. Data entered on a client's computer is generally already known to the user who is entering it; hence, securing data while it is on the client's computer really isn't a significant concern. However, once data leaves a client's computer and is transported over the Web to the web server, it can be intercepted by anyone using an HTTP packet sniffer or other similar mechanism.

In order to secure data while it is transported over the Web, the data is encrypted before it leaves the client machine and unencrypted when it reaches the web server, and vice versa. Many methods are used in the software industry to encrypt data; however, the standard used on the Web for ecommerce is called *Secure Sockets Layer (SSL)*. SSL utilizes 128-bit encryption and is implemented through certificates that can be obtained from a third-party Certificate Authority (CA) such as VeriSign.

Managing User Authentication Information

All sensitive data must be handled with extreme care in order to keep it secure. User credentials are of particular importance. If valid user credentials are compromised, a malicious user can gain access to deeper levels of sensitive data managed by the application. Credentials typically take the form of a username and password and must be gathered from a user through a page or screen. Once acquired, the credentials must be passed to a method in a Web Service that can use the credentials to attempt to authenticate the user.

Most commonly, a class is used to represent the user and the user's roles and permissions within the application. Silverlight does not contain a class dedicated for this purpose. However, Silverlight does include interfaces that can be implemented by a custom class to ensure that it complies structurally with other security components of the .NET Framework. The Silverlight security interfaces include the IIdentity interface and the IPrincipal interface and are located in the System.Security.Principal namespace.

The IIdentity interface ensures that a class that implements it stores information identifying the user. The IPrincipal interface ensures that a class fully describes a user's security context by identifying not only the user's identity but also the roles that the user is a member of. The following code listing shows a class that successfully implements the members of the IIdentity interface:

```
using System;
using System.Security.Principal;

namespace L0701
{
    public class AuthenticationTicket : IIdentity
    {
        // data members.
        public string AuthenticationType { get; set; }
        public bool IsAuthenticated { get; set; }
        public string Name { get; set; }
    }
}
```

This class includes the AuthenticationType, IsAuthenticated, and Name members. The Name property stores an identifying name for the user. Generally, the Name property stores the username portion of the user's credentials, but it may also store the user's actual name or a unique alias for the user. The IsAuthenticated member is used to determine whether or not a user has been authenticated, and the AuthenticationType member is used to identify the method used to authenticate the user.

Ask the Expert

Q: **Why doesn't the class that implements the IIdentity interface store the user's password?**

A: If both the username and password are stored as data members in the class, it makes the class that implements the IIdentity interface a real security risk. Any malicious user who gains access to the class at runtime will be able to retrieve the user's credentials. By not storing the password in the class, the security risk is mostly mitigated. The class that implements the IIdentity interface is typically instantiated and populated after the user has been authenticated; hence, it is not necessary to store the password or the actual username in the class.

The following listing illustrates Silverlight code that calls a web method to authenticate a user and, if the user is successfully authenticated, creates an instance of the AuthenticationTicket class and populates it:

```
using System;
using System.Collections.Generic;
using System.Linq;
using System.Net;
using System.Windows;
using System.Windows.Controls;
using System.Windows.Documents;
using System.Windows.Input;
using System.Windows.Media;
using System.Windows.Media.Animation;
using System.Windows.Shapes;

namespace L0701
{
    public partial class Page : UserControl
    {

        UserServices.UserServicesSoapClient svc =
new UserServices.UserServicesSoapClient();
```

```
public Page()
{
    InitializeComponent();

    svc.AuthenticateCompleted +=
    new EventHandler<L0701.UserServices
    .AuthenticateCompletedEventArgs>
    (svc_AuthenticateCompleted);
}

private void btnLogIn_Click(object sender, RoutedEventArgs e)
{

    svc.AuthenticateAsync(txtUserName.Text, txtPassword.Text);
}

public void svc_AuthenticateCompleted
    (object sender, UserServices.AuthenticateCompletedEventArgs e)
{

    if (e.Result) {

        AuthenticationTicket ticket = new AuthenticationTicket();
        ticket.Name = txtUserName.Text;
        ticket.IsAuthenticated = true;
    }
}
}
}
}
```

Service-Oriented Architecture (SOA) Security

A Web Service is a class that is available over the Web. A Web Service contains methods that are exposed over the Web to be called by any type of client application. In many scenarios, a web method will provide access to a server database so that a client application can retrieve data. With that in mind, standards had to be put into place so that calls made to web methods could be authenticated prior to execution, in essence securing the Web Service.

Web Service standards, just like all other web standards, are constantly evolving to keep up with technological advances. Maintaining a secure environment over the Web is not an easy task. To add to the complexity, bear in mind that the Web is a stateless environment. Communications between web clients and web methods are handled in the same manner as communications between web clients and websites. Each request is isolated from all other requests. A method of maintaining state between requests to a web method is necessary so that a client does not have to be authenticated with each request.

In the simplest example, user credentials can be passed to a web method with each request so that the request can be authenticated. However, formal standards have been created for authenticating user requests to web methods. In a nutshell, the default mechanism used to transport data to and from a web method, SOAP, is constructed very similar to an HTML document. The SOAP document is referred to an *envelope,* and it includes a head section and a body section. The head section is optional but can be used to transport additional information and parameters that are intended to be utilized by the processing engine. When information is transported in the SOAP header, the SOAP message is said to contain a "custom SOAP header." User credentials are one example of information that can be passed in a custom SOAP header. The following markup listing illustrates user credentials stored in a SOAP header:

```
POST /myService.asmx HTTP/1.1
Host: localhost
Content-Type: application/soap+xml; charset=utf-8
Content-Length: 300
<?xml version="1.0" encoding="utf-8"?>
<soap:Envelope xmlns:soap="http://schemas.xmlsoap.org/soap/envelope/">
  <soap:Header>
    <myHeader xmlns="http://www.myDomain.com">
      <UserName>ShanTheMan</UserName>
      <PasswordHash>jd4y5u6i2!ej#556</PasswordHash>
    </myHeader>
  </soap:Header>
  <soap:Body>
    ...
  </soap:Body>
</soap:Envelope>
```

Notice in this markup that the SOAP message is contained inside an HTTP packet. Beyond simply storing user credentials in a SOAP header, more formal Web Service–related security standards have been drafted, such as WS-Security. For more information on WS-Security, visit the WS-Security specification page located in the MSDN library at http://msdn.microsoft.com/en-us/library/ms951273.aspx.

REST Security

REST is an acronym for Representational State Transfer, and it was created by the developers of the HTTP standard as a succinct method for sending and receiving data and commands over the Web. REST has become extremely popular in recent months because the amount of data being transported back and forth pales in comparison to the amount of data being transported using SOAP. Hence, communication using REST is typically much more efficient.

An HTTP packet is similar in structure to a SOAP message in that it contains a head section and a body section. The premise behind using REST is to eliminate the HTTP payload, or the body section, in order to make communications more efficient. Therefore, the logical location for storing user credentials while in transit in a "RESTful" message is in the HTTP header.

In most scenarios, a REST message will be sent to the server that contains a GET or POST command. The GET or POST command will be used to call a method stored in a service that is hosted on the server. The GET or POST call to the method can include parameters to pass to the method, such as a username and password. The username and password parameters may be secured using cryptography prior to the REST call and unsecured on the server, or the entire communication can be secured using SSL.

Using REST will significantly reduce the amount of metadata being transported over the Web in communications between a client computer and the Web server.

Silverlight Security Functionality

It should be reiterated that Silverlight applications execute on the client's machine and communications with a server occur only when initiated manually from the Silverlight application. Calls to a server from a Silverlight application are made asynchronously to a Web Service. Microsoft may include controls and functionality to assist in performing related security tasks; however, at this time, security features and functionality included in Silverlight are minimal. The minimal security offering is also by design. Silverlight applications execute in an isolated and secure environment known as a *sandbox*. The sandbox prevents a Silverlight application from directly interacting with the user's file system and, in turn, also prevents most malicious activity. Hence, more advance security functionality is not really necessary. Additionally, because Silverlight executes on the client machine and not the server, Silverlight includes no code access security (CAS) features or enterprise-level security features.

Cryptography

Although security features included in Silverlight are thin, Silverlight does include classes to assist in cryptography. Cryptography is the process of obscuring data to make it more secure by converting it into a different format or data representation. Two common cryptography processes are encryption and hashing, and both require a key or algorithm to determine how data should be converted or obscured. The Silverlight cryptography classes are included in the System.Security.Cryptography namespace.

Encryption

Encryption is a bidirectional process. When data is encrypted, it is intended to be decrypted. Data is encrypted by using an encryption key. There are many encryption standards available and varying strengths of encryption keys. Some of the encryption standards that have been used throughout history are known to be cracked, but the .NET Framework and Silverlight utilize modern encryption standards that have been proven as secure when used to encrypt data for transport over the Web.

Any sensitive data that is to be transported over the Web should first be encrypted to protect it. On the receiving end, the data can then be decrypted. The standard used for encrypting and decrypting sensitive data in transit over the Web is called Secure Sockets Layer (SSL), and it employs 128-bit encryption.

Hashing

Hashing is a unidirectional process. When data is hashed, it cannot be "un-hashed." In fact, there is no such thing as "un-hashing" or "de-hashing." Hashing is useful for obscuring data values when the original value is not as important as is the ability to ensure that a consistent seed value is supplied. With hashing, if the same hashing algorithm is used, a consistent seed value will always generate a consistent resultant hashed value. Hashing is a perfect fit for obscuring passwords supplied by a user for authentication. When a user supplies a password, it can be hashed prior to being transported over the Web. If the password hash falls into malicious hands, the original seed password value can never be arrived at; hence, the password hash is not of value to a malicious user.

Silverlight 3 includes the SHA1 hashing algorithm, which is the accepted and most commonly used hashing standard on the Web. The following code snippet shows an updated version of the btnLogIn_Click event handler that now hashes the password supplied by the user before sending it over the Web:

```
private void btnLogIn_Click(object sender, RoutedEventArgs e)
{

    byte[] passwordBytes = Encoding.UTF8.GetBytes
        (txtPassword.Text);
    SHA1Managed hash = new SHA1Managed();
    byte[] passwordHashed = hash.ComputeHash(passwordBytes);
    svc.AuthenticateAsync
        (txtUserName.Text, Convert.ToBase64String(passwordHashed));
}
```

This code snippet will hash the supplied password; for instance, a supplied password of "P@55w0rd" will be converted to "0NKdvLTjMMElX0ADkcjUqe59Qsg=". As you can see, the resultant hashed value in no way resembles the value of the given input value. If a hashing algorithm is used consistently, an input value will always result in the same hash value. Hence, if the user's password was hashed when entered by the user and stored with the user's profile, when the user attempts to supply a password to log in, the resultant hash value should match the stored hash value.

Microsoft has published a white paper that reinforces the topics presented in this chapter and recommends some best practices for security in Silverlight. You can download the white paper at http://www.microsoft.com/downloads/details.aspx?displaylang=en&FamilyID= 7cef15a8-8ae6-48eb-9621-ee35c2547773.

Conclusion

Due to Silverlight executing in an isolated environment on the client, the Silverlight framework does not include as extensive security functionality and features as a server-side technology such as ASP.NET. Silverlight is able to communicate with and integrate with ASP.NET security features. Using a combination of SSL and cryptography, data being managed by a Silverlight application can be secured while in transit between the Silverlight application and a Web Service.

Chapter 8

Designing Silverlight User Interfaces

Key Concepts & Skills

- Learn about the types of controls available in Silverlight

- Explore Silverlight user interface controls

- Understand the importance of good user interface design using Silverlight controls

- Observe how to create control styles and templates

- Work with the Expression Blend Visual State Manager (VSM)

Although it is vitally important to understand how to network using Silverlight, the primary focus of Silverlight is to create RIAs where a user can be presented with an elaborate UI. As such, it is imperative that a developer or a designer understands the tools available for creating user interfaces using Silverlight. Silverlight version 1 did not include user interface controls; however, when Microsoft released Silverlight 2, they included a gamut of user interface controls as well as the ability to create custom controls and the ability to customize existing controls.

Layout Controls

The current version of Silverlight includes several layout controls. Layout controls were introduced with Windows Presentation Foundation (WPF) and serve as a container for other controls. Layout controls are used to manage the layout, sizing, and positioning of the controls contained in them.

Canvas Control

The Canvas control was available in previous versions of Silverlight and served as the document element in a Silverlight XAML document. Due to its use in the past, a Silverlight design surface is now generically referred to as a "Silverlight canvas." In the current version of Silverlight, the document element is now a UserControl element, and a Canvas control is used to absolutely position other controls on a canvas.

When controls are contained within a Canvas layout control, the Canvas.Left property and the Canvas.Top property are used to absolutely position the contained controls within the space of the containing Canvas control. The following XAML markup illustrates a Canvas control that contains an Ellipse with a gradient fill applied:

```
<UserControl x:Class="L0801.Page"
    xmlns="http://schemas.microsoft.com/winfx/2006/xaml/presentation"
    xmlns:x="http://schemas.microsoft.com/winfx/2006/xaml"
    xmlns:d="http://schemas.microsoft.com/expression/blend/2008"
    xmlns:mc="http://schemas.openxmlformats.org/markup-
        compatibility/2006"
    mc:Ignorable="d"
    d:DesignHeight="300" d:DesignWidth="400">
    <Canvas x:Name="LayoutRoot" Background="White">
        <Ellipse Height="123" Width="188" Canvas.Left="77"
        Canvas.Top="56" Stroke="#FF38720B">
            <Ellipse.Fill>
                <LinearGradientBrush EndPoint="0.5,1"
                    StartPoint="0.5,0">
                    <GradientStop Color="#FF74EE15"/>
                    <GradientStop Color="#FFFFFFFF" Offset="0.571"/>
                </LinearGradientBrush>
            </Ellipse.Fill>
        </Ellipse>
    </Canvas>
</UserControl>
```

Figure 8-1 illustrates the result of this markup as displayed in Firefox.

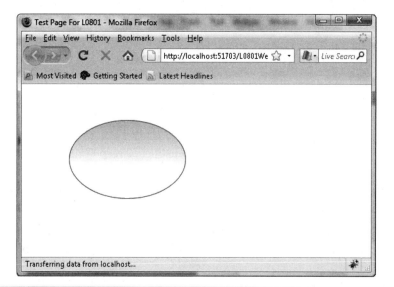

Figure 8-1   An ellipse contained in a Canvas control

StackPanel Control

The StackPanel control was introduced in Silverlight 2. As mentioned, in previous versions, the document element of a Silverlight canvas was the Canvas control; therefore, controls in Silverlight could only be absolutely positioned. The StackPanel control is a true dynamic layout control in that it dynamically manages the positioning, sizing, and layout of the controls it contains.

Contained controls are "stacked" on top of each other. The StackPanel control may be configured to stack controls horizontally or vertically. The StackPanel control originated in WPF and made its way into Silverlight. The following XAML markup illustrates the use of the StackPanel control:

```
<UserControl x:Class="L0802.Page"
    xmlns="http://schemas.microsoft.com/winfx/2006/xaml/presentation"
    xmlns:x="http://schemas.microsoft.com/winfx/2006/xaml"
    xmlns:d="http://schemas.microsoft.com/expression/blend/2008"
    xmlns:mc="http://schemas.openxmlformats.org/markup-
        compatibility/2006"
    mc:Ignorable="d"
    d:DesignHeight="300" d:DesignWidth="400">
    <StackPanel x:Name="LayoutRoot" Background="White">
        <RadioButton Height="Auto" Width="Auto"
        Content="English" GroupName="language"/>
        <RadioButton Height="Auto" Width="Auto"
        Content="French" GroupName="language"/>
        <RadioButton Height="Auto" Width="Auto"
        Content="Chinese" GroupName="language"/>
        <RadioButton Height="Auto" Width="Auto"
        Content="German" GroupName="language"/>
        <RadioButton Height="Auto" Width="Auto"
        Content="Spanish" GroupName="language"/>
        <RadioButton Height="Auto" Width="Auto"
        Content="Russian" GroupName="language"/>
    </StackPanel>
</UserControl>
```

Figure 8-2 shows the result of this markup listing, as displayed in Safari.

DockPanel Control

The DockPanel control is similar to the StackPanel control in that it dynamically manages the sizing and layout for controls contained within it. However, the DockPanel control is used to "dock" contained controls to a border in the same manner that toolbars and other

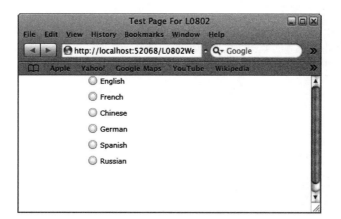

Figure 8-2   Radio buttons contained in a StackPanel

controls are docked in other Windows applications. The following markup illustrates a DockPanel control that contains a single Button control:

```
<UserControl
    xmlns="http://schemas.microsoft.com/winfx/2006/xaml/presentation"
    xmlns:x="http://schemas.microsoft.com/winfx/2006/xaml"
    xmlns:d="http://schemas.microsoft.com/expression/blend/2008"
    xmlns:mc="http://schemas.openxmlformats.org/markup-
        compatibility/2006"
    mc:Ignorable="d"
    xmlns:controls="clr-namespace:System.Windows.Controls;assembly=
    System.Windows.Controls" x:Class="L0803.Page"
    d:DesignHeight="300" d:DesignWidth="400">
    <Grid x:Name="LayoutRoot" Background="White">

      <controls:DockPanel LastChildFill="False" >
          <Button Margin="0,28,-104,107" Content="click me" />
      </controls:DockPanel>

    </Grid>
</UserControl>
```

Figure 8-3 illustrates a Button control contained in a DockPanel control. The Button control is docked to the left side of the control.

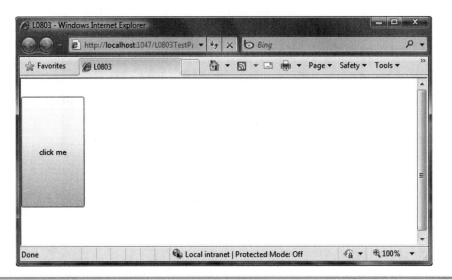

Figure 8-3   A Button control contained in a DockPanel control

WrapPanel Control

The WrapPanel control is similar to the StackPanel control and the DockPanel control but is used to automatically wrap controls to the next line if there is not enough space to keep controls on the lines where they are currently positioned. The WrapPanel control wraps contained controls in the same way that Microsoft Word wraps words when they no longer fit on the current line. The following markup illustrates a DockPanel control that contains eight Button controls:

```
<UserControl
    xmlns="http://schemas.microsoft.com/winfx/2006/xaml/presentation"
    xmlns:x="http://schemas.microsoft.com/winfx/2006/xaml"
    xmlns:d="http://schemas.microsoft.com/expression/blend/2008"
    xmlns:mc="http://schemas.openxmlformats.org/markup-
        compatibility/2006"
    mc:Ignorable="d"
    xmlns:controls="clr-namespace:System.Windows.Controls;assembly=
    System.Windows.Controls" x:Class="L0804.Page"
    d:DesignHeight="300" d:DesignWidth="400">
    <Grid x:Name="LayoutRoot" Background="White">

      <controls:WrapPanel >
          <Button Content="Button1"/>
          <Button Content="Button2"/>
```

Figure 8-4   A WrapPanel control that contains eight Button controls

```
            <Button Content="Button3"/>
            <Button Content="Button4"/>
            <Button Content="Button5"/>
            <Button Content="Button6"/>
            <Button Content="Button7"/>
            <Button Content="Button8"/>
        </controls:WrapPanel>

    </Grid>
</UserControl>
```

Figure 8-4 illustrates the behavior of the WrapPanel control when the browser sized is reduced so that the eight buttons cannot be displayed on a single line.

TabControl Control

The TabControl contains one or more "tabs" and is analogous to a physical file folder. TabControls have been commonly used in applications for years. Each tab in a TabControl may contain an assortment of controls that can be categorized and visually isolated from the controls on another tab. The following markup illustrates the use of a TabControl control:

```
<UserControl
    xmlns="http://schemas.microsoft.com/winfx/2006/xaml/presentation"
    xmlns:x="http://schemas.microsoft.com/winfx/2006/xaml"
    xmlns:d="http://schemas.microsoft.com/expression/blend/2008"
    xmlns:mc="http://schemas.openxmlformats.org/markup-
        compatibility/2006"
    mc:Ignorable="d"
    xmlns:controls="clr-namespace:System.Windows.Controls;assembly=
    System.Windows.Controls" x:Class="L0805.Page"
```

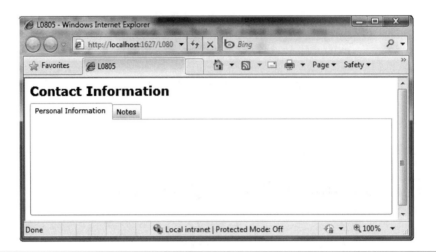

Figure 8-5 A TabControl control that contains two TabItem controls

```
d:DesignHeight="300" d:DesignWidth="400">
<Grid x:Name="LayoutRoot" Background="White">

  <controls:TabControl Margin="8,39,8,8">
      <controls:TabItem Header="Personal Information">
          <Grid/>
      </controls:TabItem>
      <controls:TabItem Header="Notes">
          <Grid/>
      </controls:TabItem>
  </controls:TabControl>
  <TextBlock Height="27" Margin="8,6,8,0"
  VerticalAlignment="Top" Text="Contact Information"
  TextWrapping="Wrap" FontWeight="Bold" FontSize="20"/>

  </Grid>
</UserControl>
```

Figure 8-5 illustrates a TabControl control that contains two TabItems.

Grid Control

The Grid control was available in Silverlight 1 and is used to lay out controls via a grid. The Grid control is very similar in functionality to an HTML table and consists of rows and columns. The Grid control should be used to display data in a tabular format, but it does not offer advanced data-editing capabilities like the DataGrid control does. The following XAML markup illustrates use of the Grid control:

```
<UserControl x:Class="L0806.Page"
    xmlns="http://schemas.microsoft.com/winfx/2006/xaml/presentation"
    xmlns:x="http://schemas.microsoft.com/winfx/2006/xaml"
    xmlns:d="http://schemas.microsoft.com/expression/blend/2008"
    xmlns:mc="http://schemas.openxmlformats.org/markup-
        compatibility/2006"
    mc:Ignorable="d"
    d:DesignHeight="300" d:DesignWidth="400">
    <Grid HorizontalAlignment="Stretch"
    Margin="8,8,8,8" VerticalAlignment="Stretch">
        <Grid.RowDefinitions>
            <RowDefinition/>
            <RowDefinition Height="3*"/>
            <RowDefinition/>
        </Grid.RowDefinitions>
        <Grid.ColumnDefinitions>
            <ColumnDefinition/>
            <ColumnDefinition Width="4*"/>
        </Grid.ColumnDefinitions>
        <Rectangle HorizontalAlignment="Stretch"
        Margin="0,0,0,0" VerticalAlignment="Stretch"
        Grid.ColumnSpan="2" Stroke="#FF000000">
            <Rectangle.Fill>
                <LinearGradientBrush
                EndPoint="0.916999995708466,0.458000004291534"
                StartPoint="0.108999997377396,0.470999985933304">
                    <GradientStop Color="#FF0C2D0C"/>
                    <GradientStop Color="#FFFFFFFF" Offset="0.969"/>
                    <GradientStop Color="#FF808080" Offset="0.778"/>
                </LinearGradientBrush>
            </Rectangle.Fill>
        </Rectangle>
        <Rectangle HorizontalAlignment="Stretch"
        Margin="8,0,8,8" VerticalAlignment="Bottom" Stroke="#FF000000"
        Height="56.8" Grid.ColumnSpan="2" Grid.Row="2">
            <Rectangle.Fill>
                <LinearGradientBrush
                EndPoint="0.916999995708466,0.458000004291534"
                StartPoint="0.108999997377396,0.470999985933304">
                    <GradientStop Color="#FF0C2D0C"/>
                    <GradientStop Color="#FFFFFFFF" Offset="0.969"/>
                    <GradientStop Color="#FF808080" Offset="0.778"/>
                </LinearGradientBrush>
            </Rectangle.Fill>
```

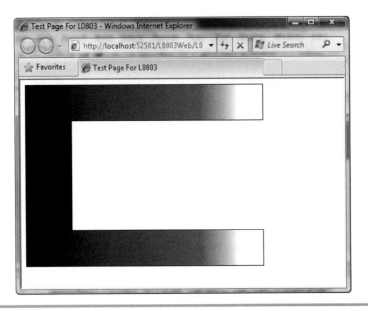

Figure 8-6 Rectangles displayed in a Grid control

```
        </Rectangle>
        <Rectangle HorizontalAlignment="Left"
        Margin="8,65,0,64.8000030517578" VerticalAlignment="Stretch"
        Width="76" Fill="#FF0C2D0C" Stroke="#FF000000"/>
    </Grid>
</UserControl>
```

Figure 8-6 shows the result of this markup, as displayed in Internet Explorer.

Border Control

A Border control acts as a container control for other controls. However, a Border control is typically used to dress up a portion of a Silverlight application. Each side of a Border control may be displayed, or not displayed, independent of other sides of the control. Additionally, a background color may be selected. The following markup illustrates the Border control with the BorderBrush and BorderThickness properties configured:

```
<UserControl x:Class="L0807.Page"
    xmlns="http://schemas.microsoft.com/winfx/2006/xaml/presentation"
    xmlns:x="http://schemas.microsoft.com/winfx/2006/xaml"
    xmlns:d="http://schemas.microsoft.com/expression/blend/2008"
    xmlns:mc="http://schemas.openxmlformats.org/markup-
        compatibility/2006"
```

```
    mc:Ignorable="d"
    d:DesignHeight="300" d:DesignWidth="400">
    <Grid x:Name="LayoutRoot" Background="White">
        <Border Margin="8,8,8,109" Background="#FFE0D8D8
        BorderBrush="#FF4F4B4B" BorderThickness="0.5,0.5,0.5,0.5"/>
    </Grid>
</UserControl>
```

User Interface Controls

Silverlight includes a multitude of controls that are used to interact with and gather data from users.

Button Control

A Button control is the most commonly used Silverlight control. It is used to submit a form of data or to perform other actions within an application. The most commonly used event of a Button control is the Click event. The following markup illustrates a simple Button control:

```
<UserControl x:Class="L0808.Page"
    xmlns="http://schemas.microsoft.com/winfx/2006/xaml/presentation"
    xmlns:x="http://schemas.microsoft.com/winfx/2006/xaml"
    xmlns:d="http://schemas.microsoft.com/expression/blend/2008"
    xmlns:mc="http://schemas.openxmlformats.org/markup-
        compatibility/2006"
    mc:Ignorable="d"
    d:DesignHeight="300" d:DesignWidth="400">
    <Grid x:Name="LayoutRoot" Background="White">
        <Button Content="click me" Height="23"
        HorizontalAlignment="Left" Margin="70,50,0,0"
        Name="button1" VerticalAlignment="Top" Width="75" />
    </Grid>
</UserControl>
```

Figure 8-7 illustrates the Button control.

Calendar Control

The Calendar control is used to display a graphical calendar to the user. Typical uses for the Calendar control include allowing the user to graphically select a date from the calendar and to navigate scheduled events using the calendar. All aspects of the Calendar control can be customized. Generally, a Calendar control is displayed at all times in a user interface.

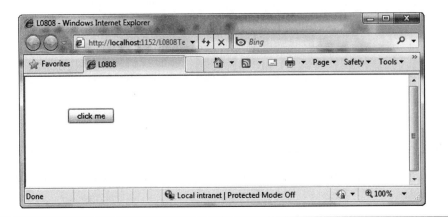

Figure 8-7 A simple Button control

For a calendar that should only be displayed quickly so that the user can select a date and move on, you should use the DatePicker control instead. The following markup illustrates a Calendar control:

```
<UserControl
    xmlns="http://schemas.microsoft.com/winfx/2006/xaml/presentation"
    xmlns:x="http://schemas.microsoft.com/winfx/2006/xaml"
    xmlns:d="http://schemas.microsoft.com/expression/blend/2008"
    xmlns:mc="http://schemas.openxmlformats.org/markup-
        compatibility/2006"
    mc:Ignorable="d"
    xmlns:controls="clr-namespace:System.Windows.Controls;
    assembly=System.Windows.Controls" x:Class="L0809.Page"
    d:DesignHeight="300" d:DesignWidth="400">

    <Grid x:Name="LayoutRoot" Background="White">

      <controls:Calendar Margin="8,8,0,123"
      Width="181" HorizontalAlignment="Left"/>

    </Grid>
</UserControl>
```

Figure 8-8 illustrates a Calendar control as displayed using Internet Explorer.

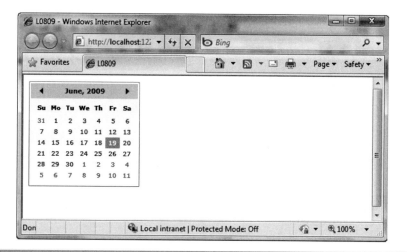

Figure 8-8 A Calendar control

CheckBox Control

A CheckBox control is used to make a yes or no (or true or false) type of decision. A CheckBox control includes the property IsThreeState. If IsThreeState is set to true, the CheckBox control toggles between three states instead of two. The third state is a null, or unknown, state. This way, a question that requires a yes or no answer is not provided a no answer by default but can be provided an unknown answer instead by default. The following markup illustrates a configured CheckBox control:

```
<UserControl x:Class="L0810.Page"
    xmlns="http://schemas.microsoft.com/winfx/2006/xaml/presentation"
    xmlns:x="http://schemas.microsoft.com/winfx/2006/xaml"
    xmlns:d="http://schemas.microsoft.com/expression/blend/2008"
    xmlns:mc="http://schemas.openxmlformats.org/markup-
        compatibility/2006"
    mc:Ignorable="d"
    d:DesignHeight="300" d:DesignWidth="400">
    <Grid x:Name="LayoutRoot" Background="White">
        <CheckBox Height="Auto" Margin="8,8,172,0"
        VerticalAlignment="Top" Content="Default Mailing Address?"
        IsThreeState="True" IsChecked="True"/>
    </Grid>
</UserControl>
```

Figure 8-9 illustrates a CheckBox control displayed using Internet Explorer.

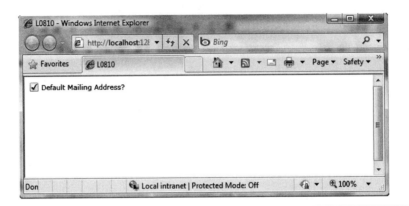

Figure 8-9 A CheckBox control

Combobox Control

The Combobox control is used to display a list of options as well as accommodate the user adding new options to the list. The Combobox can be configured to display a read-only list of options, thus serving the same purpose as a DropdownListbox in most other development environments. However, the Combobox is called a "combo" due to the ability to add new items to the list. If a single selection is to be made from the list, a Combobox is the control that should be used. If the user is able to make multiple selections from the list, the Listbox control should be used. The following markup illustrates a Combobox that displays mixed martial arts disciplines:

```
<UserControl x:Class="L0811.Page"
    xmlns="http://schemas.microsoft.com/winfx/2006/xaml/presentation"
    xmlns:x="http://schemas.microsoft.com/winfx/2006/xaml"
    xmlns:d="http://schemas.microsoft.com/expression/blend/2008"
    xmlns:mc="http://schemas.openxmlformats.org/markup-
        compatibility/2006"
    mc:Ignorable="d"
    d:DesignHeight="300" d:DesignWidth="400">

    <Grid x:Name="LayoutRoot" Background="White">
        <ComboBox Height="23" HorizontalAlignment="Left"
        Margin="12,39,0,0" Name="comboBox1" VerticalAlignment="Top"
        Width="249">
            <ComboBoxItem Content="Boxing" />
            <ComboBoxItem Content="Muay Thai" />
```

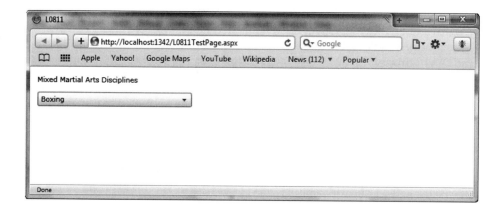

Figure 8-10   A Combobox displayed using Safari

```
            <ComboBoxItem Content="Brazilian Jiu Jitsu" />
            <ComboBoxItem Content="Grappling" />
            <ComboBoxItem Content="Wrestling" />
            <ComboBoxItem Content="Other (tae kwon do, karate, etc)" />
        </ComboBox>
        <TextBlock Height="21" HorizontalAlignment="Left"
        Margin="12,12,0,0" Text="Mixed Martial Arts Disciplines"
        VerticalAlignment="Top" Width="209" />
    </Grid>
</UserControl>
```

Figure 8-10 illustrates the Combobox displayed using Safari with the option Boxing selected.

DataGrid Control

The DataGrid control is used to display data in a tabular format. The DataGrid control supports the inline editing of data, the sorting of data by clicking a column header, and the paging of data. The DataGrid is one of the more complex controls, but you can quickly populate and display it by simply assigning it a DataSource with the AutoGenerateColumns property configured to True. The following markup illustrates a simple DataGrid control that is bound to a generic list of names:

```
<UserControl
    xmlns="http://schemas.microsoft.com/winfx/2006/xaml/presentation"
    xmlns:x="http://schemas.microsoft.com/winfx/2006/xaml"
    xmlns:d="http://schemas.microsoft.com/expression/blend/2008"
    xmlns:mc="http://schemas.openxmlformats.org/markup-
        compatibility/2006"
```

```
mc:Ignorable="d"
xmlns:data="clr-namespace:System.Windows.Controls;
assembly=System.Windows.Controls.Data" x:Class="L0812.Page"
d:DesignHeight="300" d:DesignWidth="400">
<Grid x:Name="LayoutRoot" Background="White">

    <data:DataGrid x:Name="dgNames" Margin="8,8,8,8"/>

    </Grid>
</UserControl>
```

The following code illustrates the simple generic collection that is bound and displayed using the DataGrid control:

```
using System;
using System.Collections.Generic;
using System.Linq;
using System.Net;
using System.Windows;
using System.Windows.Controls;
using System.Windows.Documents;
using System.Windows.Input;
using System.Windows.Media;
using System.Windows.Media.Animation;
using System.Windows.Shapes;

namespace L0812
{
    public partial class Page : UserControl
    {
        public Page()
        {
            InitializeComponent();

            List<string> names = new List<string>();
            names.Add("Benny Madrid");
            names.Add("Brad Peterson");
            names.Add("Matt Howard");
            names.Add("Carlos Farias");

            dgNames.ItemsSource = names;
        }
    }
}
```

Finally, Figure 8-11 shows the DataGrid when displayed using Internet Explorer.

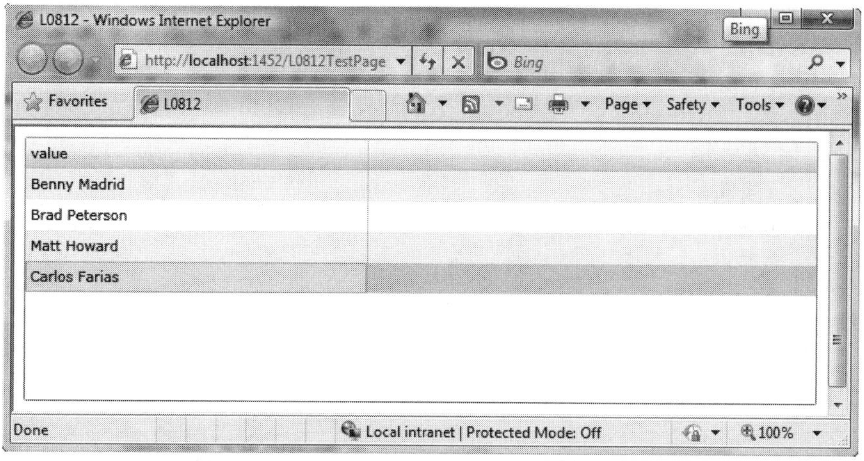

Figure 8-11   A DataGrid control displaying the contents of a simple generic list of string values

DatePicker Control

The DatePicker control is used to display a Calendar control to the user for the selection of a date value. The calendar displayed by the DatePicker is shown only when the user clicks the DatePicker control. Once the user makes a selection from the displayed Calendar control, the selected value is returned and the calendar is hidden. The DatePicker is intended to be used for a single date value selection, so as to not consume the user interface real estate necessary to display a full Calendar control. The following markup illustrates the use of a DatePicker control:

```
<UserControl
    xmlns="http://schemas.microsoft.com/winfx/2006/xaml/presentation"
    xmlns:x="http://schemas.microsoft.com/winfx/2006/xaml"
    xmlns:d="http://schemas.microsoft.com/expression/blend/2008"
    xmlns:mc="http://schemas.openxmlformats.org/markup-
        compatibility/2006"
    mc:Ignorable="d"
    xmlns:controls="clr-namespace:System.Windows.Controls;
    assembly=System.Windows.Controls" x:Class="L0813.Page"
    d:DesignHeight="300" d:DesignWidth="400">
    <Grid x:Name="LayoutRoot" Background="White">
      <controls:DatePicker Height="23" Margin="8,8,0,0"
      VerticalAlignment="Top" Width="147" HorizontalAlignment="Left"/>


    </Grid>
</UserControl>
```

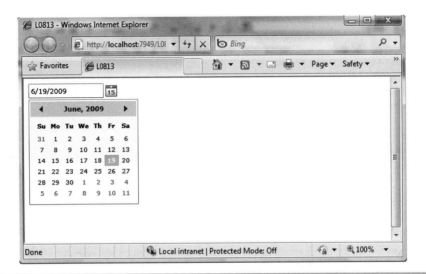

Figure 8-12 A DatePicker control with the calendar displayed

Figure 8-12 shows a DatePicker control with the calendar displayed in Internet Explorer.

Expander Control

The Expander control is typically used for user interface organization and navigation purposes. The Expander control displays a header with a caption that describes its contents. The Expander control also displays a button in the header that expands and collapses the contained region. The Expander control is useful for integrating controls and sections into a user interface that may not be used as often. The following markup illustrates an Expander control:

```
<UserControl
    xmlns="http://schemas.microsoft.com/winfx/2006/xaml/presentation"
    xmlns:x="http://schemas.microsoft.com/winfx/2006/xaml"
    xmlns:d="http://schemas.microsoft.com/expression/blend/2008"
    xmlns:mc="http://schemas.openxmlformats.org/markup-
        compatibility/2006"
    mc:Ignorable="d"
    xmlns:controls="clr-namespace:System.Windows.Controls;
    assembly=System.Windows.Controls" x:Class="L0814.Page"
    d:DesignHeight="300" d:DesignWidth="400">

    <Grid x:Name="LayoutRoot" Background="White">

        <controls:Expander Margin="8,8,198,62"
```

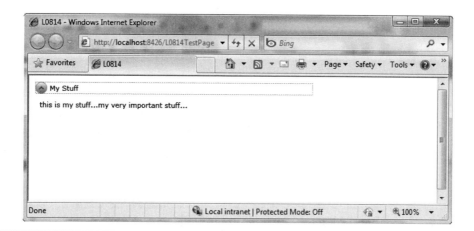

Figure 8-13   An Expander control that contains a TextBlock

```
Header="My Stuff" ToolTipService.ToolTip="this is my
stuff that i only display when i choose to"
IsExpanded="False" UseLayoutRounding="True">
     <TextBlock Text="this is my stuff...my
     very important stuff..." TextWrapping="Wrap"
     Margin="8,8,6,12" UseLayoutRounding="False"/>
</controls:Expander>

     </Grid>
</UserControl>
```

Figure 8-13 shows an Expander control that is expanded. The Expander control contains a TextBlock control.

HyperlinkButton Control

A HyperlinkButton control is displayed like a standard HTML hyperlink but has an associated Click event so that it behaves like a standard Button control. The hyperlink button also behaves like a standard HTML hyperlink if its NavigateUri property is set to a valid URL, as shown in the following markup:

```
<UserControl x:Class="L0815.Page"
    xmlns="http://schemas.microsoft.com/winfx/2006/xaml/presentation"
    xmlns:x="http://schemas.microsoft.com/winfx/2006/xaml"
    xmlns:d="http://schemas.microsoft.com/expression/blend/2008"
    xmlns:mc="http://schemas.openxmlformats.org/markup-
        compatibility/2006"
    mc:Ignorable="d"
```

Figure 8-14 A HyperlinkButton control displayed in FireFox

```
    d:DesignHeight="300" d:DesignWidth="400">
    <Grid x:Name="LayoutRoot" Background="White">
        <HyperlinkButton Height="Auto" Margin="8,8,54,0"
VerticalAlignment="Top" Content="Microsoft Web Site"
NavigateUri="http://www.microsoft.com"/>
    </Grid>
</UserControl>
```

Figure 8-14 shows a HyperlinkButton control that links to the Microsoft home page as displayed in FireFox.

Image Control

An Image control is used to display an image. Silverlight supports the display of popular web image formats, including JPG and PNG. However, due to legalities, it does not support the display of GIF files. The following markup illustrates the use of an Image control:

```
<UserControl x:Class="L0816.Page"
    xmlns="http://schemas.microsoft.com/winfx/2006/xaml/presentation"
    xmlns:x="http://schemas.microsoft.com/winfx/2006/xaml"
    xmlns:d="http://schemas.microsoft.com/expression/blend/2008"
    xmlns:mc="http://schemas.openxmlformats.org/markup-
        compatibility/2006"
    mc:Ignorable="d"
    d:DesignHeight="300" d:DesignWidth="400">
    <Grid x:Name="LayoutRoot" Background="White">
        <Image Height="200" Source="babyPigs.jpg" />
    </Grid>
</UserControl>
```

Figure 8-15 shows an Image control in Internet Explorer displaying an image of baby pigs.

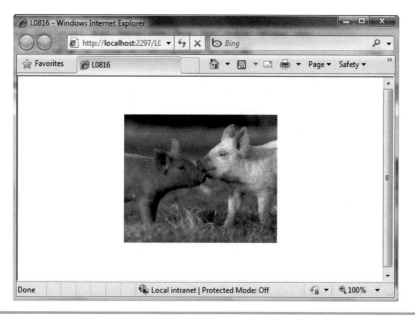

Figure 8-15   An Image control displayed using Internet Explorer

Label Control

A Label control is simply a text string displayed in an application. A Label control
differs from a TextBlock control in its intended use. Most user interface controls have
a descriptive label next to and associated with them that identifies the intended purpose
of the control. Prior to Silverlight 3, user interface control labels were created using a
TextBlock control. Silverlight 3 introduces the Label control designed for this use. The
Label control is a simple control but includes some properties and behavior that lend to
easier user interface navigation.

Listbox Control

The Listbox control is identical to the Combobox control except that the Listbox is not a
dropdown control; instead, it remains expanded. Additionally, the Listbox control does not
include functionality to automatically accommodate a user adding new options to the list.
The following markup illustrates a Listbox control:

```
<UserControl x:Class="L0817.Page"
    xmlns="http://schemas.microsoft.com/winfx/2006/xaml/presentation"
    xmlns:x="http://schemas.microsoft.com/winfx/2006/xaml"
    xmlns:d="http://schemas.microsoft.com/expression/blend/2008"
```

```
xmlns:mc="http://schemas.openxmlformats.org/markup-
    compatibility/2006"
mc:Ignorable="d"
d:DesignHeight="300" d:DesignWidth="400">
<Grid x:Name="LayoutRoot" Background="White">
    <ListBox Height="276" HorizontalAlignment="Left"
    Margin="12,12,0,0" Name="listBox1" VerticalAlignment="Top"
    Width="376">
        <ListBoxItem Content="Shannon" />
        <ListBoxItem Content="Patricia" />
        <ListBoxItem Content="Nashly" />
        <ListBoxItem Content="Abbi" />
        <ListBoxItem Content="London" />
        <ListBoxItem Content="Ladybird" />
        <ListBoxItem Content="Peanut" />
    </ListBox>
</Grid>
</UserControl>
```

Figure 8-16 displays a Listbox control in Internet Explorer.

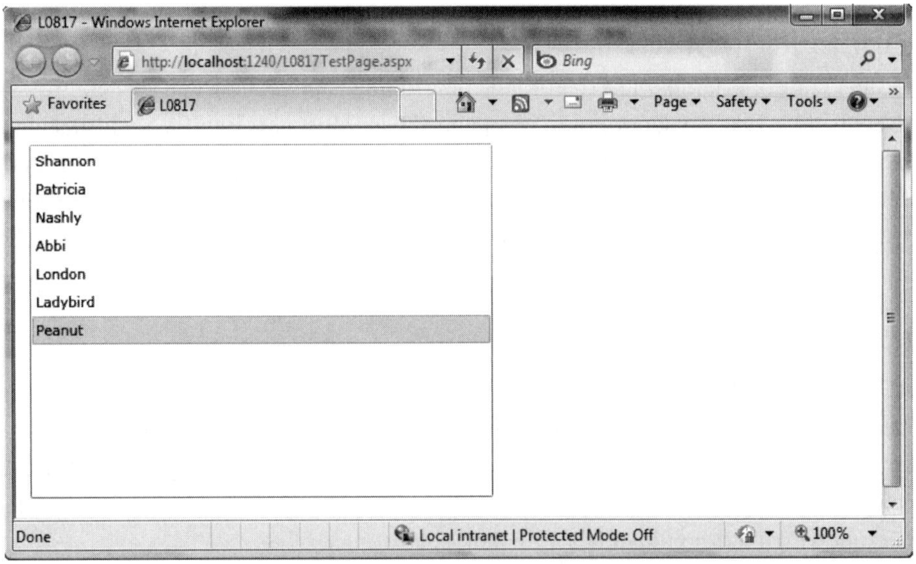

Figure 8-16 A Listbox control displaying names

PasswordBox Control

The PasswordBox control is a Textbox control that is designed to mask input so that it is not evident what input value is being entered. Bear in mind that the PasswordBox does not protect or encrypt input in any way but simply masks the input values. The following markup illustrates a PasswordBox control and a TextBlock control. When the PasswordBox control loses focus, it displays the input password value in the TextBlock control.

```
<UserControl x:Class="L0818.Page"
    xmlns="http://schemas.microsoft.com/winfx/2006/xaml/presentation"
    xmlns:x="http://schemas.microsoft.com/winfx/2006/xaml"
    xmlns:d="http://schemas.microsoft.com/expression/blend/2008"
    xmlns:mc="http://schemas.openxmlformats.org/markup-
        compatibility/2006"
    mc:Ignorable="d"
    d:DesignHeight="123" d:DesignWidth="400">
    <Grid x:Name="LayoutRoot" Background="White" Height="116">
        <PasswordBox Height="23" HorizontalAlignment="Left"
        Margin="12,12,0,0" Name="passwordBox1" VerticalAlignment="Top"
        Width="170" LostFocus="passwordBox1_LostFocus" />
        <TextBlock Height="61" HorizontalAlignment="Left"
        Margin="12,41,0,0" Name="tbPassword" Text=""
            VerticalAlignment="Top"
        Width="376" />
    </Grid>
</UserControl>
```

Figure 8-17 shows the PasswordBox control displayed in Internet Explorer.

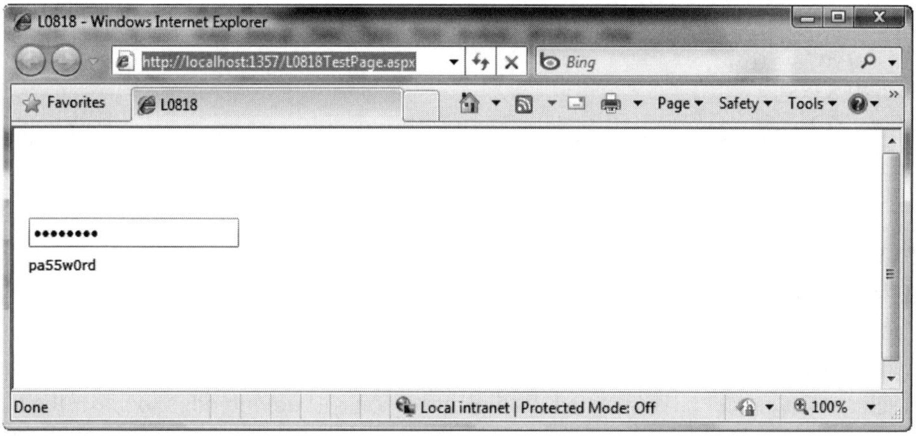

Figure 8-17   A PasswordBox control

ProgressBar Control

The ProgressBar control is used to visually track the progress of a process and is common to practically all application platforms. A common use of the ProgressBar control is to track the progress of a copy operation. The ProgressBar control includes Minimum and Maximum properties that define the lower and upper boundaries, respectively, of the value assigned to the Value property. The Minimum property cannot be configured to a value less than 0, and the Maximum property cannot be configured to a value greater than 100. Generally, the Minimum and Maximum properties are configured to 0 and 100, respectively, which are their default values. The value assigned to the Value property indicates the percentage of the process that has been completed.

The following markup illustrates the use of a ProgressBar control:

```
<UserControl x:Class="L0819.Page"
    xmlns="http://schemas.microsoft.com/winfx/2006/xaml/presentation"
    xmlns:x="http://schemas.microsoft.com/winfx/2006/xaml"
    xmlns:d="http://schemas.microsoft.com/expression/blend/2008"
    xmlns:mc="http://schemas.openxmlformats.org/markup-
        compatibility/2006"
    mc:Ignorable="d"
    d:DesignHeight="300" d:DesignWidth="400" Loaded="UserControl_
        Loaded">

    <Grid x:Name="LayoutRoot" Background="White">
      <ProgressBar Height="22" Margin="8,8,8,0"
        VerticalAlignment="Top" Name="pbSample" />
      <TextBlock Height="18" Margin="8,34,150,0"
        VerticalAlignment="Top" Text="progress of a random process..."
        TextWrapping="Wrap"/>

    </Grid>
</UserControl>
```

Figure 8-18 shows a ProgressBar control with a Value property configuration of 45 displayed using Internet Explorer.

RadioButton Control

A RadioButton control is included in a group with other RadioButton controls. Each RadioButton control is used to make a selection out of a group of options. A single RadioButton control should not be displayed to a user because once a single RadioButton is selected, it cannot be deselected. RadioButton controls are intended to allow the user to make a mutually exclusive selection out of a group of possible selections. RadioButton controls should be displayed as a group to the user.

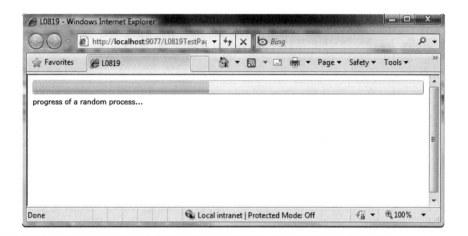

Figure 8-18 A ProgressBar control configured to 45

Each RadioButton control includes a property named GroupName. The GroupName property is assigned a user-defined string that represents the name of the group to which RadioButton should belong. All RadioButtons that belong to the same group will portray the available list of options for a user to choose from. The following markup listing illustrates the use of a RadioButton control:

```
<UserControl x:Class="L0820.Page"
    xmlns="http://schemas.microsoft.com/winfx/2006/xaml/presentation"
    xmlns:x="http://schemas.microsoft.com/winfx/2006/xaml"
    xmlns:d="http://schemas.microsoft.com/expression/blend/2008"
    xmlns:mc="http://schemas.openxmlformats.org/markup-
        compatibility/2006"
    mc:Ignorable="d"
    d:DesignHeight="300" d:DesignWidth="400">
    <StackPanel x:Name="LayoutRoot" Background="White">
        <RadioButton Height="Auto" Width="Auto"
        Content="English" GroupName="language"/>
        <RadioButton Height="Auto" Width="Auto"
        Content="French" GroupName="language"/>
        <RadioButton Height="Auto" Width="Auto"
        Content="Chinese" GroupName="language"/>
        <RadioButton Height="Auto" Width="Auto"
        Content="German" GroupName="language"/>
        <RadioButton Height="Auto" Width="Auto"
        Content="Spanish" GroupName="language"/>
        <RadioButton Height="Auto" Width="Auto"
        Content="Russian" GroupName="language"/>
    </StackPanel>
</UserControl>
```

Figure 8-19 Several RadioButton controls

Figure 8-19 illustrates several RadioButton controls as displayed using Apple Safari.

RepeatButton Control

A RepeatButton control is used to repeat the action associated with a Click event while the button is held down. The RepeatButton includes properties to control the speed and interval the button uses to determine how fast to repeat the Click action. The Delay property indicates in milliseconds how long the button control should delay after the user clicks the button before it should begin repeating the Click action. The Interval property indicates how many milliseconds should pass between iterations of the Click action. The following markup listing illustrates use of the RepeatButton control:

```
<UserControl x:Class="L0821.Page"
    xmlns="http://schemas.microsoft.com/winfx/2006/xaml/presentation"
    xmlns:x="http://schemas.microsoft.com/winfx/2006/xaml"
    xmlns:d="http://schemas.microsoft.com/expression/blend/2008"
    xmlns:mc="http://schemas.openxmlformats.org/markup-
        compatibility/2006"
    mc:Ignorable="d"
    d:DesignHeight="300" d:DesignWidth="400">
    <Grid x:Name="LayoutRoot" Background="White">
      <RepeatButton Height="25" Click="RepeatButton_Click"
        HorizontalAlignment="Left" Margin="8,8,0,0"
        VerticalAlignment="Top" Width="134" Content="click me to
            repeat"/>
      <TextBlock x:Name="tbTarget" Margin="8,37,8,8" Text=""
        TextWrapping="Wrap"/>

    </Grid>
</UserControl>
```

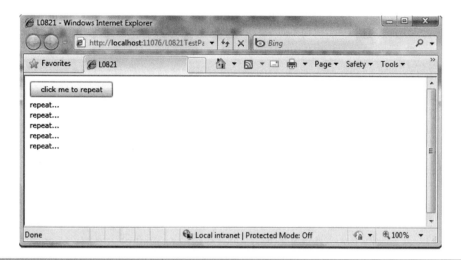

Figure 8-20 A RepeatButton that adds to the Text property of a TextBlock

Figure 8-20 illustrates a RepeatButton displayed using Internet Explorer that adds to the Text property of a TextBlock control each time it is clicked.

ScrollViewer Control

A ScrollViewer control serves as a container control for other controls. Most commonly, a Textbox control is placed within a ScrollViewer control to create a text box that supports multiple lines of text. The ScrollViewer provides a scrollable portal that accommodates the scrolling and viewing of all content in the contained text box. The following markup listing illustrates a ScrollViewer control that contains a Textbox control:

```
<UserControl x:Class="L0822.Page"
    xmlns="http://schemas.microsoft.com/winfx/2006/xaml/presentation"
    xmlns:x="http://schemas.microsoft.com/winfx/2006/xaml"
    xmlns:d="http://schemas.microsoft.com/expression/blend/2008"
    xmlns:mc="http://schemas.openxmlformats.org/markup-
        compatibility/2006"
    mc:Ignorable="d"
    d:DesignHeight="300" d:DesignWidth="400" Loaded="UserControl_
        Loaded" >
    <Grid x:Name="LayoutRoot" Background="White">
      <ScrollViewer Margin="8,8,8,0" VerticalAlignment="Top"
          Height="128">
          <TextBlock Height="Auto" Width="Auto"
          TextWrapping="Wrap" Name="tbAbe"/>
```

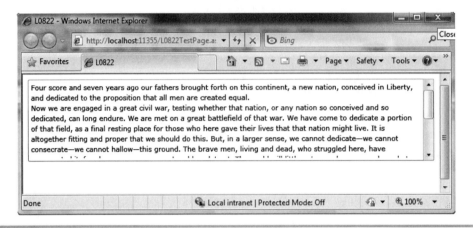

Figure 8-21 A ScrollViewer control that contains a Textbox control

```
        </ScrollViewer>
    </Grid>
</UserControl>
```

Figure 8-21 shows the results of this markup listing.

Slider Control

A Slider control is used to slide across a range of values. The minimum and maximum values to slide across as well as the increment to be used when sliding across the span of values are configured using the control properties. The Slider control includes an event named ValueChanged that can be used to take an action in response to the user adjusting the Slider control. The following markup illustrates a Slider control:

```
<UserControl x:Class="L0823.Page"
    xmlns="http://schemas.microsoft.com/winfx/2006/xaml/presentation"
    xmlns:x="http://schemas.microsoft.com/winfx/2006/xaml"
    xmlns:d="http://schemas.microsoft.com/expression/blend/2008"
    xmlns:mc="http://schemas.openxmlformats.org/markup-
        compatibility/2006"
    mc:Ignorable="d"
    d:DesignHeight="300" d:DesignWidth="400">
    <Grid x:Name="LayoutRoot" Background="White">
        <Slider Height="22" HorizontalAlignment="Left"
        Margin="12,12,0,0" Name="sldrTemp" ValueChanged="sldrTemp_
        ValueChanged" VerticalAlignment="Top" Width="376" />
        <TextBlock Height="21" HorizontalAlignment="Left"
        Margin="12,40,0,0" Name="tbTarget" VerticalAlignment="Top"
        Width="376" />
    </Grid>
</UserControl>
```

The following is code used to handle the ValueChanged event:

```
using System;
using System.Collections.Generic;
using System.Linq;
using System.Net;
using System.Windows;
using System.Windows.Controls;
using System.Windows.Documents;
using System.Windows.Input;
using System.Windows.Media;
using System.Windows.Media.Animation;
using System.Windows.Shapes;

namespace L0823
{
    public partial class Page : UserControl
    {
        public Page()
        {
            InitializeComponent();
        }

        private void sldrTemp_ValueChanged(object sender,
        RoutedPropertyChangedEventArgs<double> e)
        {

            if (e.NewValue < 5)
            {

                tbTarget.Text = "brrr, it's cold in here...";
            }
            else if (e.NewValue > 8)
            {

                tbTarget.Text = "wow, it is HOT in here...";
            }
            else
            {

                tbTarget.Text = "aaahhhhh, just right...";
            }
        }
    }
}
```

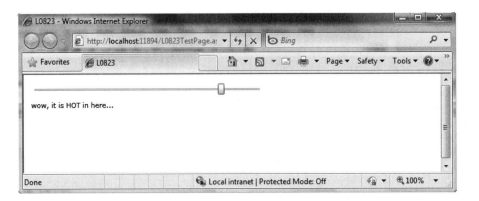

Figure 8-22 A Slider control as displayed using Internet Explorer

Figure 8-22 shows a Slider control displayed using Internet Explorer. The Slider control simulates a thermostat. When the Slider control is adjusted, the value of the TextBlock is updated to reflect the temperature setting.

TextBlock Control

A TextBlock control is used to display a string literal value to the user. Silverlight does not support writing text directly to most control types. Instead, text must be contained in a TextBlock control, a Label control, or a similar control.

Textbox Control

A Textbox control is used to gather text data from a user and is the most commonly used data-entry control across all software platforms.

ToggleButton Control

A ToggleButton control functions like a CheckBox control in that it is used to make a yes or no selection. However, a ToggleButton control looks like a standard Button that remains depressed once a user clicks it until the user clicks it again. As with a CheckBox control, a ToggleButton control supports the IsThreeState property. The following markup listing illustrates the use of a ToggleButton control:

```
<UserControl x:Class="L0824.Page"
    xmlns="http://schemas.microsoft.com/winfx/2006/xaml/presentation"
    xmlns:x="http://schemas.microsoft.com/winfx/2006/xaml"
    xmlns:d="http://schemas.microsoft.com/expression/blend/2008"
```

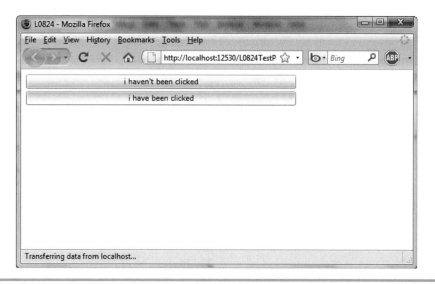

Figure 8-23   Two ToggleButton controls displayed using Firefox

```
xmlns:mc="http://schemas.openxmlformats.org/markup-
    compatibility/2006"
mc:Ignorable="d"
d:DesignHeight="300" d:DesignWidth="400">
<Grid x:Name="LayoutRoot" Background="White">
  <ToggleButton Height="Auto" Margin="8,8,190,0"
  VerticalAlignment="Top" Content="i haven't been clicked"
  IsChecked="False"/>
  <ToggleButton Height="Auto" Margin="8,34,190,0"
  VerticalAlignment="Top" Content="i have been clicked"
  IsChecked="True"/>

</Grid>
</UserControl>
```

Figure 8-23 shows two ToggleButton controls in Firefox. The first ToggleButton is not depressed while the second has been depressed.

Designing User Interfaces

With Silverlight still in its infancy, formal user interface design standards have not yet been compiled. However, many standards are being implemented in the industry by those who are creating applications using Silverlight. In a nutshell, the design standards recommended by Microsoft follow the User Experience (UX) guidelines for Windows Vista. The UX guidelines are documented in the MSDN document titled "Guidelines," located at http://msdn.microsoft.com/en-us/library/aa511440.aspx.

Create Control Skins and Templates

The controls that are shipped with WPF and now Silverlight are created and assembled using a collection of shapes and images that are grouped together. In most other development technologies, the controls that are included may or may not be extendable beyond the form in which they are provided out of the box. However, most controls used in other development technologies cannot be broken down into smaller parts. Conversely, the controls provided with WPF and Silverlight can be "ungrouped" or broken down in order to gain access to the smaller collective parts. Each smaller part of a control can be modified so that the appearance is changed. Modifying the appearance of a user interface control in Silverlight is referred to as "skinning the control."

Silverlight 3 and Expression Blend 3 support skinning controls. Any control, including custom controls, in Silverlight may be skinned to give it a custom appearance. For example, Figure 8-24 shows a standard button in a Silverlight control in Expression Blend.

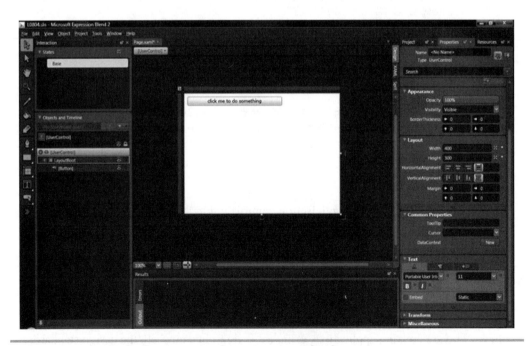

Figure 8-24 A standard Button control in Expression Blend

Try This Create a Control Skin

To skin a Silverlight control, follow these steps:

1. Start or open Expression Blend.

2. When prompted, create a new Silverlight project. Assign the project a name, select a location to create the new project, and then click OK.

3. From the toolbox on the left side of Blend, drag a control such as a TextBox and drop it onto the Silverlight design area.

4. To create a template or skin for the control, right-click the control and select Edit Control Parts (Template) | Edit a Copy from the context menu.

5. When the Create Style Resource dialog box is displayed, assign the template a name and determine where to define the template. If the template is defined in "This Document," it is created as a template in the current XAML document and it is only available within the current document. If the template is defined at the Application level, it is created as a template in the App.xaml file and it is available throughout the entire application. The Create Style Resource dialog is then displayed, as shown in Figure 8-25.

6. When you click OK on the Create Style Resource dialog, the new control template is displayed in the Objects and Timeline pane, and the various states that the control may exist in are displayed using the Visual State Manager in the Interaction pane. Select any items in the Objects and Timeline pane to customize the appearance of the control. As an example, the standard Button control was modified to appear as shown in Figure 8-26.

Figure 8-25   The Expression Blend Create Style Resource dialog

(continued)

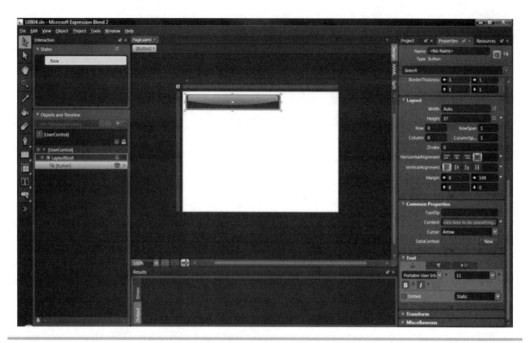

Figure 8-26 The newly created control template

> **NOTE**
>
> As shown in Figure 8-26, modifications to a control template can affect the behavior of the control. In this example, a gradient layer was removed; hence, some of the animations built into the standard Button control are no longer valid and were automatically removed. Click the Return Scope button to exit the template-editing mode and begin utilizing the customized ("skinned") control.

7. When you modify the display of a control, Expression Blend adds custom XAML behind the scenes to render the custom control. The result of the preceding modification is shown in the following XAML listing.

8. Exit Expression Blend.

```
<UserControl x:Class="L0804.Page"
    xmlns="http://schemas.microsoft.com/winfx/2006/xaml/presentation"
    xmlns:x="http://schemas.microsoft.com/winfx/2006/xaml"
    Width="400" Height="300"
xmlns:vsm="clr-namespace:System.Windows;assembly=System.Windows">
    <UserControl.Resources>
        <Style x:Key="myButton" TargetType="Button">
            <Setter Property="IsEnabled" Value="true"/>
            <Setter Property="IsTabStop" Value="true"/>
            <Setter Property="Background" Value="#FF003255"/>
```

```
                        <Setter Property="Foreground" Value="#FF313131"/>
                        <Setter Property="MinWidth" Value="5"/>
                        <Setter Property="MinHeight" Value="5"/>
                        <Setter Property="Margin" Value="0"/>
                        <Setter Property="HorizontalContentAlignment"
                        Value="Center"/>
                        <Setter Property="VerticalContentAlignment"
                        Value="Center"/>
                        <Setter Property="Cursor" Value="Arrow"/>
                        <Setter Property="TextAlignment" Value="Left"/>
                        <Setter Property="TextWrapping" Value="NoWrap"/>
                        <Setter Property="FontSize" Value="11"/>
                        <Setter Property="Template">
                                <Setter.Value>
                                        <ControlTemplate TargetType="Button">
                                                <Grid>
                                                        <Grid.Resources>

<Color x:Key="LinearBevelLightStartColor">#FCFFFFFF</Color>

<Color x:Key="LinearBevelLightEndColor">#F4FFFFFF</Color>

<Color x:Key="LinearBevelDarkStartColor">#E0FFFFFF</Color>

<Color x:Key="LinearBevelDarkEndColor">#B2FFFFFF</Color>

<Color x:Key="MouseOverLinearBevelDarkEndColor">#7FFFFFFF</Color>

<Color x:Key="HoverLinearBevelLightStartColor">#FCFFFFFF</Color>

<Color x:Key="HoverLinearBevelLightEndColor">#EAFFFFFF</Color>

<Color x:Key="HoverLinearBevelDarkStartColor">#D8FFFFFF</Color>

<Color x:Key="HoverLinearBevelDarkEndColor">#4CFFFFFF</Color>

<Color x:Key="CurvedBevelFillStartColor">#B3FFFFFF</Color>

<Color x:Key="CurvedBevelFillEndColor">#3CFFFFFF</Color>

<SolidColorBrush x:Key="BorderBrush" Color="#FF000000"/>

<SolidColorBrush x:Key="AccentBrush" Color="#FFFFFFFF"/>

<SolidColorBrush x:Key="DisabledBrush" Color="#A5FFFFFF"/>

<LinearGradientBrush x:Key="FocusedStrokeBrush"
EndPoint="0.5,1" StartPoint="0.5,0">
```

(continued)

```xml
<GradientStop Color="#B2FFFFFF" Offset="0"/>

<GradientStop Color="#51FFFFFF" Offset="1"/>

<GradientStop Color="#66FFFFFF" Offset="0.325"/>

<GradientStop Color="#1EFFFFFF" Offset="0.325"/>
                                        </LinearGradientBrush>
                                      </Grid.Resources>

    <vsm:VisualStateManager.VisualStateGroups>

<vsm:VisualStateGroup x:Name="CommonStates">

    <vsm:VisualStateGroup.Transitions>

<vsm:VisualTransition Duration="0:0:0.2" To="MouseOver"/>

<vsm:VisualTransition Duration="0:0:0.1" To="Pressed"/>

    </vsm:VisualStateGroup.Transitions>

<vsm:VisualState x:Name="Normal"/>

<vsm:VisualState x:Name="MouseOver">

                                        <Storyboard/>
                                      </vsm:VisualState>

<vsm:VisualState x:Name="Pressed">

                                        <Storyboard>

    <DoubleAnimationUsingKeyFrames Duration="0"
    Storyboard.TargetName="DownStroke"
    Storyboard.TargetProperty="Opacity">

    <SplineDoubleKeyFrame KeyTime="0" Value="1"/>

    </DoubleAnimationUsingKeyFrames>

                                        </Storyboard>
                                      </vsm:VisualState>

<vsm:VisualState x:Name="Disabled">

                                        <Storyboard>

    <DoubleAnimationUsingKeyFrames Duration="0"
```

```
                    Storyboard.TargetName="DisabledVisual"
                    Storyboard.TargetProperty="Opacity">

                    <SplineDoubleKeyFrame KeyTime="0" Value="1"/>

                    </DoubleAnimationUsingKeyFrames>

                                                        </Storyboard>
                                                    </vsm:VisualState>
                                                </vsm:VisualStateGroup>

<vsm:VisualStateGroup x:Name="FocusStates">

<vsm:VisualState x:Name="Focused">

                                                    <Storyboard>

                    <ObjectAnimationUsingKeyFrames Duration="0"
                    Storyboard.TargetName="FocusVisual"
                    Storyboard.TargetProperty="Visibility">

                    <DiscreteObjectKeyFrame KeyTime="0">

                    <DiscreteObjectKeyFrame.Value>

                    <Visibility>Visible</Visibility>

                    </DiscreteObjectKeyFrame.Value>

                    </DiscreteObjectKeyFrame>

                    </ObjectAnimationUsingKeyFrames>

                                                        </Storyboard>
                                                    </vsm:VisualState>
                                                    <vsm:VisualState
                    x:Name="Unfocused">

                                                        <Storyboard>

                    <ObjectAnimationUsingKeyFrames Duration="0"
                    Storyboard.TargetName="FocusVisual"
                    Storyboard.TargetProperty="Visibility">

                    <DiscreteObjectKeyFrame KeyTime="0">

                    <DiscreteObjectKeyFrame.Value>

                    <Visibility>Collapsed</Visibility>

                    </DiscreteObjectKeyFrame.Value>
```

(continued)

```
        </DiscreteObjectKeyFrame>

      </ObjectAnimationUsingKeyFrames>
                                          </Storyboard>
                                      </vsm:VisualState>
                                  </vsm:VisualStateGroup>

    </vsm:VisualStateManager.VisualStateGroups>
                                    <Rectangle
    x:Name="Background" Fill="{TemplateBinding Background}"
    RadiusX="4" RadiusY="4"/>
                                    <Grid Margin="2"
    x:Name="CurvedBevelScale">
                                      <Grid.RowDefinitions>
                                        <RowDefinition
Height="7*"/>

                                        <RowDefinition
Height="3*"/>
                                      </Grid.RowDefinitions>
                                      <Path
Margin="3,0,3,0" x:Name="CurvedBevel" Stretch="Fill"
Data="F1 M 0,0.02 V 0.15 C
0.15,0.22 0.30,0.25 0.50,0.26 C 0.70,0.26 0.85,0.22 1,0.15 V 0.02 L 0.97,
0 H 0.02 L 0,0.02 Z">
                                        <Path.Fill>

<LinearGradientBrush EndPoint="0.5,1" StartPoint="0.5,0">

<GradientStop Color="{StaticResource CurvedBevelFillStartColor}"
Offset="0"/>

<GradientStop Color="{StaticResource CurvedBevelFillEndColor}"
Offset="1"/>

</LinearGradientBrush>
                                        </Path.Fill>
                                      </Path>
                                    </Grid>
                                    <Rectangle Margin="1"
x:Name="Accent" Stroke="{StaticResource AccentBrush}"
StrokeThickness="1"
RadiusX="3" RadiusY="3"/>
                                    <Grid
x:Name="FocusVisual" Visibility="Collapsed">
                                      <Rectangle
Margin="2" Stroke="{StaticResource AccentBrush}" StrokeThickness="1"
RadiusX="3" RadiusY="3"/>
```

```xml
<Rectangle Stroke="{TemplateBinding Background}" StrokeThickness="2"
RadiusX="3" RadiusY="3"/>
                                                    <Rectangle
Stroke="{StaticResource FocusedStrokeBrush}" StrokeThickness="2"
RadiusX="3"
RadiusY="3"/>
                                        </Grid>
                                        <Grid x:Name="DownStroke"
Opacity="0">
                                                <Rectangle
Margin="1,2,1,1" Opacity="0.05" Stroke="{TemplateBinding Background}"
StrokeThickness="1" RadiusX="3" RadiusY="3"/>
                                                <Rectangle
Margin="1,1.75,1,1" Opacity="0.05" Stroke="{TemplateBinding
Background}"
StrokeThickness="1" RadiusX="3" RadiusY="3"/>
                                                <Rectangle
Margin="1,1.5,1,1" Opacity="0.05" Stroke="{TemplateBinding
Background}"
StrokeThickness="1" RadiusX="3" RadiusY="3"/>
                                                <Rectangle
Margin="1,1.25,1,1" Opacity="0.05" Stroke="{TemplateBinding
Background}"
StrokeThickness="1" RadiusX="3" RadiusY="3"/>
                                                <Rectangle Margin="1"
Opacity="1" Stroke="{TemplateBinding Background}" StrokeThickness="1"
RadiusX="3" RadiusY="3"/>
                                                <Rectangle
Margin="1" StrokeThickness="1" RadiusX="4" RadiusY="4">
                                                        <Rectangle.Stroke>

<LinearGradientBrush EndPoint="0.5,1" StartPoint="0.5,0">

<GradientStop Color="#A5FFFFFF" Offset="0"/>

<GradientStop Color="#FFFFFFFF" Offset="1"/>

</LinearGradientBrush>

                                                        </Rectangle.Stroke>
                                                </Rectangle>
                                        </Grid>
                                        <ContentPresenter
Margin="4,5,4,4" HorizontalContentAlignment="{TemplateBinding
HorizontalContentAlignment}" Padding="{TemplateBinding Padding}"
VerticalContentAlignment="{TemplateBinding VerticalContentAlignment}"
Content="{TemplateBinding Content}" ContentTemplate="{TemplateBinding
ContentTemplate}" TextAlignment="{TemplateBinding TextAlignment}"
TextDecorations="{TemplateBinding TextDecorations}"
```

(continued)

```
TextWrapping="{TemplateBinding TextWrapping}"/>
                                        <Rectangle
x:Name="DisabledVisual" IsHitTestVisible="false" Opacity="0"
Fill="{StaticResource DisabledBrush}" RadiusX="4" RadiusY="4"/>
                                </Grid>
                        </ControlTemplate>
                    </Setter.Value>
                </Setter>
            </Style>
        </UserControl.Resources>
        <Grid x:Name="LayoutRoot" Background="White">

        <Button Height="37" HorizontalAlignment="Stretch"
Margin="8,8,149,0" Style="{StaticResource myButton}"
VerticalAlignment="Top" Content="click here to do something..."/>

        </Grid>
</UserControl>
```

Notice in this XAML listing that the style created has a key of "myButton" assigned. The style is applied to a control using the Style attribute and the StaticResource directive.

Visual State Manager

Nearly all Silverlight controls exist in multiple states, or appearances, while they are instantiated. For example, a Button control includes a default state (appearance) that is shown when the button is initially displayed. When a user moves the mouse pointer over the Button control, by default it changes color somewhat to highlight the button. The highlighted appearance represents a different visual state in which the Button control exists. Each type of control may include several visual states. Expression Blend includes an interface, called the Visual State Manager (VSM), for easily managing the various visual states of a control.

To access the VSM, open a Silverlight control in Expression Blend. Right-click the control that visual states should be modified for and select Edit Control Parts (Template) | Edit a Copy to create a template copy of the control. Notice the VSM highlighted in Figure 8-27.

In order to use the VSM, select the desired state to change from the VSM panel, modify the control with that state selected, and then save the control. The Visual State Manager also provides access to the visual states of a control programmatically.

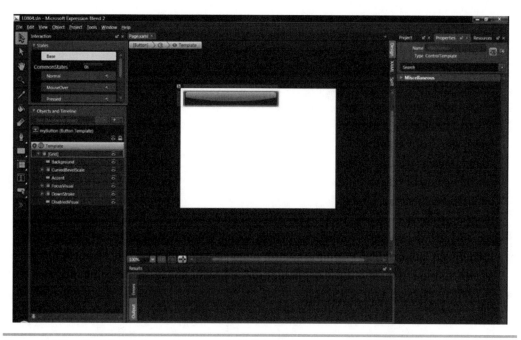

Figure 8-27   The Visual State Manager (VSM) Expression Blend interface

Conclusion

The .NET Framework is the leading development environment in the industry. A key selling point for teams adopting Silverlight as a development platform is that the armies of existing .NET developers can almost immediately leverage their existing knowledge to create Silverlight applications. Silverlight development teams may have the final user interface for an application designed prior to developing the actual user interface. However, by using control templates, a developer can quickly build and prototype an application user interface and then later adjust and refine the look and feel of the user interface. Additionally, via control templates, the user interface of a Silverlight application can be quickly modified. What's more, users can select a custom skin to use when viewing a Silverlight application.

Chapter 9
Working with Data in Silverlight

Key Concepts & Skills

- Gain an understanding of how to work with data programmatically

- Observe how to use Silverlight to access data stored as XML

- Learn how to use Language Integrated Query (LINQ) in Silverlight applications

- Explore the use of Silverlight Isolated Storage for storing data locally on the client machine

Data is imperative to business applications. Silverlight is commonly compared to other popular RIA technologies. However, due to the armies of existing .NET developers who will be developing applications using Silverlight, Silverlight will commonly be used to create business applications. As such, knowledge of working with data in Silverlight is a vital skill for a Silverlight developer.

Working with Data in Code

All data to be displayed to the user must first be dealt with programmatically. When you're working with data programmatically, data is typically stored in memory for later reference, while other operations are carried out, or while it is being manipulated. Data may be entered by a user, retrieved from a data source, or created programmatically.

Variables

The most basic means of storing data in memory is through the use of variables. All programming languages support some form of variables. A *variable* is a named location in memory used to store data. Most programming languages share a common means of storing data as variables; however, the specifics of how data is stored and managed in memory is particular to a programming language. Strongly typed programming languages are very strict about what type of data can be stored in a variable. Weakly typed programming languages are not strict about what type of data can be stored in a variable. Strongly typed programming languages are generally more efficient than weakly typed programming languages.

Silverlight may be coded using several languages. Some of the languages used in Silverlight (such as JavaScript) are weakly typed, whereas others (such as C#) are strongly typed. Developers must thoroughly understand how to work with variables in the language they use when working with Silverlight. The following code snippet illustrates the declaration and initialization of a simple string type variable named "name":

```
// simple variable.
string name = "shannon horn";
```

Collections

In addition to storing a single piece of data in memory, most programming languages also support storing multiple pieces of data in a named location in memory. A *collection* is a named location in memory, similar to a variable, that is structured for storing multiple pieces of data. Depending on the programming language used, multiple types of collections may be supported. For example, C# supports simple arrays, ArrayLists, Stacks, Queues, and HashTables. Each type of collection supported is structured for storing and retrieving data in a different fashion.

In C#, collections are stored in memory as reference types instead of value types and are located in the System.Collections namespace. The following code snippet illustrates the declaration and initialization of a standard string array named "athleteNames."

```
// store athlete information in an ArrayList.
string[] athleteNames = new string[3];
athleteNames[0] = "Shannon Horn";
athleteNames[1] = "Benny Madrid";
athleteNames[2] = "Edwin Dewees";
```

Generics

Collections are versatile and simplify data storage in code by making it easier to store and transport multiple data items and objects. However, standard collections have some drawbacks. A standard collection—including an array, ArrayList, Stack, Queue, and HashTable—stores data internally as a simple object. By storing data as a simple object, you can use a standard collection to store any type of data. In a nutshell, in C#, a standard collection is a weakly typed construct that exists in a strongly typed language. The internal storage design of a standard collection affects performance and type safety negatively.

When a data item is stored in a standard collection, it must be converted to a simple object type. When a data item stored in a standard collection is removed from the collection, it must be converted from a simple object type to the destination type.

The process of converting data to and from a simple object degrades performance. Additionally, a simple object can be converted to any more complex type. However, there is no guarantee that the data stored as a simple object will be correctly represented when removed from the standard collection and converted to a more complex type. For example, a complex object that represents data about an athlete may be stored in a collection and then removed from the collection and converted to a string. The code written to perform the operation should compile but will, more than likely, cause errors to occur at runtime. Thus, type safety is lost.

Generic collections are available only in more advanced languages, such as C#. In the .NET Framework, generic collections are located in the System.Collections.Generic namespace. A generic collection is a strongly typed collection and requires that the data type to be used for storage be specified at the time the collection is instantiated. Here is an example:

```
// a generic collection for storing athlete names as strings.
List<string> athleteNames = new List<string>(3);
athleteNames.Add("Shannon Horn");
athleteNames.Add("Benny Madrid");
athleteNames.Add("Edwin Dewees");
```

In this code snippet, the athleteNames generic collection will store only string values; however, the collection could be configured to store and manage any valid .NET type.

TIP
Microsoft strongly recommends using generic collections in lieu of using standard collections and arrays. Generic collections are strongly typed and type-safe, thus ensuring the consistency of the contents stored in the collection.

Working with Data Stored in XML

The Extensible Markup Language (XML) was released by the World Wide Web Consortium (W3C; http://www.w3.org) in 1999 as a standardized means of storing and transporting data over the Web. XML has proliferated web development technologies, and virtually all software development platforms support some form of XML interaction. The .NET Framework contains a gamut of classes for working with XML data in the System. Xml namespace.

Silverlight contains a subset of XML functionality in the System.Xml namespace. XML data can be read using the XmlReader class, and XML data can be written using the XmlWriter class. Additionally, Silverlight includes the XmlWriterSettings class, which is used to specify configuration settings to be used when writing XML data. If configuration settings are not specified using the XmlWriterSettings class, default configuration settings are used. In the following code listing, the XmlReader class, the XmlWriter class, and the XmlWriterSettings class are used to read in a well-formed XML string, parse it, and write the contents to a TextBlock:

```
using System;
using System.Collections.Generic;
using System.Linq;
using System.Net;
using System.Windows;
using System.Windows.Controls;
using System.Windows.Documents;
using System.Windows.Input;
using System.Windows.Media;
using System.Windows.Media.Animation;
using System.Windows.Shapes;
using System.Xml;
using System.Text;
using System.IO;

namespace L0904
{
    public partial class Page : UserControl
    {
        public Page()
        {
            InitializeComponent();
        }

        private void UserControl_Loaded(object sender, RoutedEventArgs e)
        {

            // store names as XML.
            string names = "<?xml version='1.0'
            encoding='utf-8' ?>
                <Names><Name>Shannon Horn</Name>
                <Name>Benny Madrid</Name>
                <Name>Edwin Dewees</Name></Names>";

            // create a reader.
            XmlReader reader = XmlReader.Create(new StringReader(names));
            XmlWriterSettings settings = new XmlWriterSettings();
            settings.Indent = true;
            settings.ConformanceLevel = ConformanceLevel.Auto;
            StringBuilder output = new StringBuilder();
            XmlWriter writer = XmlWriter.Create(output, settings);
```

```
        // display the names.
        while (reader.Read())
        {

            if (reader.NodeType == XmlNodeType.Text)
            {

                writer.WriteString(reader.Value + Environment
                    .NewLine);
            }
        }

        reader.Close();
        writer.Close();
        tbNames.Text = output.ToString();
    }
  }
}
```

The results of this code listing are shown in Figure 9-1.

TIP

For more information on the Extensible Markup Language and related technologies, visit the W3C tutorial website located at http://www.w3schools.com.

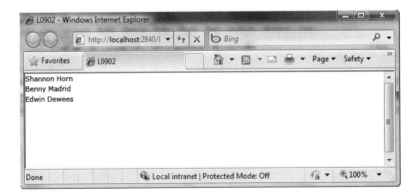

Figure 9-1 The result of reading and writing XML data

Language Integrated Query (LINQ)

A major addition to the .NET Framework in version 3.5 was Language Integrated Query (LINQ). Most seasoned developers have mastered or are adequately familiar with the Structured Query Language (SQL). SQL is used to query relational database data. However, in many cases, SQL queries that pull data from a relational database schema are abstracted away from business logic and middle-tier code.

Data may also be stored in formats other than a relational database such as an XML file or a consumed Web Service. Typically, in each data storage scenario, a specialized language is used to retrieve and query the contained data. Furthermore, data is generally represented at the business logic and code level through objects, arrays, and collections. Developers regularly have to search these constructs by using tailor-made loops.

Many programmers have long requested a language for querying data stored in programming constructs and object-oriented mechanisms. SQL is a stable and well-entrenched industry standard. It would be an insurmountable task to attempt to extend SQL so that it could be used to query programming constructs and other data sources. However, Microsoft was determined to make things easier for programmers by creating a standard for querying data stored in multiple data-storage mechanisms and coding constructs. The result of their efforts was a new query language that targets data stored in objects and collections, called Language Integrated Query (LINQ). LINQ was also extended to be able to query relational data stored in databases, XML data, and other data sources. However, data queried by using LINQ must be stored as objects. If data is queried from a relational data source using LINQ, it must first be represented using an object model.

LINQ is capable of querying any object programmatically that implements the IEnumerable interface. LINQ will present an entirely new programming paradigm to experienced .NET developers, but its new functionality and benefits should be quickly enjoyed and adapted by most. To summarize, the primary benefits of using LINQ are a single, consistent language for querying data across any type of data source and a means of doing so that is type-safe and supported by the most popular .NET Framework programming languages.

LINQ has grown into an extensive query language. Additionally, in order to make LINQ relevant and a valid solution into the future, Microsoft designed LINQ to be extensible, meaning it can be extended by Microsoft or third-party vendors to support additional data sources. Comprehensive coverage of LINQ is beyond the scope of this book. However, as an example, we will create a simple LINQ query instance here using Silverlight. Silverlight supports LINQ using classes in the System.Linq namespace.

Try This Create a LINQ Query

1. Start or open Visual Studio 2010.

2. Select File | New | Project to create a new Silverlight project.

3. When prompted with the New Project dialog, under the programming language of your choice listed in the pane on the left side of the dialog, select the Silverlight node.

4. In the Templates pane on the right side of the dialog, select the Silverlight Application template.

5. Assign the new project a name, select a location to create the project, and then click OK.

6. When prompted with the Add Silverlight Application dialog, click the OK button to accept the default settings.

7. When the Page.xaml file is displayed, in the XAML code at the bottom of the screen there should be a blank line inside the <Grid> control at approximately line 6. At the blank line, enter a new control as follows:

```
<TextBlock Name="tbOutput" />
```

8. Right-click the XAML visual design area at the top of the screen and select View Code.

9. In the Page() class constructor and after the call to the InitializeComponent() method, create a new string array and store some names in it as shown next. The new string array will serve as a programmatic data source.

```
string[] namesList = new string[3] { "Shannon Horn","Benny Madrid",
"Edwin Dewees"};
```

10. Create a LINQ query to query all names that begin with the letter *E*, as shown here:

```
var names =
from name in namesList
where name.Substring(0, 1) == "E"
select name;
```

11. Using a foreach loop, iterate through the results returned by the LINQ query, as shown next, and display the results in the tbOutput TextBlock:

```
foreach (string name in names) {

tbOutput.Text = name;
}
```

12. Press F5 to test the application in the default browser.

13. When prompted with the Debugging Not Enabled dialog, click the OK button to accept the default setting.

14. When you are done viewing the application, close the browser. Feel free to experiment with the names in the array and the LINQ query.

15. Close Visual Studio 2010.

The first step in working with LINQ is to identify a data source. In the example created here, we store a list of names in a simple string array. The second step in working with LINQ is to create the LINQ query. A LINQ query uses concepts and vocabulary very similar to a SQL query; however, the clauses are presented in a different order. Finally, the third step in working with LINQ is to execute the query. A LINQ query is executed using a foreach loop in C#. The following code snippet illustrates a simple LINQ query against a list of names in a string array. The following LINQ query uses the where clause to filter out all names except those that begin with the letter *E*.

```
// obtain the data source.
// list of names.
string[] namesList = new string[3] { "Shannon Horn","Benny Madrid",
"Edwin Dewees"};

// create the query.
var names =
from name in namesList
where name.Substring(0, 1) == "E"
select name;

// execute the query.
foreach (string name in names) {

tbOutput.Text = name;
}
```

The results of this code snippet are shown in Figure 9-2.

TIP

For more information about Language Integrated Query (LINQ), visit the MSDN article "Language-Integrated Query (LINQ)," located at http://msdn.microsoft.com/en-us/library/bb397926.aspx.

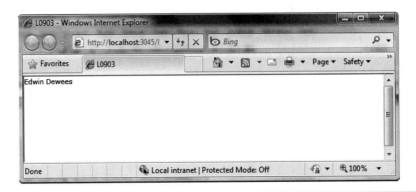

Figure 9-2 The result of a LINQ query

Isolated Storage

Due to the security constraints placed on a Silverlight application (the "sandbox" that it operates in), a Silverlight application, on its own accord, cannot write directly to or read directly from the file system on the client's machine. In an effort to allow developers to store some data local to the client, Microsoft designed Silverlight to read data from and write data to a virtual file system called Isolated Storage. Isolated Storage is instantiated by using cookies.

You need to be aware of a few things when working with Isolated Storage in Silverlight. First, as mentioned previously, Isolated Storage is available in Silverlight only if the client has cookies enabled. Hence, if cookies are not enabled, a Silverlight application cannot utilize Isolated Storage. Additionally, data that must persist should not be stored in Isolated Storage but should be stored in a server-side database. At any point in time, a client may delete cookies and, thus, delete data stored in Isolated Storage. Isolated Storage should be used to store inconsequential data, such as user preferences, that may be retrieved from the server if necessary or may be re-created by the user.

Silverlight Isolated Storage is currently limited to a 1MB capacity, and the classes used to work with Isolated Storage are located in the System.IO.IsolatedStorage namespace. The following code snippet illustrates saving a user's login credentials to Isolated Storage in a file named UserCredentials.txt:

```
// remember the user's credentials for next time.
if (chkRememberMe.IsChecked == true) {

using (IsolatedStorageFile
```

```
isoStore = IsolatedStorageFile.GetUserStoreForApplication()) {

using (IsolatedStorageFileStream isoStream =
new IsolatedStorageFileStream("UserCredentials.txt", FileMode.Create,
isoStore)) {

using (StreamWriter writer = new StreamWriter(isoStream)) {

writer.Write(user.UserName + "|" + user.PasswordHash);
}
}
}
}
```

The preceding code snippet illustrates using the IsolatedStorageFile class and the IsolatedStorageFileStream class to work with Isolated Storage. The following code snippet illustrates using the same classes to determine if the UserCredentials.txt file exists in Isolated Storage. If it does exist, the contents of the file are read.

```
// determine if the user's credentials exist in isolated storage.
using (IsolatedStorageFile isoStore = IsolatedStorageFile.GetUserStore
ForApplication()) {

using (IsolatedStorageFileStream isoStream =
new IsolatedStorageFileStream("UserCredentials.txt", FileMode.Open,
isoStore)) {

using (StreamReader reader = new StreamReader(isoStream)) {

// read the credentials.
string[] sb = reader.ReadLine().Split('|');

// do we have credentials?
if (sb.Length > 0) {

// if the credentials exist, parse them out and authenticate them.
user.UserName = sb[0];
user.Password = sb[1];

// authenticate.
svc.AuthenticateUserAsync(user.UserName, user.Password);
}
}
}
}
```

Save As File and Open File Dialogs

The preceding section mentioned that Silverlight, on its own accord, cannot access the user's local file system. This behavior is a security precaution to prevent malicious scripts from taking advantage of a user's machine through the Silverlight plug-in. Silverlight 3 introduces a Save As File dialog that can be used to save files to the user's local file system. Silverlight includes a companion Open File dialog that can be used to, not surprisingly, open files from the user's local file system.

Upon first glance, this may seem like a contradiction of the IO interaction security precaution taken with isolated storage. However, the Save As File dialog and the Open File dialog can be displayed only through user interaction, such as the user clicking a button to initiate the save/open file process. Additionally, the Save As File dialog and the Open File dialog do not expose any information about the user's file system to a Silverlight application but simply provide a stream for writing data to and reading data from based on the user's selection.

The Save As File dialog and the Open File dialog are not utilized in Silverlight XAML but are controlled programmatically. In the following markup, a simple form displays text contents in a Textbox and displays two buttons—one for opening a file and one for saving a file:

```
<UserControl x:Class="L0905.Page"
    xmlns="http://schemas.microsoft.com/winfx/2006/xaml/presentation"
    xmlns:x="http://schemas.microsoft.com/winfx/2006/xaml"
    xmlns:d="http://schemas.microsoft.com/expression/blend/2008"
    xmlns:mc="http://schemas.openxmlformats.org/markup-
        compatibility/2006"
    mc:Ignorable="d" d:DesignWidth="400" Height="88">
    <Grid x:Name="LayoutRoot" Background="White"
    Height="88" VerticalAlignment="Top">
        <ScrollViewer Margin="8,8,8,33"
            d:LayoutOverrides="VerticalAlignment">
                <TextBox x:Name="txtData" Height="Auto"
                Width="Auto" Text="" TextWrapping="Wrap"/>
        </ScrollViewer>
        <Button x:Name="btnOpen" Height="Auto"
        Margin="0,0,91,7" VerticalAlignment="Bottom"
        Width="91" Content="open" HorizontalAlignment="Right"
        RenderTransformOrigin="0.486,-0.045" Click="btnOpen_Click"
        d:LayoutOverrides="VerticalAlignment" />
        <Button x:Name="btnSave" Height="Auto"
        Margin="0,0,8,7" VerticalAlignment="Bottom" Content="save"
        Width="79" HorizontalAlignment="Right" Click="btnSave_Click"
        d:LayoutOverrides="VerticalAlignment" />
    </Grid>
</UserControl>
```

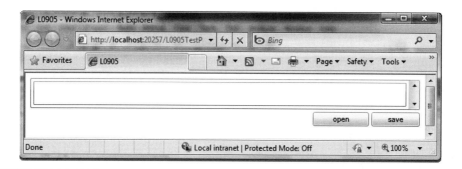

Figure 9-3 A simple form that includes options to open and save local files

The code used to open a file from the file system is shown in the following code listing. The Silverlight form is shown in Figure 9-3.

```
private void btnOpen_Click(object sender, RoutedEventArgs e)
{
    OpenFileDialog dialog = new OpenFileDialog()
    {
        Filter = "Text Files|*.txt|All Files|*.*",
        FilterIndex = 1
    };
    if (dialog.ShowDialog() == true)
    {
        FileInfo openFile = dialog.File;
        StreamReader reader = openFile.OpenText();
        txtData.Text = reader.ReadToEnd();
        reader.Close();
    }
}
```

Finally, the code used to save the contents of the form Textbox to a local text file is shown here:

```
private void btnSave_Click(object sender, RoutedEventArgs e)
{
    SaveFileDialog dialog = new SaveFileDialog()
    {
        DefaultExt = ".txt",
        Filter = "Text Files|*.txt|All Files|*.*",
        FilterIndex = 1
    };

    if (dialog.ShowDialog() == true)
    {
```

```
                        using (Stream saveStream = dialog.OpenFile())
                        {

                            // write the data
                            byte[] data = Encoding.Unicode.GetBytes
                                (txtData.Text);
                            saveStream.Write(data, 0, data.Length);
                            saveStream.Close();
                        }
                    }
                }
```

Data Binding in Silverlight

Silverlight 3 provides multiple methods for binding user interface controls and components directly to business objects and data sources. This is known as "data binding." Under the data binding umbrella, the user interface component is called the "target," whereas the data source is called the "source."

A key user interface control used to display tabular data to users, the DataGrid control, was illustrated in Chapter 8. The DataGrid control can be easily "data bound" by assigning the data source to the ItemsSource property of the DataGrid control. A few other user interface controls may also be easily and directly data bound to a source, including the Listbox control and the Combobox control.

XAML Element Data Binding

Silverlight 3 simplifies data binding somewhat by allowing target controls to be bound directly to the value of a property of another user interface control using XAML. In Silverlight 2, target controls could be partially bound to the value of a property of another control using XAML. However, in order for a control to be fully data bound to the value of a property of another control, the name of the control and the name of the property must be configured using XAML. Silverlight 2 only accommodated setting the name of the property but not the name of the source control.

Silverlight 3 accommodates setting the name of the source control as well as the name of the property to bind to in XAML. This form of data binding is called "element-to-element binding" and is implemented using XAML {Binding} expressions. A {Binding} expression accepts three parameters: the property name, the element name, and the binding mode value. The following markup illustrates a TextBlock control and a Slider control. The Slider control is bound to the Angle property of the tbTransform

RotateTransform element for the TextBlock. Due to the binding, as the Slider control is moved, the TextBlock automatically rotates with no code required.

```
<UserControl x:Class="L0906.Page"
    xmlns="http://schemas.microsoft.com/winfx/2006/xaml/presentation"
    xmlns:x="http://schemas.microsoft.com/winfx/2006/xaml"
    xmlns:d="http://schemas.microsoft.com/expression/blend/2008"
    xmlns:mc="http://schemas.openxmlformats.org/markup-
        compatibility/2006"
    mc:Ignorable="d" d:DesignWidth="400" Height="187">
    <Grid x:Name="LayoutRoot" Background="#FFE4DFDF">
        <TextBlock Margin="8,8,8,83" Text="superion"
          TextWrapping="Wrap" Height="Auto" FontSize="72"
          TextAlignment="Center" FontFamily="Arial Unicode MS"
          FontWeight="Bold" d:LayoutOverrides="Height"
          RenderTransformOrigin="0.5,0.5">
            <TextBlock.RenderTransform>
                <TransformGroup>
                    <RotateTransform x:Name="tbTransform" />
                </TransformGroup>
            </TextBlock.RenderTransform>
            <TextBlock.Foreground>
                <LinearGradientBrush EndPoint="0.5,1"
                    StartPoint="0.5,0">
                  <GradientStop Color="#FF7A7676"
                      Offset="0.412"/>
                  <GradientStop Color="#FFF26414" Offset="1"/>
                </LinearGradientBrush>
            </TextBlock.Foreground>
        </TextBlock>
        <Slider Height="Auto" Margin="8,0,8,27"
          Maximum="360" VerticalAlignment="Bottom"
          Value="{Binding Angle, ElementName=tbTransform,
          Mode=TwoWay}" />
    </Grid>
</UserControl>
```

Figure 9-4 illustrates a TextBlock control that is rotated by adjusting the value of a Slider control.

The BindingMode value is pulled from the BindingMode enumeration. Here are the possible values:

● **OneTime** One-time binding is used to pull the value from the source and provide it to the target one time. This setting is optimal for data that will be displayed but not be modified, such as a heading.

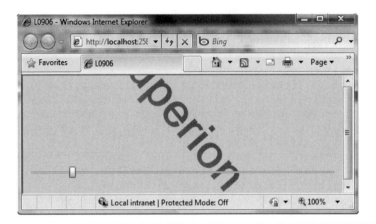

Figure 9-4   A TextBlock being rotated through element-to-element binding to a Slider

- **OneWay**   One-way binding is used to pull the value from the source and provide it to the target and keep it updated as the source changes. This setting is optimal for read-only data being displayed.

- **TwoWay**   Two-way binding is used to keep the source and the target synchronized. As the value of the source changes, the target is updated, and as the value of the target changes, the source is updated.

Conclusion

Silverlight applications execute in a remote environment on the client's workstation that is isolated from the client's file system by the security sandbox. Silverlight includes the ability to work with data coming from server-side databases as well as data stored in XML. Silverlight includes classes located in the System.Xml namespace for working with XML data. Silverlight also includes classes located in the System.IsolatedStorage namespace that enable storing minimal data locally on the client's workstation. Be aware that only disposable data should be stored in Isolated Storage. Finally, Silverlight supports querying all types of data by using Language Integrated Query (LINQ).

Chapter 10

Retrieving Server Resources

Key Concepts & Skills

- Compare synchronous to asynchronous programming techniques
- Learn how to use the WebClient class to download resources from a web server

A pplications typically display files to a user that are large in size, such as images and media files. If a single image, such as a company logo, is to be displayed to a user, it may be best to embed that image in the Silverlight application so that it is available on the client machine without any additional effort.

However, what if many images or media files are to be displayed to the user, or what if a variable number of files are to be displayed? For instance, if a Silverlight control displays a list of products to the user, and the user selects a product to display details for, there is no way to determine which product the user will select and want to view the details and a photo of. It would be incredibly inefficient and unwieldy to attempt to package photos of all products in the Silverlight application.

Hence, it is imperative that Silverlight has the ability to dynamically download resources from a server for use in an application.

Synchronous vs. Asynchronous Processing

Computers that contain a single processor are only capable of performing a single task at a time. Most laptops that are running Windows, for example, have a single processor (CPU) and are only capable of performing a single task on the computer at a time. If that is the case, how does an elaborate operating system such as Windows seemingly perform many concurrent tasks as well as host multiple applications in memory simultaneously, with each application also performing tasks? The answer is that the operating system manages the time that the processor allocates to performing each task very efficiently. The operating system allocates an incredibly small slice of the processor's time to each application and task that is in memory. The applications and tasks are then cycled through, with each performing a small amount of work. The processor cycles through the applications and tasks very quickly, thus giving the illusion that multiple tasks are being performed simultaneously.

Each application that is loaded into memory is referred to as a *process*. Each process typically attempts to perform a single task, so each process is assigned a single thread of execution (a slice of the processor's time) to use to complete the task. Most code is written to perform a single task at a time and to complete the task at hand before continuing on to execute the next task. This type of processing is referred to as *synchronous processing*. In most scenarios, synchronously executing code is accomplished very quickly and will suffice. Additionally, in most scenarios, most tasks being performed in code are reliant on the previous task being completed before they can be performed. For example, when you query a database, the query cannot be executed until a connection to the database is open. Hence, the database commands must be performed in a particular order, and synchronous processing is a perfect fit.

However, occasionally tasks are performed in code that are not reliant upon other tasks to be completed first. When tasks that can be performed independently can be identified, performance would be increased if the task could be performed in parallel to other tasks being performed by the application. This is possible by intentionally writing code that spawns another thread of execution so that the process (application) is allocated more than one slice of the processor's time. If multiple tasks are performed in parallel by an application, the application is said to be "multithreaded" (that is, it utilizes more than a single thread to perform its work). When tasks are performed in parallel, the call in code from the initial thread that initiates a task to be performed on another thread doesn't have to wait around for the additional task to complete before continuing on. If it did wait for additional threads to complete their work, the tasks would still be performed in series and there would be no benefit to utilizing multiple threads of execution.

When an additional task is performed in parallel on a separate thread, it is referred to as *asynchronous processing*. Asynchronous processing is more complex than synchronous processing. When a task is performed synchronously, the code that initiated the synchronous task waits on the task to complete before continuing. However, when a task is performed asynchronously, the code that initiated the asynchronous task continues execution immediately and does not wait on the asynchronous task to complete. So what happens when the asynchronous task completes?

When code initiates an asynchronous task, it also directs the asynchronous task to execute a method or function (known as a *callback method)* once it completes its work.

Asynchronous processing is a perfect fit for time-consuming tasks that can be performed independently. Asynchronous processing is utilized in most of the recent web technologies. For example, in AJAX (which stands for Asynchronous JavaScript and XML), an asynchronous call is made to the server behind the scenes. The call is independent of the thread that is processing the web page and interacting with the user; thus, UI performance is increased and the user does not have to wait on the call to the server to complete but will see the results when they are returned.

The WebClient Class

Silverlight includes a class—called the WebClient class—that is used to directly download resources from a web server. The WebClient class was formerly called the HTTP Downloader. The WebClient class is best suited to directly downloading larger resources from a web server that may take time to download, including images and media files. All networking calls made in Silverlight are asynchronous calls; hence, all calls made by the WebClient class are asynchronous.

A few steps are involved in using the WebClient class. Walking through an example is the best way to illustrate the WebClient class. The example shown here starts with a simple piece of XAML that includes a single Image control that will display dynamically downloaded images:

```
<UserControl x:Class="L1001.Page"
    xmlns="http://schemas.microsoft.com/winfx/2006/xaml/presentation"
    xmlns:x="http://schemas.microsoft.com/winfx/2006/xaml"
    Width="400" Height="300" Loaded="UserControl_Loaded">
    <Grid x:Name="LayoutRoot" Background="White">
      <Image Height="59" HorizontalAlignment="Left"
          Margin="26,27,0,0" VerticalAlignment="Top" Width="56"
          x:Name="imgWeather"/>
    </Grid>
</UserControl>
```

The starting Silverlight project includes four small JPG files, as shown in Figure 10-1.

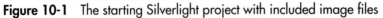

Figure 10-1   The starting Silverlight project with included image files

Notice in Figure 10-1 that the images are all shown as separate files. The WebClient class is capable of downloading a single file at a time from a server but is also capable of downloading a collection of files from the server that has been compressed into a zip file.

The first step necessary in using the WebClient class is to create an instance of the class. Generally, an instance of the WebClient class will be created as a class-level member. The syntax to create an instance is shown in the following code snippet:

```
// create an instance of the WebClient class
WebClient downloader = new WebClient();
```

The next step in the process of using the WebClient class is to assign a callback handler to the OpenReadCompleted event. A callback handler is normally assigned in the constructor of the class in the code-behind file for the Silverlight control. The following code snippet illustrates assigning a callback handler:

```
// assign a callback handler
downloader.OpenReadCompleted +=
new OpenReadCompletedEventHandler(downloader_OpenReadCompleted);
```

The WebClient class is now ready for use. In order to make a call to retrieve resources from a server, use the OpenReadAsync method. The next code snippet illustrates making a call to the server to retrieve a file named Images.zip. An instance of the Uri class is created to indicate where the request resource resides in relation to the Silverlight application. Finally, the third parameter that can be passed to the OpenReadAsync is used to identify the file to extract from the zip file package if one is requested. In the following code snippet, the file sunny.jpg is extracted. If a single file is to be downloaded instead of a package, the name of the file is used as the first parameter instead of the package name and then the third parameter is omitted.

```
// download images
downloader.OpenReadAsync(new Uri("images.zip",
UriKind.Relative), sunny.jpg);
```

The next step in using the WebClient class is to write code in the callback handler to determine what to do with the requested resource once it arrives. The following code snippet displays the image that is returned in the WebClient request:

```
// display the image
StreamResourceInfo photosDownloaded = new StreamResourceInfo(e.Result
as Stream, null);
string photoToGrab = e.UserState.ToString();
StreamResourceInfo photoStream =
```

```
Application.GetResourceStream(photosDownloaded, new Uri(photoToGrab,
UriKind.Relative));
BitmapImage bitmap = new BitmapImage();
bitmap.SetSource(photoStream.Stream);
imgWeather.Source = bitmap;
```

The result of the code in the callback method is shown in Figure 10-2.

Refer to the entire code listing, shown next, to gain a full understanding of using the
WebClient class:

```
using System;
using System.Collections.Generic;
using System.Linq;
using System.Net;
using System.Windows;
using System.Windows.Controls;
using System.Windows.Documents;
using System.Windows.Input;
using System.Windows.Media;
using System.Windows.Media.Animation;
using System.Windows.Shapes;
using System.Windows.Resources;
using System.IO;
using System.Windows.Media.Imaging;
```

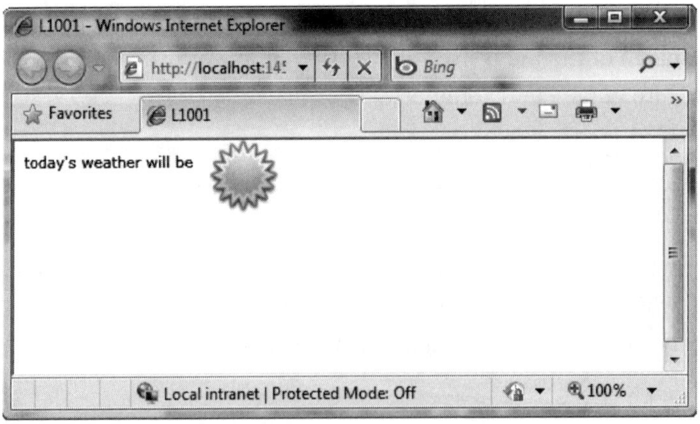

Figure 10-2 The dynamically downloaded image displayed

```
namespace L1001
{
     public partial class Page : UserControl
     {

          // create an instance of the WebClient class
          WebClient downloader = new WebClient ( );

          public Page ( )
          {
               InitializeComponent ( );

               // assign a callback handler.
               downloader.OpenReadCompleted +=
                    new penReadCompletedEventHandler (
                    downloader_OpenReadCompleted );
          }

          void downloader_OpenReadCompleted (
          objectsender, OpenReadCompletedEventArgs e )
          {

               // display the image
               StreamResourceInfo photosDownloaded = new
               StreamResourceInfo ( e.Result as Stream, null );
               string photoToGrab = e.UserState.ToString ( );
               StreamResourceInfo photoStream =
               Application.GetResourceStream ( photosDownloaded,
               new Uri ( photoToGrab, UriKind.Relative ) );
               BitmapImage bitmap = new BitmapImage ( );
               bitmap.SetSource ( photoStream.Stream );
               imgWeather.Source = bitmap;
          }

          private void UserControl_Loaded
               ( object sender, RoutedEventArgs e )
          {

               // download images
               downloader.OpenReadAsync(new
               Uri("images.zip",UriKind.Relative), "sunny.jpg");
          }
     }
}
```

Additional Threading Classes

Most communication tasks are completed asynchronously, such as a call to a service or the use of the WebClient class. However, occasionally code must complete a task that may be long running but should not interfere with user interface responsiveness. Such a task should be carried out asynchronously using an additional thread. Silverlight tasks can be performed on a separate thread by using the BackgroundWorker class. The BackgroundWorker class performs a task on a secondary thread that executes "in the background" and is located in the System.ComponentModel namespace.

Try This ## Complete a Time-Consuming Process Using the BackgroundWorker Class

1. Start or open Visual Studio 2010.

2. Create a new Silverlight 3 project.

3. Design the Silverlight user interface to include a Button control and a TextBlock control. The Button control will be clicked to perform a fictitious background process and then write a string to the Text property of the TextBlock control.

4. Create a Click event handler for the Button control.

5. In the code-behind file, include the System.ComponentModel namespace by adding the following line of code to the using statement collection:

```
using System.ComponentModel;
```

6. Create an instance of the BackgroundWorker class as a class-level member, as shown in the following line of code:

```
BackgroundWorker backgroundWorker = new BackgroundWorker ( );
```

7. In the page constructor, wire up event handlers for the DoWork event and the RunWorkerCompleted event, as shown here:

```
public Page ( )
{
       InitializeComponent ( );

       // wire up event handlers
       backgroundWorker.DoWork += new
       DoWorkEventHandler(backgroundWorker_DoWork);
```

```
backgroundWorker.RunWorkerCompleted +=
new RunWorkerCompletedEventHandler(backgroundWorker_
RunWorkerCompleted);
}
```

8. Write code for the DoWork event handler, as shown next. The DoWork event handler performs the actual background worker process.

```
private void backgroundWorker_DoWork ( object sender,
   DoWorkEventArgs e )
{

      // do something time consuming...
      System.Threading.Thread.Sleep ( 500 );
}
```

9. Write code for the RunWorkerCompleted event handler. The RunWorkerCompleted event handler is executed after the DoWork event hander is complete. The following RunWorkerCompleted event handler writes a string to the TextBlock control:

```
private void backgroundWorker_RunWorkerCompleted ( object sender,
RunWorkerCompletedEventArgs e )
{

      // when done, report to the user
      this.tbLabel.Text = "Done!";
}
```

10. Finally, write code in the Click event of the Button control to kick off the background worker process by calling the RunWorkerAsync method, as shown here:

```
private void btnWriteLabel_Click ( object sender, RoutedEventArgs e )
{

      // kick off the background process when the button is clicked
      backgroundWorker.RunWorkerAsync ( );
}
```

The BackgroundWorker class can also be configured to report the progress of the process and to allow the process to be cancelled by the user.

Silverlight applications have access to additional, more advanced threading classes such as the Thread class and the ThreadPool class. Threading classes are located in the System.Threading namespace.

Additional Performance Tips

In addition to the techniques illustrated above, the following tips are recommended by Microsoft to further improve performance of Silverlight applications.

- Test on multiple platforms and browsers.

- Set EnableFrameRateCounter to True during development.

- Use the transparent background for a Silverlight plug-in sparingly.

- When animating the opacity or transform of a UIElement, set its CacheMode.

- While animating text, set TextRenderingMode to RenderForAnimation.

- Avoid using Windowless mode.

- Use Visibility instead of Opacity whenever possible.

- In full-screen mode, hide unused objects.

- Do not use Width and Height with MediaElement objects.

- Do not use Width and Height with Path objects.

- Break up CPU-intensive work into smaller tasks.

- Break up large application packages.

- Use Double.ToString(CultureInfo.InvariantCulture) rather than Double.ToString().

Conclusion

A basic premise of creating an application that will execute in a client/server environment or over the Web is to minimize network traffic to improve performance. To minimize network traffic, only data that is actually needed should be requested. If 1,000 images exist on the server, but only a single image out of the 1,000 needs to be displayed, then only the single image should be requested from the server. The WebClient class can be used to request a single file from a server or a packaged group of files.

Chapter 11

Debugging and Deploying Silverlight Applications

Key Concepts & Skills

- Learn about the types of errors that occur in software

- Gain an understanding of exceptions and exception handling

- Explore the Visual Studio 2010 debugger

- Observe how to deploy a Silverlight application to the Windows Live Silverlight Streaming Service and to a local web server

Debugging is a process that must be performed by all software developers. Debugging can be skipped, but the quality and stability of the resultant application will be shaky and questionable, at best. Silverlight is built on the same architecture as WPF and other .NET Framework applications and has the full power of the Visual Studio debugger at its disposal.

Silverlight applications can also be easily deployed to a free service available from Microsoft or to any local web server.

Error Handling Overview

When writing code, it is vital that you plan to handle any potential errors that could occur when the application is running. Although an application may function perfectly when used by a developer in a development environment, countless errors could occur in an application once it is deployed. An application being used by its developer in its development environment is an optimal scenario. However, once an application is deployed, there's no way to calculate how a user may attempt to utilize the application and what other applications installed on the client machine or resource factors may affect the application performance.

As a result, most programming languages include facilities for handling errors if they occur. Errors generally occur when an application is dependent on something controlled or provided externally. For example, a user may provide invalid data to an application or an attempt to connect to a database, or a resource may fail if the database or resource is unavailable. Error-handling code should be placed in code at any point where an error could possibly occur.

There are three categories of application errors: compilation errors, runtime errors, and logic errors. Compilation errors typically occur due to syntax errors in code and are called "compilation errors" because they are caught during application compilation. Because an application won't compile while compilation errors exist, they are corrected before an application is deployed to users. A runtime error is an error that occurs only at runtime, such as the example given previously, where a database is not available when an attempt is made to connect to it. Finally, a logic error is generally the most difficult to identify; it's an error that may not cause an application to stop executing but may cause an application to produce unexpected results. For example, you may have a Boolean expression in an if statement in code that is used to determine whether or not a user should have permission to execute a piece of code. If the Boolean expression is checking for false when it should be checking for true, the result will be the opposite of what is expected but the behavior may not cause an error to occur.

Most .NET-compliant programming languages provide try, catch, and finally blocks. JavaScript also provides try, catch, and finally blocks. When code inside a try block encounters an error, application execution stops and the application begins searching for a catch block that is designed to handle the type of error that occurred. When it finds one, it executes the code in the catch block. A finally block is optional but is used to provide code that is executed whether or not the code in the try block executes successfully. A finally block generally includes cleanup code.

More advanced languages create an object at runtime that fully describes the error condition that occurred. The object created is referred to as an *exception*. Hence, for error conditions that occur within the scope of try, catch, and finally blocks, the object describing the error condition is referred to as an exception.

Debugging and Testing

Debugging and testing code written in a Silverlight application is fairly straightforward and may occur in one of two given scenarios. The first scenario is a Silverlight application that executes only on the client, whereas the second is a Silverlight application that makes calls to a Web Service. Previous modules have covered thoroughly how to set up and configure the environment for testing a Silverlight application that calls a Web Service by using Visual Studio 2010.

The Visual Studio 2010 debugger is incredibly powerful—one of the leading, if not the leading, debugger in the industry—and includes more features than most developers will ever make use of. However, the simplest and most useful feature of the debugger is the ability to set breakpoints in code. When a breakpoint is set in code and execution of code

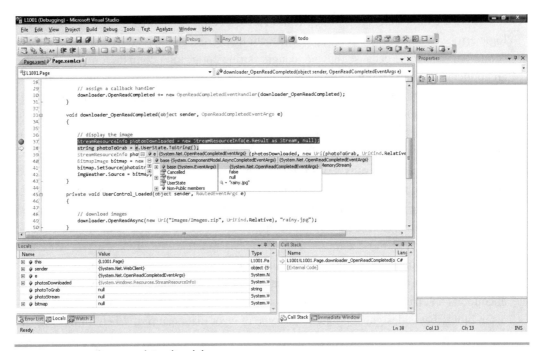

Figure 11-1 The Visual Studio debugger

encounters the breakpoint, execution halts at that point and every facet of code execution can be analyzed in depth. In Figure 11-1, the Visual Studio 2010 debugger is displayed with a breakpoint set in the example used in the previous module.

An application should be put through several levels and rounds of testing prior to being released to users in a production environment. In fact, just as application security should be considered early on and a formal security plan should be created during the planning phase of the application design cycle, a formal testing plan should also be created. The testing plan will document the levels of testing that should be performed on an application as well as who will be performing the testing. The various levels of testing include unit testing, regression testing, load testing, and integration testing.

Unit testing is typically performed first and, in many cases, performed by the developer. A unit test is generally composed of a small script that can be automated to simulate user interaction with an application. Visual Studio 2010 can be used to automate unit testing by iterating through a collection of unit test scripts a specified number of times. The result of unit testing can be reviewed by the developer.

TIP

To start debugging in Visual Studio 2010, press F5, select the Start Debugging (green play) button in the Visual Studio 2010 toolbar, or select Start Debugging from the Debug menu. Occasionally, you may need to run an application to test it and determine the cause of an error that is occurring. When in that scenario, press CTRL+F5 to run the application without debugging enabled. When an application is run without debugging enabled, the .NET Framework will display the raw exception message directly to the developer when the error is encountered.

The Silverlight Unit Test Framework

A large percentage of developers create application code and consider testing that code to be the next step in the development life cycle. Thoroughly testing code prior to deployment is crucial to application success. Some developers consider testing to be an afterthought or may never test their code at all. Testing can be treated as a separate phase in the development life cycle; however, a popular practice is to design unit tests prior to creating the code or at the same time. This design paradigm is referred to as "test-driven development" or "test-first design." A complete framework, called the Silverlight Unit Test Framework, was created to enable the creation of unit tests in Silverlight as well as the implementation of test-driven development in Silverlight.

The Silverlight Unit Test Framework is available on Microsoft CodePlex, located at http://code.msdn.microsoft.com/silverlightut. As its name implies, the Silverlight Unit Test Framework can be used to create and execute unit tests as well as asynchronous integration tests and can be integrated into the Visual Studio 2010 project templates.

Deploying

Once an application has been fully tested and is confirmed to be stable, the application is ready to be deployed. *Deployment* is the process of installing the application and configuring it for production use. Deployment may consist of simply copying the application files to a production location or may consist of creating an installation program that users can download and install. A formal deployment plan should also be created during the planning phase of the application design cycle.

In most cases, a Silverlight application simply needs to be copied to a web server where users can access it over the Web.

Windows Live Silverlight Streaming Service

In an effort to support Silverlight developers and designers, Microsoft created a space online to host Silverlight applications under the Windows Live suite of tools and services.

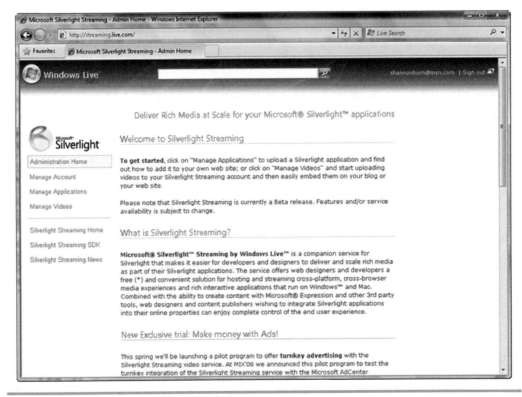

Figure 11-2 The Windows Live Silverlight Streaming Service

The Windows Live Silverlight Streaming Service is free to use and is located at
http://silverlight.live.com/.

The Windows Live Silverlight Streaming Service home page is shown in Figure 11-2.

Uploading a Silverlight Application

The first step in the process of utilizing the Silverlight Streaming Service is to obtain
an account ID and key. To obtain an account with the Silverlight Streaming Service,
you'll need a Windows Live ID. If you have one, you can simply log into the Silverlight
Streaming Service and generate your account ID and key. If you do not have a Windows
Live ID, you can sign up for one at the streaming service website. Figure 11-3 shows the
key-generation page.

Figure 11-3   The Silverlight Streaming Service key-generation page

Once you have obtained an account ID and key, you are ready to prepare your application for upload to the service. The Silverlight Streaming Service was very cumbersome to use in its infancy; however, using the service is now straightforward and simple—not much preparation is necessary.

The basic steps of using the service are to create a new application in the service, assign the application a unique name, and upload the Silverlight XAP file for the application. Once a Silverlight application XAP file has been uploaded to the streaming service, a configuration file can be created to direct the streaming service on how it should handle and manage your new Silverlight application. The configuration file is an XML file called the "application manifest." In previous versions of the streaming service, the manifest had to be uploaded as part of the deployment process. The streaming service will now create the manifest for you and offers you options to configure the manifest after the XAP file has been uploaded.

A Silverlight application manifest resembles the following markup:

```
<?xml version="1.0" encoding="utf-8" ?>
<SilverlightApp>
<source>Page.xaml</source>
<version>1.0</version>
<width>100%</width>
<height>100%</height>
<inplaceInstallPrompt>false</inplaceInstallPrompt>
<background>#FFFFFF</background>
<framerate>24</framerate>
<isWindowless>false</isWindowless>
</SilverlightApp>
```

Once a Silverlight application is deployed to the streaming service, the service provides a test page and links for using the Silverlight application remotely.

Try This   Deploy a Silverlight Application to the Windows Live Silverlight Streaming Service

1. Ensure that the Silverlight application you want to deploy to the Silverlight Streaming Service has been built using Visual Studio 2010 or Expression Blend and is ready to deploy.

2. Start Microsoft Internet Explorer or your browser of choice.

3. Navigate to the Windows Live Silverlight Streaming Service located at http://streaming.live.com.

4. Click the Sign In link to sign into the service using your Windows Live ID.

5. Click the Manage Applications link and then click the Upload an Application link.

6. In the Application Name text box, assign a name to the new application and click the Create button.

7. Click the Browse button and navigate to the .xap file for the Silverlight application you want to upload.

8. Click the Upload button.

9. Under the Configure This Application section, click the Create link to create the application manifest.

10. Verify the manifest details for the application and click the Update button.

11. Click the Launch Application Test Page link to test the uploaded application.

Web Server Deployment

Deploying a Silverlight application to a web server is also a simple process. The first step in the process is to create a virtual folder for the new Silverlight application to reside in. A Silverlight application may also be an integrated part of another web application. A Silverlight XAP file typically resides inside a subfolder named ClientBin. Hence, when you deploy a Silverlight application, the Silverlight XAP file should reside in the ClientBin subfolder. Additionally, any files or resources that are used by the Silverlight application should be placed relatively in the same location where they existed in the Silverlight project.

As mentioned in Chapter 1, web server requirements for hosting a Silverlight application are minimal because the server does not process Silverlight but simply downloads it to the client machine for processing.

Conclusion

Once an application is created, it must be thoroughly debugged and tested to ensure that it is bug free and performs as intended. Furthermore, although an application may perform perfectly, it must be deployed to a server or client location in order to be useful to a client.

Chapter 12

Developing Line of Business (LOB) Applications

Key Concepts & Skills

- Learn how to apply common industry-standard software design patterns in a Silverlight application

- Explore features and functionality that can be applied to extend a Silverlight application

- Investigate integrating a Silverlight application with .NET RIA Services

Microsoft Silverlight has impressed the masses with the features and functionality it offers in a package built around the .NET Framework. To add to this, Microsoft promises more functionality, improvements, and enhancements in future versions. However, with a multitude of .NET developers focusing on business applications, it is imperative to have an understanding of how to use Silverlight to develop line of business (LOB) applications.

Architecture

Most applications, particularly business applications, contain at least three tiers:

- A source for storing and retrieving data (such as Microsoft SQL Server)

- Code that performs logic required in the application (such as code written using C#)

- Some form of interface that allows users to interact with the application (such as a Silverlight control)

Twenty years ago, software applications would commonly handle all three tiers using a single technology. This design is called *single tier*. As computer networks advanced, client/server computing became popular. Applications that utilize client/server computing store data in a separate location from the code and user interface technologies. Separation of the tiers is implemented to improve performance and security. Three-tier design takes things a step further by storing the data, code, and user interface on separate machines, and each can be created using the best technology for that tier. For example, Microsoft SQL Server might be used to manage data, C# might be used to create code for an application, and Silverlight might be used to create the user interface.

If an application is carefully designed, the various tiers of the application can be much more flexible as well. For example, a well-designed application may be able to access data stored in both Microsoft SQL Server and Oracle or provide user interfaces using both Silverlight and Windows Forms. In order for an application design to be this flexible, each tier must be very modular and must not be coupled to other tiers. In other words, each tier must make generic calls to other tiers without concern for or knowledge of the technology used to create the internal structure of the tier being called. Note that the tier storing the data is the bottom tier, or the *back end.* The tier storing the code is the middle tier, and it knows how to communicate only with the bottom tier. Finally, the tier storing the user interface is the top tier, or the *front end,* and it does not communicate directly with the bottom tier but knows how to communicate only with the middle tier.

Creating tiers of an application to be extremely flexible, modular, and loosely coupled is increasingly important in modern applications that generally use the Web as a primary means of data transport. Additionally, user interface technologies are becoming increasingly complex. To compensate for user interface complexity and to ensure that the user interface is not tightly coupled to middle-tier technologies, well-documented and proven design patterns are commonly implemented. Common design patterns used in Silverlight applications are the Model-View-Controller (MVC) pattern and the Model-View-View Model (MVVM) pattern.

Model-View-Controller

The Model-View-Controller (MVC) pattern focuses on communication details between the user interface and the middle tier (business tier). Three components exist in the MVC pattern:

- **Model**   The model represents the middle tier, or the *business tier,* and contains the code that determines how to store and retrieve data managed by the application and the code that performs the logic of the application.

- **View**   The view represents the user interface and is responsible for simply presenting user interface controls and displaying data to the user.

- **Controller**   The controller serves as the proxy object between the view and the model and determines how the two will interact.

Model-View-View Model

The Model-View-View Model pattern is a fairly recent development that extends the Model-View-Controller pattern. In the MVC pattern, the controller contains logic that determines how user interface events are handled and how data in the model is displayed in the view.

Silverlight includes the ability to directly bind controls to data sources and automatically keep the data being displayed synchronized with the underlying data source. The Model-View-View Model pattern is designed to take advantage of this new data-binding capability. In MVVM, the controller is replaced by a view model that the controls displayed in the view can directly bind to. A view model exposes properties that reflect underlying data values.

Creating a Data-Entry Form

Most software applications created are either business applications or games. The most common functionality presented in a business application is the ability for a user to view and edit data stored by the application. Once a design pattern has been implemented, a user interface can be assembled to serve as the view to present data to the user. A user interface can be constructed piece by piece using Silverlight controls, and this may be the solution required in some scenarios. However, some third-party utilities can be used to expedite building Silverlight user interfaces for business applications.

Additionally, Silverlight ships with the DataForm control. The DataForm control is bound to a single business object or a collection of business objects and automatically displays a user interface to display the data exposed by the properties in the object. If the DataForm control is bound to a single object, it displays a single user interface, using text box controls to display string properties, check box controls to display Boolean properties, and so on. If the DataForm control is bound to a collection of controls, it displays the data for the first control but also offers buttons to navigate the collection, add a new instance to the collection, edit an instance, and delete an instance.

The DataForm control is very easy to use and can be bound to underlying objects using code or XAML, but it might not be the answer for every user interface. The following "Try This" exercise illustrates using a DataForm to display data stored in a simple object.

Try This Display Data in Silverlight Using the DataForm Control

Designing line-of-business data forms can be a complex and redundant process. The DataForm control takes some of the pain out of creating data forms in Silverlight.

1. Start or open Visual Studio 2010.

2. Create a new Silverlight 3 project.

3. Right-click the Page.xaml file and select the option Open in Expression Blend.

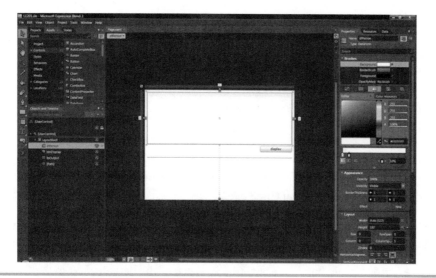

Figure 12-1   DataForm control user interface designed using Expression Blend

4. Use Expression Blend to drop a DataForm control onto the Silverlight design surface. Also, add a Button control and a TextBlock control so that the DataForm control resembles Figure 12-1.

5. Back in Visual Studio 2010, right-click the Silverlight project and add a new class. Design the class as you see fit. The sample class shown here stores simple personal information for an athlete:

```
using System;

namespace L1201
{
    public class Person
    {

        // data members
        public int Id {get;set;}
        public string FirstName {get; set;}
        public string LastName {get;set;}
        public bool Athlete { get; set; }
        public string Notes { get; set; }

        public Person (int id, string firstName,
        string lastName, bool athlete, string notes)
```

(continued)

```
        {
                this.Id = id;
                this.FirstName = firstName;
                this.LastName = lastName;
                this.Athlete = athlete;
                this.Notes = notes;
        }
    }
}
```

6. In the Silverlight XAML file, add an event handler for the UserControl Loaded event and a handler for the Button Click event.

7. In the Silverlight code-behind file, create an instance of the Person class as a class-level member.

8. In the Loaded event handler, assign the instance of the Person class to the CurrentItem property of the DataForm control.

9. In the Click event handler, concatenate the Person object member values and display them in the TextBlock control, as shown in the following code:

```
using System;
using System.Windows;
using System.Windows.Controls;

namespace L1201
{
    public partial class Page : UserControl
    {

        Person fighter = new Person ( 115, "Benny", "Madrid", true,
        "Benny has an incredible career in MMA ahead of him..." );

        public Page ( )
        {
            InitializeComponent ( );
        }

        private void UserControl_Loaded ( object sender,
            RoutedEventArgs e )
        {

            dfPerson.CurrentItem = fighter;
        }
```

```
        private void btnDisplay_Click ( object sender,
            RoutedEventArgs e )
        {

            tbOutput.Text = fighter.FirstName + " " +
            fighter.LastName + ( fighter.Athlete ? " is " :
                " is not " ) +
            " an athlete. " + fighter.Notes;
        }
    }
}
```

10. The Silverlight XAML is shown in the following markup:

```
<UserControl
    xmlns="http://schemas.microsoft.com/winfx/2006/xaml/presentation"
    xmlns:x="http://schemas.microsoft.com/winfx/2006/xaml"
    xmlns:d="http://schemas.microsoft.com/expression/blend/2008"
    xmlns:mc="http://schemas.openxmlformats.org/
        markup-compatibility/2006"
    mc:Ignorable="d"
    xmlns:dataFormToolkit="clr-namespace:System.Windows.Controls;
    assembly=System.Windows.Controls.Data.DataForm.Toolkit"
    x:Class="L1201.Page" d:DesignWidth="538"
    Loaded="UserControl_Loaded" Height="385">

    <Grid x:Name="LayoutRoot" Background="White">

        <dataFormToolkit:DataForm x:Name="dfPerson"
        Margin="8,8,8,0" Height="182" VerticalAlignment="Top"/>
        <Button x:Name="btnDisplay"
        HorizontalAlignment="Right" Margin="0,0,8,169"
        VerticalAlignment="Bottom" Width="115" Content="display"
        Click="btnDisplay_Click"/>
        <TextBlock x:Name="tbOutput" Height="125" Margin="8,0,8,8"
        VerticalAlignment="Bottom" TextWrapping="Wrap"/>
        <Path Fill="White" Stretch="Fill" Stroke="Black"
        Height="1" Margin="8,0,7,148" VerticalAlignment="Bottom"
        UseLayoutRounding="False" Data="M8,235 L530,236"
        StrokeThickness="0.5"/>
    </Grid>
</UserControl>
```

11. Press F5 or select the option Start Debugging. The resultant user interface is shown in Figure 12-2.

(continued)

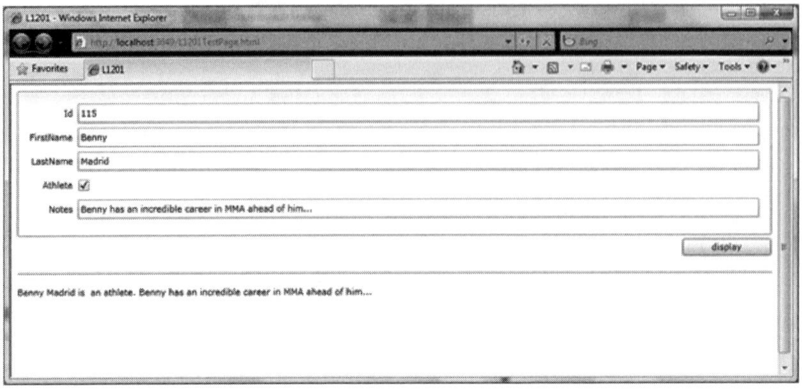

Figure 12-2 A user interface displayed using the DataForm control

Test the user interface by modifying the data values and clicking the button.

Navigation

Silverlight has been used to create some incredible controls and user interfaces. However, one point of confusion for many new Silverlight developers is how to navigate from one Silverlight control to another so that a cohesive user experience can be created that consists of more than a single control. The Silverlight Navigation Framework was created to facilitate navigating between Silverlight controls and it integrates with the browser history.

Silverlight 3 applications cannot rely on home-cooked navigation managed from a server, where each Silverlight control resides on a separate web page that is presented to the user. First off, designing Silverlight navigation in this manner totally defeats the purpose of using Silverlight because a full postback is required between each Silverlight control. Secondly, if a Silverlight application is configured by the user to be stored and run offline and the user machine cannot access the server, the application will not function.

The premise behind Silverlight navigation is that an entire Silverlight application is presented to the user on a single page or a very minimal number of pages. Optimally, using a single page for presentation, a master Silverlight control is displayed that is capable of loading smaller, composite Silverlight controls and XAML.

The Silverlight Navigation Framework contains two primary components: a frame and a page. A frame contains other frames or pages and serves as the primary Silverlight object being displayed to the user. A page is a smaller, composite control displayed in a frame or a container of XAML markup. A frame contains a few key properties, including the Source property, which identifies the initial page that will be loaded, and the JournalOwnership property, which identifies how the Silverlight frame integrates with browser history.

Generally, navigation among a collection of Silverlight controls is not integrated into the browser history. Any links created will point to the page displaying the Silverlight controls and the first control displayed instead of a deeper navigated control. By integrating Silverlight navigation controls into the browser history, you can create links to navigated controls. This process is known as *deep linking*. Integration into browser history also aids in search engine optimization of content displayed on deeply linked Silverlight controls.

Follow these steps to create a Silverlight Navigation Application:

Try This Create a Silverlight Navigation Application

1. Start or open Visual Studio 2010.

2. Create a new Silverlight Navigation Application. It is not mandatory to start with a Silverlight Navigation Application template, but the template wires up the basic plumbing for navigation, which can then be modified to suit your needs.

3. Press F5 or select the option Start Debugging. Figure 12-3 shows the basic navigation application created.

Figure 12-3   A basic Silverlight Navigation Application template displayed using Safari

(continued)

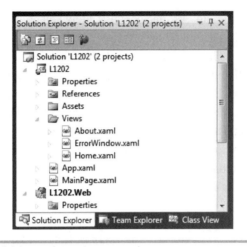

Figure 12-4   The Views folder in the Solution Explorer

4. Close the browser.

5. Modify the template to suit your needs. Figure 12-4 shows the Views folder displayed in the Solution Explorer. The content for each page may be modified and additional pages may be added.

Interacting with HTML

You can utilize the Silverlight plug-in on a web page by incorporating the HTML object tag or by using JavaScript. Silverlight versions 1.0 and 2 also shipped with ASP.NET controls for integrating the Silverlight plug-in into a web page, but these controls do not ship with Silverlight 3. Developers are now encouraged to integrate Silverlight 3 with a web page using either the HTML object tag or JavaScript.

Additionally, Silverlight controls can access containing HTML; conversely, JavaScript can be used to access and control a Silverlight control from a containing HTML page. The integration of Silverlight properties and values and those of containing HTML and JavaScript is called *HTML Bridge*. The HTML Bridge classes are contained in the System. Windows.Browser namespace. The three primary classes a Silverlight control will use to access and manipulate containing HTML are HtmlPage, HtmlDocument, and HtmlElement.

HtmlPage is a static class that represents the containing page. HtmlDocument is an instance reference to the containing page. HtmlElement represents HTML elements on the containing document.

Try This Writing a String to HTML

Silverlight controls are contained within HTML pages. However, there may be scenarios where interaction between a Silverlight control and the containing HTML is useful.

1. Start or open Visual Studio 2010.

2. Create a new Silverlight project.

3. In the Solution Explorer, double-click the TestPage.html page to open it.

4. Add an input control to the HTML and ensure that it is assigned a unique ID value similar to txtFromSL.

5. Open the Page.xaml.cs code-behind file.

6. Add the following statement to the top of the file:

```
using System.Windows.Browser;
```

7. In the page constructor, create a reference to the containing HTML page using the following line of code:

```
HtmlDocument doc = HtmlPage.Document;
```

8. Get a reference to the HTML input control using the following line of code:

```
HtmlElement targetInput = doc.GetElementById ( "txtFromSL" );
```

9. Assign a string to the value property of the input control using the following line of code:

```
targetInput.SetAttribute ( "value", "this came from Silverlight..." );
```

10. Press F5 or select the option Start Debugging. Figure 12-5 shows the modified input control.

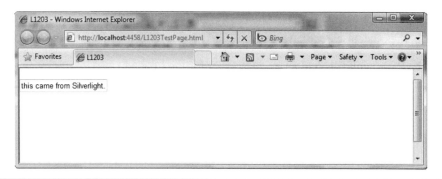

Figure 12-5 An HTML page modified using HTML Bridge

Dynamically Loading XAML

There may be scenarios where a Silverlight control, stored in a separate XAML file, should be loaded into memory and displayed to the user. Dynamically displaying a Silverlight control is a fairly simple process using the System.Windows.Markup .XamlReader.Load() method. The Load() method can load a Silverlight control defined in a separate XAML file or dynamically create a Silverlight control from a string of XAML.

Try This Dynamically Loading an XAML Button

Silverlight utilizes dynamic programming languages. A key feature of a dynamic language is the ability to dynamically load content and process it. Silverlight can dynamically load XAML files and utilize them.

1. Start or open Visual Studio 2010.

2. Create a new Silverlight project.

3. In the Solution Explorer, right-click the Silverlight project and select the option to add a new Silverlight control.

4. Add markup similar to the following to the newly added Silverlight control to render a simple customized control:

```
<Button xmlns="http://schemas.microsoft.com/client/2007"

Width="100" Height="100" Content="click me"></Button>
```

5. Save the newly added Silverlight control.

6. In the Solution Explorer, select the newly added Silverlight control. Then, in the Properties sheet, select the value Embedded Resource for the Build Action property.

7. In the Page.xaml file, add an event handler for the Loaded UserControl event.

8. In the Page.xaml.cs file, add a line of code to the Loaded event handler to retrieve the newly added Silverlight control using the namespace and control name, as shown here:

```
Stream stream = this.GetType ( ).Assembly

.GetManifestResourceStream ( "L1204.myButton.xaml" );
```

9. Add a line of code to read the contents of the Silverlight control into a string, as shown here:

```
string xaml = new StreamReader ( stream ).ReadToEnd ( );
```

10. Using the Load method, convert the contents of the string variable into a Button control, as shown next:

```
Button myButton = ( Button ) XamlReader.Load ( xaml );
```

11. Add the new control to the LayoutRoot container control, as shown here:

```
LayoutRoot.Children.Add ( myButton );
```

12. Press F5 or select the option to Start Debugging. The loaded Silverlight control should display as shown in Figure 12-6.

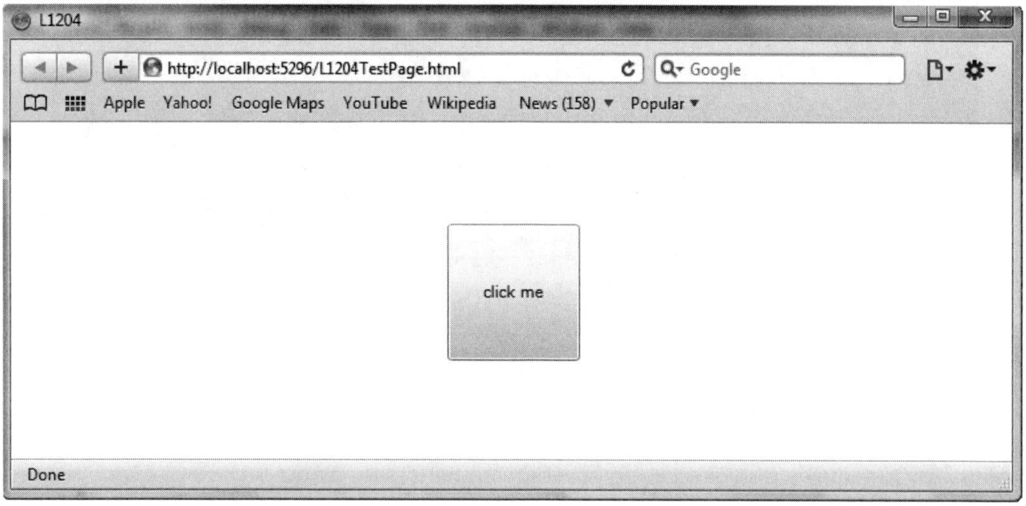

Figure 12-6 A dynamically loaded Silverlight control displayed in Safari

Full-Screen Mode

A nice feature supported by Silverlight is the ability to display in full-screen mode so that the Silverlight application is the only application shown. Full-screen mode is very useful when displaying graphic intensive and immersive applications such as movie and media players or games. The System.Windows.Interop namespace contains the Content class that includes a Boolean property named IsFullScreen. Assigning a value of true to the IsFullScreen property causes the application to display in full-screen mode. Alternatively, when a value of false is assigned to the IsFullScreen property, the application will display in normal browser mode. Figure 12-7 shows a Silverlight control in full-screen mode.

NOTE

Silverlight, by design, prevents an application from displaying in full-screen mode by default and on its own accord. An application can be displayed in full-screen mode only in response to user interaction.

Figure 12-7   A movie displayed using Silverlight in full-screen mode

Search Engine Optimization (SEO)

Search engines are the most commonly used tool on the Web today and have become the world's primary directory service. Search engines have replaced the yellow pages used years ago. Most search engines present the top 10 to 20 hits to the user when a search is completed. The vast majority of users will refine or modify their search if they do not see what they are looking for on the initial page displayed by a search engine. If Web content is not indexed by a search engine or is not ranked highly, a user searching may never find that content using a search engine.

Most search engines utilize search engine crawlers to search the Web and locate and index web content. Search engines are very efficient at indexing text-based content but have traditionally had a very difficult time indexing dynamic content stored in databases, content stored in script files, and content presented by plug-in technologies, including Silverlight.

Silverlight web applications should be designed in such a way to account for users who do not have the Silverlight plug-in installed, who are using browsers or operating systems not supported by the Silverlight plug-in, and who require accessible web content. When content is designed to be accessible to these users, it is referred to as *down-level content*.

The most basic approach (and what is considered by most to be the best approach) is to design a Silverlight web application using ASP.NET or simple web technologies that support virtually all users so that any user can view the content. Once this is in place, you can build a Silverlight experience on top of the basic web design. When you use this approach, users who have the Silverlight plug-in installed will be presented with the Silverlight experience, whereas all other users will be presented the down-level content.

When designing for down-level users, you can duplicate content in the basic web application and the Silverlight application; however, this is more difficult to manage and maintain, particularly when the content is updated. HTML Bridge may also be used in the Silverlight application to pull content in from the down-level user interface so that only a single copy of the content exists. This is a better approach but does require more effort.

The obvious benefit to designing a Silverlight application in this manner is that the content of the web application resides in a text format and is ready to be indexed by search engines. Additionally, a Silverlight application can take advantage of extended functionality in the underlying web technologies, such as the globalization and localization features inherent in ASP.NET.

Here are some other tips for creating content that is quickly and easily indexed by search engines:

- Use descriptive titles for pages.

- Add description metadata.

- Use a meaningful application name.

- Use the HTML Object tag.

- Specify alternative content for Silverlight so that down-level users are accommodated.

- Use CreateObject when using Silverlight.js.

- Thoroughly test down-level experiences and content.

Printing and Reporting

Most robust LOB applications offer the ability to visualize data managed by the application using graphs, charts, diagrams, and reports. Microsoft has worked hard to deliver the tools, features, and functionality necessary to build LOB applications in Silverlight 3. However, a major feature missing in Silverlight 3 is the ability to print Silverlight content. Some reports from Microsoft claim that the decision to exclude printing capability from the Silverlight release was an effort to reinforce "green" applications that do not waste paper.

Although direct printing functionality is not included in Silverlight, data presented in a Silverlight application can be visualized in detail using graphs, charts, diagrams, images, media, and animation. However, integration with a more sophisticated reporting solution such as SQL Server Reporting Services is not yet supported directly in Silverlight 3.

With that said, it may appear that there is no good news about printing and reporting in a Silverlight 3 application. However, tools and functionality are included so that a Silverlight application can be integrated with a Microsoft Office application. Hence, a Silverlight application can use Microsoft Word or Microsoft Excel to generate advanced reports that are ready to print.

Globalization

Globalization is the process of creating an application that can be presented to users from different cultures and locales. For example, a globalized application may present data in English to users from the United States while presenting data in Chinese to users from China. An additional term that is commonly used when discussing globalization is *localization.* Localization takes globalization one step further and creates very specific settings for a particular locale. For example, although an application may display content in Spanish for users in Mexico and users in Spain, many settings will differ between Mexico and Spain, such as the date and time settings, monetary settings, and so on.

Silverlight supports a subset of the globalization and localization features available in the .NET Framework using classes in the System.Globalization namespace. Silverlight globalization is somewhat limited in comparison to the .NET Framework, though. Silverlight supports the following:

- Unicode data using UTF-8 and UTF-16

- Custom cultures and globalization data as supported by the client OS

NOTE
Creating globalized and localized Silverlight applications can be complex and is beyond the scope of this book. For more information on Silverlight globalization, visit the MSDN Silverlight Deployment and Localization page located at http://msdn .microsoft.com/en-us/library/cc189057(VS.95).aspx.

Out-of-Browser (OOB) Support

Among the gamut of new features available in Silverlight 3 is the ability to install a Silverlight application locally on a user's machine and run it in an offline mode. When a Silverlight application is installed locally on a user's machine, it is referred to as an *out-of-browser (OOB) application.* Once enabled for offline support, a Silverlight application may be installed on a user's machine in response to a mouse or keyboard gesture or programmatically, but the user must initiate the offline installation. Given offline support, Silverlight applications may be created to be always connected, always disconnected, or occasionally connected.

Try This   Enable Silverlight Out-of-Browser Support

Enabling a Silverlight 3 application for out-of-browser support is a fairly easy process. Here are the steps to follow:

1. Start or open Visual Studio 2010.

2. Create a new Silverlight application.

3. Design some type of Silverlight user experience similar to that shown in Figure 12-8.

4. In the Solution Explorer, right-click the Silverlight project and select Properties from the context menu.

(continued)

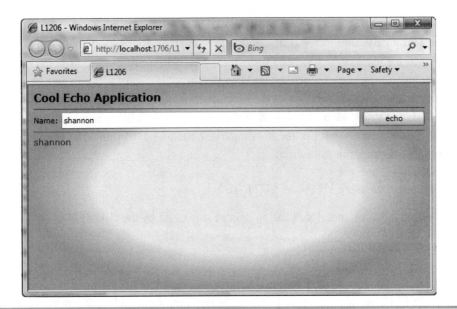

Figure 12-8 A simple Silverlight user experience

5. From the Silverlight tab of the Project Properties dialog, select the Enable Running the Application Out of the Browser option and then click the Out-of-Browser settings button.

6. Configure the settings in the Out-of-Browser Settings dialog as shown in Figure 12-9.

7. Click OK and then close the Project Properties dialog.

8. Press F5 or select the Start Debugging option to start the application.

9. When the application is displayed in the browser, right-click the application and select Install <your application> onto this computer... .

10. The Install Application dialog should be displayed, as shown in Figure 12-10. Click OK.

11. The application should be displayed out of the browser. Test the application.

12. Close the browser and the application.

13. From the Start menu or desktop shortcut, start the application out of the browser and test it again.

14. To uninstall the application, start the application, right-click it, and select Remove This Application. Click OK.

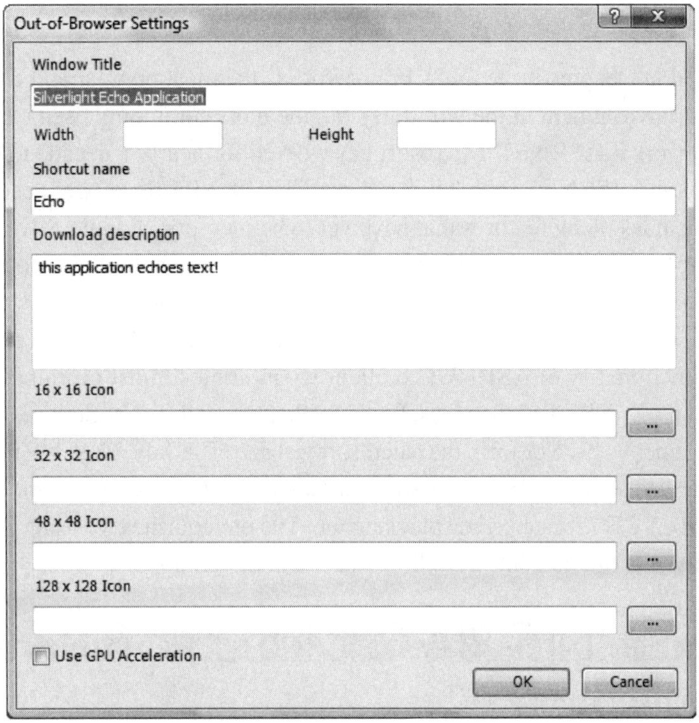

Out-of-Browser Settings

Window Title

Silverlight Echo Application

Width   Height

Shortcut name

Echo

Download description

this application echoes text!

16 x 16 Icon

32 x 32 Icon

48 x 48 Icon

128 x 128 Icon

☐ Use GPU Acceleration

OK   Cancel

Figure 12-9   The Out-of-Browser Settings dialog

Install application

You are installing **Echo** from **http://localhost**

Please confirm the locations for the shortcuts.

☑ Start menu
☐ Desktop

More Information   OK   Cancel

Figure 12-10   The Install Application dialog

RIA Services

As mentioned in Chapter 1, the .NET Framework is the most popular and commonly used development environment in the world. By far, the most commonly used technology in the .NET Framework is ASP.NET. Microsoft has worked for nearly a decade to build essential functionality into ASP.NET so that most, if not all, ASP.NET developer needs are met. ASP.NET includes many features that have yet to be incorporated into Silverlight, including data validation, authentication, and roles. Instead of creating a duplicate code base so that this additional functionality could be added to Silverlight, Microsoft has developed *.NET RIA Services*, which is a set of Web Services hosted on Microsoft web servers that offers the functionality of ASP.NET to client technologies, most prominently Silverlight.

To begin using .NET RIA Services, first download the .NET RIA Services installer from the Silverlight.net website or from the Microsoft website. The July 2009 .NET RIA Services installer is located at http://www.microsoft.com/downloads/details.aspx?FamilyID=76bb3a07-3846-4564-b0c3-27972bcaabce&displaylang=en. The prerequisites for using .NET RIA Services are Visual Studio 2008 with SP1 or later and Silverlight 3.

Try This Utilize .NET RIA Services in a Silverlight Application

To enable integration of .NET RIA Services into a Silverlight application, follow these steps:

1. Start or open Visual Studio 2010.

2. Create a new Silverlight application.

3. When presented with the New Silverlight Application dialog, ensure that the Enable .NET RIA Services check box is selected and click OK, as shown in Figure 12-11.

4. To expose data from a database using .NET RIA Services, right-click the ASP.NET web test harness project in the Solution Explorer and select Add New Item.

5. Select ADO.NET Entity Data Model from the Add New Item dialog, name the model, and then click Add.

6. Add tables from a database to the data model and save the data model as shown in Figure 12-12.

7. Right-click the ASP.NET web harness project in the Solution Explorer and select Add New Item.

Figure 12-11   The Enable .NET RIA Services check box

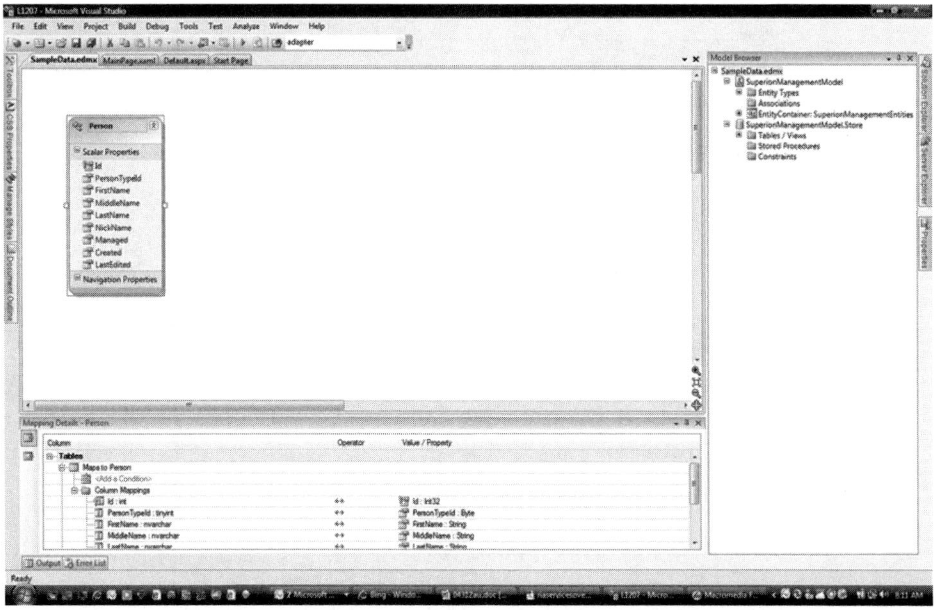

Figure 12-12   A table added to an ADO.NET entity data model

(continued)

8. From the Add New Item dialog, select Domain Service Class, name the class, and then click Add.

9. From the Add New Domain Service Class dialog, name the service and select the option Enable Client Access. From the Available Data Contexts dropdown, select the entity data model created previously, select the entity to expose, and then click OK (see Figure 12-13).

10. Add a DataGrid to the Silverlight Page.xaml file to display data from the data model.

11. Open the Page.xaml code-behind file.

12. Add two using statements to the top of the code-behind file, as shown here:

```
using L1207.Web;
using System.Windows.Ria.Data;
```

13. Create an instance of the data model context class as a class-level variable.

14. In the page constructor or in the Loaded event handler, call the generic LoadOperation and load the data entities.

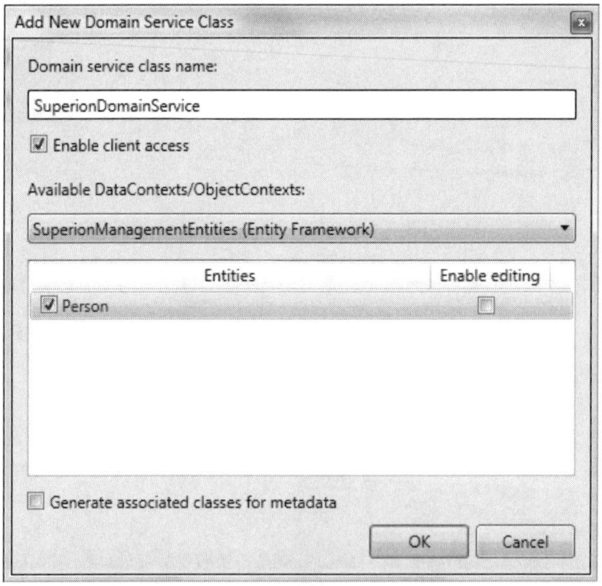

Figure 12-13 The configured Add New Domain Service Class dialog

15. Assign the entities to the ItemSource of the DataGrid. The code-behind file should resemble that shown in the following listing:

```
using System;
using System.Collections.Generic;
using System.Linq;
using System.Net;
using System.Windows;
using System.Windows.Controls;
using System.Windows.Documents;
using System.Windows.Input;
using System.Windows.Media;
using System.Windows.Media.Animation;
using System.Windows.Shapes;

using L1207.Web;
using System.Windows.Ria.Data;

namespace L1207
{
    public partial class MainPage : UserControl
    {

        private SuperionDomainContext dc = new
            SuperionDomainContext();

        public MainPage()
        {
        }

        private void UserControl_Loaded(object sender,
            RoutedEventArgs e)
        {

            LoadOperation<Person>
            persons = this.dc.Load(this.dc.GetPersonQuery());
            dgPerson.ItemsSource = persons.Entities;
        }
    }
}
```

16. Press F5 or select the option Start Debugging to review the data displayed in the DataGrid.

Conclusion

Silverlight has come a long way since its initial beta and version 1.0. Silverlight 3 can now be used to create LOB applications. Silverlight is no longer just an advanced method of integrating media into web applications but is now a full-fledged competitor in the RIA application market. It is poised to become the leading technology used to create RIA applications.

Index